HOW TO FORM AND OPERATE
A LIMITED LIABILITY COMPANY

HOW TO FORM AND OPERATE
A LIMITED LIABILITY COMPANY
A do-it-yourself guide

Gregory C. Damman, J.D.

Self-Counsel Press Inc.
a subsidiary of
International Self-Counsel Press Ltd.
U.S.A.　　　Canada
(Printed in Canada)

Copyright © 1995, 1998 by Self-Counsel Press Inc.

All rights reserved.

No part of this book may be reproduced or transmitted in any form by any means — graphic, electronic, or mechanical — without permission in writing from the publisher, except by a reviewer who may quote brief passages in a review.

Printed in Canada

First edition: October 1995
Second edition: March 1998

Cataloguing in Publication Data
Damman, Gregory C., 1963-
    How to form and operate a limited liability company

    (Self-counsel legal series)
    ISBN 1-55180-182-5

    1. Private companies — United States. 2. Limited partnership — United States.
I. Title. II. Series.
KF1380.Z9D35 1998   346.73′0668   C98-910281-5

Cover photography by Terry Guscott, ATN Visuals, Vancouver, B.C.

Self-Counsel Press Inc.
1704 N. State Street
Bellingham, Washington 98225
a subsidiary of
International Self-Counsel Press Ltd.
1481 Charlotte Road
North Vancouver, British Columbia
Canada   V7J 1H1

To my wife and children

CONTENTS

ACKNOWLEDGMENTS		xiii
1 WHAT IS A LIMITED LIABILITY COMPANY?		1
a. History		2
1. The Wyoming experience		2
2. The IRS reversal		2
3. The LLC explosion		2
b. The major benefits of doing business as an LLC		3
1. Limited liability		3
2. Partnership tax status		3
3. LLC flexibility		4
c. A potpourri of additional LLC benefits		4
1. International participation		4
2. Confidentiality		4
3. Estate planning		5
d. LLC disadvantages		5
1. Uncertain interstate recognition		5
2. Evolving tax status		6
e. The future of LLCs		6
1. Uniformity		6
2. Professionals		7
3. Sole proprietors		8
2 IS AN LLC THE PROPER ENTITY FOR YOUR BUSINESS?		9
a. What to consider when choosing a form of business		9
1. Nature of the business		9
2. Type of owners		9
3. Tax considerations		10
4. Management considerations		10
5. Liability considerations		10
6. Record keeping considerations		10
b. Entity comparison		10
1. Sole proprietorship versus LLC		11
2. General partnership versus LLC		11
3. S corporation versus LLC		11
4. C corporation versus LLC		12
5. Limited partnership versus LLC		12

3 HOW TO FORM AN LLC — 14
a. Filing the necessary documents (ULLCA section 202) — 14
  1. Articles of Organization — 14
  2. Drafting the Articles of Organization — 16
  3. Amendment of the Articles of Organization (ULLCA section 204) — 17
  4. LLC name and identification (ULLCA sections 105, 106, 107) — 18
b. The filing fees — 19
c. Other potential requirements — 19
d. Choosing the state in which to form an LLC — 19

4 THE OPERATING AGREEMENT — 21
a. Contents of the Operating Agreement — 21
b. Signature requirements — 22
c. Changing the Operating Agreement — 23

5 CONVERTING AN EXISTING BUSINESS INTO AN LLC — 39
a. Converting a partnership (ULLCA sections 902, 903) — 39
b. Converting a corporation — 40
  1. S corporation — 40
  2. C corporation — 40
  3. Corporate LLC conversion alternatives — 40

6 THE BASICS OF LLC MEMBERSHIP — 42
a. LLC membership in general — 42
  1. What do I get? — What do I want? — 42
  2. Who may be an LLC member? — 42
b. Are multiple members necessary? — 43
c. The nature of an LLC membership interest (ULLCA section 501) — 43
  1. Membership contributions (ULLCA sections 401, 402) — 43
  2. Membership transfers (ULLCA section 502) — 44
d. Leaving an LLC — 45
  1. Withdrawal or dissociation (ULLCA sections 601, 602(a)) — 45
  2. Wrongful dissociation (ULLCA section 602) — 46
  3. What happens when an LLC member dissociates? (ULLCA section 603) — 47

7 LIABILITY OF MEMBERS — 48
a. The nature of an LLC's "limited liability" (ULLCA sections 302, 303) — 48
b. Piercing the LLC veil — 49
  1. Inseparability — 50
  2. Undercapitalization — 50
  3. Illegal purpose — 50
  4. Lack of compliance with formalities — 50
  5. Equity and justice — 51
c. How to avoid having the LLC veil pierced — 51

8	**THE SOURCES OF MANAGEMENT RESPONSIBILITY (ULLCA SECTION 404)**	52
	a. Management provisions in the Articles of Organization	52
	b. Management provisions in the Operating Agreement	53
9	**CONDUCTING THE BUSINESS OF AN LLC (ULLCA SECTION 301(a))**	56
	a. General management considerations	56
	1. Member agents	56
	2. Selecting managers	57
	3. Manager agents	58
	b. Special responsibilities of members and managers (ULLCA section 409)	58
	c. Distributions (ULLCA sections 405, 406, 407)	60
10	**"CHECK THE BOX" TAX STATUS**	63
	a. A simplified process	63
	1. Elimination of flexible/bulletproof characterization	63
	2. Single-member LLCs	64
	3. Firms ineligible for "check the box" status	64
	b. Making the election	64
	c. Taxation of member contributions	64
	d. Possible taxation at the state level	65
11	**GENERAL LLC TAX CONSIDERATIONS**	67
	a. What tax forms must be filed?	67
	1. Due date for Form 1065	67
	2. Where to file	67
	3. Failure to file Form 1065	67
	4. Taxable year	68
	5. Tax matters member	68
	6. Signing the return	68
	7. Audits	68
	8. Accounting method	68
	b. Details of Form 1065	69
	1. Cost of goods sold	69
	2. Other information	69
	3. Partners' share of income	69
	4. Balance sheets	69
	5. Reconciliation of income	69
	6. Analysis of partners' capital accounts	69
	7. Capital gains and losses	70
	c. Self-employment taxes	70
	d. The LLC accountant	70

12	**WILL MY LLC BE RECOGNIZED IN OTHER STATES?**	77
	a. Interstate recognition of LLCs — in general	77
	b. How to avoid interstate problems	77
	1. Form a manager-managed LLC	78
	2. Include a choice of law statement in documents	78
	3. Properly identify the LLC	78
	4. Educate members and employees	78
	5. Form other entities and make them members	78
	6. Obtain adequate insurance coverage	78
	7. Register in other states	79
13	**IS MY LLC MEMBERSHIP INTEREST A SECURITY?**	80
	a. What is a security?	80
	b. LLCs and the federal securities laws	80
	c. Avoiding application of the securities laws	81
14	**WHAT TYPES OF BUSINESSES ARE FORMING AS LLCs?**	82
	a. LLCs are suitable for nearly any type of business	82
	1. Real estate ventures	82
	2. Natural resource development	83
	3. Accounting firms	84
	4. High technology firms	84
	5. Law firms	84
	6. Medical practices	84
	7. Agricultural holdings	84
	8. Family businesses: estate planning	85
	b. Some businesses may not operate as LLCs	87
15	**THE LLC LAWYER**	88
	a. Is an LLC lawyer necessary?	88
	b. How to select an LLC lawyer	88
	c. Services and fees	89
	1. Peace-of-mind service	89
	2. Start-up service	90
	3. Full service	90
16	**TERMINATING AN LLC**	91
	a. The basics of dissolution (ULLCA sections 801, 802)	91
	1. Winding up	92
	2. Filing matters	92
	3. Agency considerations (ULLCA section 804)	92
	4. Distributions	92
	b. Creditors' rights upon dissolution (ULLCA sections 807, 808)	93
	c. Terminating an LLC through merger	93

17 MISCELLANEOUS ISSUES 95
   a. LLC records 95
   b. Keeping up with LLC changes 96
   c. Annual fees and reports 96
   d. Workers' and unemployment compensation 97
   e. Is an LLP more appropriate? 97
   f. A final note 97

APPENDIXES
   1. Uniform Limited Liability Company Act 99
   2. State-By-State Directory of Information 135

SAMPLES

#1	Operating Agreement	24
#2	Form 8832	66
#3	Form 1065	71
#4	Schedule K-1	75

ACKNOWLEDGMENTS

Lawyers have a knack for making a simple subject appear complex. For example, some lawyers cannot simply refer to "a contract." A contract must be described as "the contractual arrangement dated and executed June 25, 1998, wherein the parties herein, and more fully described above, exchanged their mutual promises for good and valuable consideration as required by the laws of this state."

Some people call this type of writing *legalese*. My goal, while writing this book, was never to fall into the murky waters of the legalese ocean. Too many lawyers' clients have already drowned in legalese. If I did fall into the legalese ocean, I apologize. If I did not, you may thank the professors at the University of Kansas School of Journalism who taught me that simplicity and conciseness are virtues.

I would also like to thank several people who assisted me with this book. Terry Knoepfle, an assistant professor of Business Law at North Dakota State University, provided me with a large amount of research materials. Shelly Kidwell and Alison Alderman helped me gather research materials and forms. They also helped with typing chores.

Ruth Wilson and Natasha Young of Self-Counsel Press also deserve my thanks for their insightful comments and hard work. They, too, sought to make this book helpful and easy to understand.

Finally, I must acknowledge the possibility that this book contains errors. If it does, they are my errors, and not the errors of any of the people who assisted me.

NOTICE TO READERS

Laws are constantly changing. Every effort is made to keep this publication as current as possible. However, the author, the publisher, and the vendor make no representation or warranties regarding the outcome or the use to which the information in this book is put and are not assuming any liability for any claims, losses, or damages arising out of the use of this book.

The reader should not rely on the author or publisher of this book for any professional advice.

Note: The fees quoted in this book are correct at the date of publication. However, fees are subject to change without notice. For current fees, check with the appropriate government office nearest you.

1
WHAT IS A LIMITED LIABILITY COMPANY?

Some questions are not easily answered. What color is a chameleon? Does broccoli taste good? Questions of this type do not have clear-cut answers. Instead, the proper response is usually "it depends." Is the chameleon on a green leaf or a brown tree trunk? Is the broccoli covered with cheese sauce?

Add "what is a limited liability company?" to the list of questions that may be answered with an "it depends" response. The answer depends on questions such as: Is the limited liability company managed by all members or is it managed by elected managers? Are corporations included as members of the limited liability company? What are the terms of the limited liability company's Operating Agreement? These questions may seem confusing to you at this point, but, hopefully, by the time you've finished this book, you will understand their significance, and that of many other similar concepts.

If you do business as a limited liability company, your friends may consider you to be an expert on the topic. They will ask what a limited liability company is. Unfortunately, they won't be happy with "it depends" or a lengthy, complicated response based on what you learned from this book. You will need a good cocktail-party answer. Tell your friends that a limited liability company is a flexible form of doing business that provides members with corporate-type limited liability, yet allows them the benefit of partnership tax status.

To *really* become an expert on limited liability companies, you need to understand the concepts discussed in this book. One of the first things you must get a handle on is terminology. Limited liability companies are commonly referred to by the abbreviation *LLC*. I refer to limited liability companies as LLCs to save space and improve readability.

This book has two goals. The first is to explain LLCs in detail so that the reader understands how to form one. The second goal is to provide the reader with the basic legal and practical considerations that accompany doing business as an LLC.

You may notice that this book is liberally sprinkled with words and phrases such as "most states," "typically," "usually," "a few states," "likely," and "probably." There is a good reason for this usage. The LLC laws vary in many ways from state to state. It is impossible, at this early point in the development of LLC law, to make more than a few statements about LLCs that are true in every single state. Therefore, you should heed the advice, given numerous times throughout this book, to check your state's LLC law on a particular question. For difficult questions, consult with an experienced LLC lawyer.

For a copy of a state's LLC law, consult the Corporate Division of the secretary of state. This office is typically in charge of filing LLC documents and therefore fields many questions about LLCs. It usually keeps a current copy on hand for the public. Some offices give free copies; others charge a nominal fee. Another good source of the LLC law is your local public library. Larger public libraries usually have a current copy of its state's statutes. Look up *limited liability company* in the index. The Clerk of the State Legislature may also be a good source for locating current LLC law. Another source is the state law library, which is usually located in the state capitol building. A phone call to the reference desk may be enough to locate a copy.

Before getting into the nuts and bolts of forming and operating an LLC, you might be interested in a brief LLC history lesson. If not, skip the next section.

a. HISTORY

In all likelihood, your state enacted its LLC law after 1990. Given this fact, you may think that the LLC is a creature of the 1990s. It is not. In the United States, LLCs emerged in the seventies. Other countries have had similar laws for many years. Brazil and Portugal, for example, have long allowed firms to do business in a similar way as *limitadas*. Germany has a similar entity called the *GmbH* (Gesellschaft mit beschraenkter Haftung). The United Kingdom has the Holding Company. Saudi Arabia has limited liability partnerships. Outside of the United States, LLC-type businesses are nothing new.

1. The Wyoming experience

Despite the foreign acceptance of LLC-type business entities, no form of business similar to these foreign entities existed in the United States until 1977. Wyoming enacted its LLC law that year as special-interest legislation intended to lure Hamilton Brothers Oil Company into Wyoming. Hamilton was involved in international oil and gas exploration and had been using the LLC form in Panama.

Unfortunately, in 1980, the IRS issued proposed regulations that would have prevented members in Wyoming LLCs from qualifying for partnership tax status because no member had personal liability for the LLC's debts. The IRS's position, eliminating partnership tax status for LLCs, effectively did away with the primary advantage of operating a business as an LLC. Therefore, no other states, except Florida, enacted an LLC law throughout the early- and mid-eighties. Florida passed an LLC law simply as an attempt to attract foreign businesses.

2. The IRS reversal

In 1988, the IRS reconsidered its position on the tax status of LLCs. It decided that limited liability protection for all members should not prevent partnership tax status, as long as the entity met the other requirements for taxation as a partnership.

The IRS issued a revenue ruling concluding that a Wyoming LLC could be taxed as a partnership. This ruling opened the floodgates. Every state now has an LLC law.

LLC laws are generally the same from state to state, but there are important differences. First, there are different formation, organizational, and operational rules from state to state, and some states impose a state income tax on LLCs while others don't. Recently, the IRS passed "check the box" regulations which clarified LLC tax status by allowing an LLC to elect partnership tax status merely by checking a box on the partnership tax form.

3. The LLC explosion

Now that the LLC wave has swept the country, many people are aware that LLCs are an extremely attractive form of doing business. Given the nationwide scope of the LLC laws and the recent enactment, the current number of LLCs will certainly multiply in just a few years. More and more people want to know whether forming a new business as an LLC, or converting an existing business into an LLC, would be beneficial. In order to make that decision, a business owner must have a general understanding of the major benefits related to operating a business as an LLC.

b. THE MAJOR BENEFITS OF DOING BUSINESS AS AN LLC

Many experts list two benefits that flow from doing business as an LLC: limited liability and partnership tax status. Actually, there is a third benefit: flexibility. A general look at each of these benefits provides the foundation for a good working knowledge of LLCs. We'll start with limited liability.

1. Limited liability

Perhaps the first thing that jumps out at someone interested in operating an LLC is the name itself. *Limited liability company* sounds great! What business owner would not want limited liability? We all know about lawsuits, creditors, loans, and all the other liability-creating animals that scare business owners. Imagine the entrepreneurship, creativity, and productivity that could take place if a large portion of a business's liability concerns could be eliminated. What would happen if these liability concerns could be lessened or eliminated? Presumably, entrepreneurs would be more willing to invest their time, money, and energy into a new business because the potential for personal liability would be lessened. This basic notion is one of the reasons state legislators across the country have looked favorably on LLCs.

All members of an LLC should be thoroughly familiar with the nature of limited liability. In short, LLC members are not personally liable for the LLC's debts and obligations. The LLC limited liability umbrella does not, however, protect members from every type of liability that could rain down on them. LLC members may still be personally liable for LLC debts if they personally guarantee those debts. They are also still personally liable for their own negligence. But the liability exposure that remains after an LLC is formed does not prevent LLCs from being an attractive business entity.

LLC members are liable only up to the amount of their capital contributions and the amount they agree to contribute to the firm's capital. Of course, limited liability is not granted at the expense of creditors. Many state LLC statutes require disclosure of members' agreed-upon contributions, and will limit distributions to members so that they cannot raid the LLC assets and make it unable to pay its debts. Perhaps the best way to think about limited liability is to consider it as corporate-type limited liability. Limited liability is a valuable asset, especially when combined with partnership tax status.

2. Partnership tax status

If LLCs provided no benefits other than limited liability, there would be little incentive to form an LLC. There must be more. The "more" is partnership tax status. This is the cornerstone of the LLC. Once again, a brief terminology lesson is helpful. You might occasionally hear some people refer to the favorable tax status of LLCs as *pass-through* taxation, rather than partnership tax status. Don't be confused. The two terms mean the same thing. The phrase pass through simply means that members are not taxed twice, as they are in a corporation. In a corporation, both the corporation and the shareholder are separately taxed. In an LLC, income passes through the LLC directly to the member who is then taxed as a partner. The LLC itself is not taxed. There is a form of corporation, called an S corporation, that also provides pass-through taxation, but S corporations are subject to many limitations that are discussed more thoroughly in chapter 2.

While partnership tax status and limited liability are important financial LLC benefits, the third benefit — flexibility — is the feature that makes LLCs extremely useful, innovative, and attractive for a broad range of businesses. In fact, many experts believe that flexibility is the most important feature of LLCs.

3. LLC flexibility

LLCs are flexible for many reasons. A prime example of LLC flexibility is that they may be formed with any type of entity as a member, including corporations, partnerships, limited partnerships, individuals, and even other LLCs.

Another feature that makes LLCs flexible is that it is easy for owners to agree about the business's direction without restrictions. For example, the members may agree that all members have management capability or, in the alternative, that only a small number of members have management power. If the members later want to change the management scheme, they may do so easily.

LLCs are also flexible because there are few state and federal laws or IRS regulations that limit the way LLCs may do business. Yet another source of flexibility is the fact that LLC members may allocate gains, losses, deductions, and credits in virtually any way they see fit. For example, if one member needs to show a greater loss than other members in a certain year, the members may agree to allocate a larger portion of the LLC loss to that member. Perhaps the only limit on LLC flexibility is a lack of imagination.

c. A POTPOURRI OF ADDITIONAL LLC BENEFITS

Limited liability, partnership tax status, and flexibility are not the only benefits obtained by doing business as an LLC. They are just the primary benefits. There are several other benefits, including international participation, confidentiality, and estate planning.

1. International participation

LLCs are not limited to domestic members, but may take on international members. The business world is becoming increasingly global, and firms that participate in the global economy have an advantage over other, more restricted, business firms.

Before the existence of LLCs, foreign investors who were familiar with LLC-type entities in their own country were frustrated by the lack of a similar-type entity in the United States. Now, many foreign investors are impressed by the fact that a U.S. business is operating with the "blessing" of a state, and they feel more protected in their business affairs.

2. Confidentiality

Many states have laws that require general partnerships, limited partnerships, and corporations to file annual reports, ownership statements, and other information with the secretary of state. (From now on, when you read the phrase "secretary of state," keep in mind that it simply refers to the central filing agency, whether that agency is in fact the secretary of state or not.) Additional filing may also be required if there is a change of ownership within those entities. These filing requirements have the effect of making a substantial amount of business information available to the public. If you want to know whether a person owns shares in a corporation and the number of shares owned, just check the secretary of state's records in the state of incorporation.

The LLC laws in many states do not impose extensive filing and reporting requirements. Often, the only time an LLC must make information public is when the Articles of Organization are filed. And even then, no financial information need be disclosed.

In addition, the LLC may not need to disclose its owners if it is managed by non-owners or some other organization. LLC ownership changes also may not bring about the need to file additional documents. The lack of filing and reporting requirements makes an LLC a confidential entity. Investors or business owners who prefer to keep their interest in the business confidential may do so easily. This confidentiality, however, has received criticism.

Some people believe that LLC confidentiality could lead to widespread fraud. If fraud does occur, it is likely that legislation will be passed imposing reporting requirements on LLCs similar to those already in place for other business entities.

3. Estate planning

Yet another advantage of doing business as an LLC is the ability to structure the LLC so that it is an estate planning device. For example, assume that the owners of a family business want to arrange the business so that it continues in existence after the death of one of the family member owners. In order to do so, the family need only form an LLC and after the family member's death, agree to continue the LLC in existence. One of the tax benefits of such an arrangement is that the LLC does not dissolve. If it did, the members would recognize a taxable gain because the LLC assets would be distributed to them.

Another way that LLCs could work as an estate planning tool is by reducing inheritance taxes. If your estate is worth more than $600,000 ($1.2 million if you are married), then the amount above $600,000 is subject to a 55% inheritance tax.

Inheritance tax can be avoided by forming an LLC with your children to hold the excess assets. You could retain a small percentage interest in the LLC but retain control over your assets by listing yourself as the manager in the Operating Agreement (see chapter 4 for a detailed discussion of Operating Agreements). This way, you could still direct the LLC to loan you or your children money as needed. Upon your death, inheritance tax would be owed on your percentage interest, but that amount would come to much less than the amount that would have been paid if the LLC had not been formed. If your children are minors, their interests could be owned by an irrevocable trust.

Most states have abolished common law marriages. According to one source I checked, only 13 states recognize common law marriages. The IRS may allow spouses to take advantage of estate planning laws used by formally married spouses, but the validity of the marriage can be challenged if it was claimed primarily to gain tax benefits.

Naturally, if you are forming an LLC as an estate planning tool, you should consult your lawyer and accountant to make certain that the LLC serves the intended purpose. The tax laws are too complicated to attempt to use an LLC as a tax-saving tool without the advice of a professional.

d. LLC DISADVANTAGES

There are many benefits from doing business as an LLC, but like most things in life, LLCs are not perfect. Fortunately, there are few disadvantages, and those are not substantial. Actually, they are not so much disadvantages as they are question marks.

1. Uncertain interstate recognition

One disadvantage is that the fast and recent development of LLC laws has created some questions as to how different states may treat LLCs that venture into that state to do business. For example, if a California LLC does business in New York and is sued, will the New York courts recognize the limited liability of California LLC members? This question is especially important if one state's LLC law grants stronger liability protection to members than another state's LLC law.

The courts have not had the opportunity to address the interstate validity of LLCs. In all likelihood, LLCs engaged in interstate commerce will be treated the same as corporations engaged in interstate commerce. That is, LLC members will enjoy limited liability in every state. Until the courts actually embrace this notion, however, interstate LLCs need to be wary. (The question of interstate LLC validity is discussed more thoroughly in chapter 12.)

2. Evolving tax status

Until the recent creation of the "check the box" option, it was difficult to predict whether an LLC would enjoy partnership tax status. Now, the primary LLC tax question is whether the states will see an opportunity to generate revenue and impose a tax on LLCs?

Many other LLC tax questions need to be answered. In all likelihood, answers will flood in over the next few years; LLC owners must stay in touch with their tax advisers to keep up-to-date on tax issues.

e. THE FUTURE OF LLCs

What will the business entity landscape look like five years from now? Ten years from now? Will LLCs outnumber partnerships and corporations? Will the S corporation become extinct? People who are interested in forming an LLC want to know the answers to questions like these. They realize that there is strength in numbers. If LLCs are widely embraced, it will be very difficult for the U.S. Congress, or any other political body, to toy with the benefits of LLC ownership.

It is difficult to predict the number of LLCs that will exist in the future. It is equally difficult to predict how similar the LLC of the future will be to today's LLC. Indeed, one expert predicted, early in the LLC evolution, that for over 90% of small- and mid-sized businesses, the LLC would not be a favorable form of doing business. This same expert predicted that only a handful of businesses would operate as LLCs. His predictions were dead wrong. Even at this early point on the LLC time line, it is clear that LLCs will be a popular form for doing business and will continue to grow in popularity.

Having acknowledged the difficulty in making LLC predictions, it is probably unwise to state an opinion on what the future holds. Nevertheless, here is my prediction:

In the future, LLCs will outnumber partnerships, LLC laws will be more uniform from state to state, most professionals will be allowed to do business as LLCs, and sole proprietors will be allowed to do business as LLCs in most states.

1. Uniformity

Imagine what would happen if every McDonald's Restaurant had a different name for the Big Mac. You would walk in, order a Big Mac, and the counter worker would say, "What? Big Mac? Never heard of it." You would be forced to read the menu to learn what to order. Uniform use of the name Big Mac among all McDonald's Restaurants makes it easier for you to place your order. The same is true with legal matters. Uniform laws from state to state make it much easier for lawyers to apply the law to their clients' cases. They aren't forced to learn entirely new legal principles just because they happen to be applying the law of a different state. The benefit of legal uniformity has caused groups of legal experts to get together and draft uniform laws such as the Uniform Commercial Code, the Uniform Partnership Act, and the Model Business Corporation Act.

Once these uniform laws are drafted, state legislatures review them and decide whether to enact them in their state. Often, uniform laws are enacted with minor changes. As a result, uniform laws are not really entirely uniform, although they are similar enough from state to state to provide the intended familiarity benefit.

Given the fondness of lawyers for uniform laws, it is not surprising that a Uniform Limited Liability Company Act was drafted by the National Conference of Commissioners on Uniform State Laws. The Uniform Limited Liability Company Act will be referred to throughout this book as the *ULLCA*. Sections of the ULLCA will be referred to frequently. Do not rely on these references as the law of any particular state. The ULLCA becomes law in a particular state only if that state enacts the ULLCA, or some variation of it. Nevertheless, the ULLCA is a good example of the general framework of the typical state LLC law (see Appendix 1).

The ULLCA is based on the *freedom of contract* concept. It is also based on principles contained in the Revised Uniform Limited Partnership Act, the Revised Model Business Corporation Act, and the Revised Uniform Partnership Act. Another source of LLC uniformity is the Prototype Limited Liability Company Act. This act is the product of an American Bar Association committee. It was intended to be a tool for states to use when drafting their own LLC acts. Indeed, the Prototype Limited Liability Company Act formed the basis for the Louisiana, Idaho, Montana, Indiana, and Arkansas LLC acts.

Most states may eventually enact the Uniform Limited Liability Company Act with minor state-specific changes. That is what happened in commercial law with the Uniform Commercial Code. The resulting commercial law uniformity benefited the general business environment by allowing transactions to take place with some certainty about the transactions' legal significance. Only time will tell whether the states will embrace the Uniform Limited Liability Company Act or revised versions of it.

2. Professionals

Professionals, such as lawyers and accountants, have expressed a strong desire to practice as LLCs. This makes sense because, traditionally, professionals have been forced to practice as partnerships. The problem is that partnerships leave partners open to personal liability for partnership debts and obligations. The early LLC statutes did not address whether professionals could practice as LLCs. Later, many states enacted LLC statutes that specifically allowed professional LLCs.

Many state legislatures and consumer groups have frowned on professional LLC practice because of a perceived lack of accountability. If you are a professional, you should carefully review your state's LLC statute to determine whether you are allowed to practice as an LLC. But even if your state does not allow professional LLCs, it would be wise to check the status of any attempts to allow professional LLC practice. Several states that initially prohibited professional LLCs later reversed themselves. Your state may be on the brink of such a reversal.

Lawyers may practice as LLCs only if the agency regulating the practice of law, such as the state supreme court or state bar association, grants its approval. A lawyer practicing in an LLC will not be insulated from personal liability for his or her negligence. However, the LLC would provide a liability shield if another member/lawyer acted negligently. Another new form of doing business, the registered limited liability partnership (RLLP), is being created in numerous states. An RLLP is simply a general partnership that has registered and, as a result, obtained limited liability for the partners. A partner in an RLLP is not personally liable for partnership debts and obligations, but remains personally liable for his or her own negligence. The RLLP may end up being the lawyer's LLC in those states that do not allow professional LLCs.

Accountants are also embracing the LLC concept. In 1992, the American Institute of Certified Public Accountants approved a change allowing accountancy to be practiced in any form permitted by state law. This change allowed accountants to practice in LLCs. Some state LLC laws specifically allow accountants to practice in LLCs, while other state LLC laws are being revised to include accountants. Indeed, accountants appear to be more interested than any other profession in practicing as LLCs.

Other professionals, such as doctors, chiropractors, engineers, and architects, are also keenly interested in practicing as LLCs.

3. Sole proprietors

Most states require LLCs to have at least two members. As a result, sole proprietors are typically unable to do business as an LLC. However, a few states, such as Arkansas, Georgia, Idaho, Montana, and Texas, allow sole proprietors to form LLCs. The fact that so few states recognize sole proprietor LLCs would seem to cast doubt on their widespread future acceptance.

However, the ULLCA allows single-member LLCs. If states look to the ULLCA when beginning to revise their LLC laws, the number of states allowing sole proprietor LLCs may increase in the future. The IRS has tacitly approved one-member LLCs by passing the "check the box" regulations allowing a business to elect not to be taxed as a corporation.

2
IS AN LLC THE PROPER ENTITY FOR YOUR BUSINESS?

By now, you are aware of the LLC basics. You also know that LLCs are a popular, fast-growing, advantageous form of doing business. Should you quickly draft the necessary paperwork and rush to the secretary of state to form your LLC? Take a deep breath and relax for a moment. You need to consider several factors.

a. WHAT TO CONSIDER WHEN CHOOSING A FORM OF BUSINESS

Business advisers have all kinds of advice for people who are trying to decide which organizational form is best for their business. Some of that advice is helpful, and some is not. Several recurring considerations may be gleaned from the literature addressing choice of business entity. Those considerations include the nature of the business, the type of owners, taxation, management, liability, and record keeping.

1. Nature of the business

The nature of a business often dictates how the business is organized. For example, assume that you want to start a business selling homemade crafts at local craft shows. Your business is in your basement and you are the sole employee. The business assets total a couple thousand dollars and you expect to earn about $15,000 annually. In this situation, it makes no sense to incorporate or form a limited liability company. Indeed, you may not be able to form a limited liability company as a sole proprietor. A small business of this type is probably best run as a sole proprietorship. Record keeping and other administrative tasks can be kept to a minimum. That way, you can spend most of your time on areas of the business that earn money, with less time spent on paperwork.

On the other hand, assume that you and three associates want to start a business manufacturing trampolines. You need several employees in addition to the four owners. You also need a manufacturing facility with office space. In this situation, a business form that protects the owners from liability would be beneficial. After all, the use of the trampolines you manufacture could result in lawsuits by injured customers. A corporate-type business form would be most appropriate. Yet tax and management considerations play a large role in what type of business form you ultimately choose. In other words, more than just the type of business must be considered when choosing a business form. (See chapter 14 for more information on what types of businesses are forming LLCs.)

2. Type of owners

Business owners are of varying types. Some are new business owners who are sole proprietors and, by necessity, jacks-of-all-trades. Some are owners with precisely defined areas of involvement in a family business. Others are investor-owners who want no part in management of the business. Still others are active owners who want total control over the business.

A form of business should not be chosen solely on the basis of the type of owner, but it is an important part of the entire mix of entity-choice considerations. LLCs are a good choice for business owners who want flexibility in management and operation of the business.

3. Tax considerations

Tax considerations affect your choice of business entity. An LLC's ability to be taxed as a partnership is a great benefit because income passes through the LLC to the member. As a result, the member avoids the double taxation that occurs in a corporation.

Other tax considerations include flexibility in allocating gains and losses among business participants and self-employment taxes. Consult an accountant for advice on the tax consequences of the use of various types of business entities.

4. Management considerations

Many investors want to participate in the management and control of the business. This is not possible in a limited partnership. In a corporation, the shareholder may participate in management and control, but he or she is also subject to double taxation. In a partnership, the partners have the ability to participate in the management and control of the business and also avoid double taxation. However, all general partners are personally liable for the debts and obligations of the partnership. In other words, there is no limited liability.

In an LLC, members may participate in the management and control of the company, and they also retain limited liability and partnership tax status. Flexibility in management — one of the hallmarks of LLCs — is also an important business consideration.

5. Liability considerations

All business owners want to avoid personal liability for the debts and obligations of the business. Patrons, suppliers, competitors, and anyone else your business comes into contact with can make some sort of claim. For example, assume that you operate a coffee shop. A patron spills coffee on the floor and leaves without cleaning it up. Moments later, another customer slips on the coffee and breaks a leg. This customer might have a negligence claim against you or your business.

If you do business as a corporation or LLC, the customers may sue the corporation or LLC and recover damages from it. The corporation or LLC assets are at risk. However, the customer may not sue you personally and have your house or car sold to satisfy a judgment.

On the other hand, if you do business as a partnership or sole proprietorship, the customers could sue you personally, recover a judgment, and have your personal assets sold to satisfy the judgment. Limited liability is not always possible, but it is more easily attainable now that LLCs have been added to the list of business entities.

6. Record keeping considerations

Record keeping is necessary in all businesses. However, when you make sure that record keeping is kept to a minimum, the business is able to concentrate on other things — like making money. Record keeping does not consist solely of tax-related records. Corporations, for example, must keep records of formal action, including decisions made at meetings. Record keeping is usually not one of the more important considerations when selecting a type of business entity. Nevertheless, if all other things are equal, the smart thing to do is select the business entity with the least amount of paperwork required.

b. ENTITY COMPARISON

In order to decide whether the LLC form is best for your business, you should compare LLCs to each of the five most popular forms of doing business: sole proprietorship, general partnership, S corporation, C corporation, and limited partnership. As you read the comparisons, keep in mind that many of the concepts described are discussed more fully in later chapters.

1. Sole proprietorship versus LLC

Unlike LLCs, a sole proprietorship requires no formal filing with a central agency in order to bring the business into existence. It exists simply because an individual decided to open up shop and pursue a certain business. Sole proprietorship management differs from LLCs in that only one person makes the decisions. Many different management schemes may exist in an LLC.

LLCs provide members with limited liability. A sole proprietor has no liability protection other than the protection he or she may achieve through insurance, such as malpractice insurance. Yet, a sole proprietorship is advantageous because of its simplicity, low cost to operate, and pass-through tax status.

For many small businesses, sole proprietorship may be the best choice of entity because of the nature of the business and the possibility that the state's LLC law does not allow sole proprietor LLCs. However, as pointed out in chapter 1, the day may come when most states allow sole proprietor LLCs.

2. General partnership versus LLC

The limited liability of LLC members is the primary element distinguishing LLCs from general partnerships. Unlike LLC members, general partners may be liable for partnership debts and obligations. But general partnerships, like sole proprietorships, typically do not have to file any documents with a central state agency in order to come into existence. In fact, a general partnership may exist without any intention by the partners to create a partnership. In other words, if you are working closely in a business with another person, you may be considered to be a partner even though no formal partnership agreement exists.

This possibility is worth worrying about given the general rule that partners are responsible for partnership debts and obligations. Your unofficial partner could incur a liability for which you could ultimately be responsible.

LLCs are similar to general partnerships insofar as both entities allow free transfer of interests subject to consent of the members. Also, general partners may, like LLC members, withdraw at will and receive the full share of their interest in the business. LLCs differ somewhat with regard to withdrawal rights, though, because most states require that members give six months' notice before they withdraw.

Management of a general partnership is similar to management of an LLC. LLCs are managed directly by the members or managers who vote in proportion to their membership interest. General partnerships are managed directly by the partners. Each partner in a general partnership has an equal management vote. LLCs and general partnerships are both dissolved when a member disassociates from the firm. However, an LLC has the ability to continue in existence if the remaining members agree to the continuation. When a partner withdraws from a general partnership, the remaining partners may continue the business of the partnership, but the partnership itself no longer exists. Finally, upon dissolution, general partners must contribute to payment of the partnership's debts. LLC members have no obligation to pay LLC debts upon dissolution.

3. S corporation versus LLC

An S corporation is essentially the same as a regular corporation. It gets its name from the subchapter of the Internal Revenue Code providing for its creation. The primary difference between an S corporation and a regular C corporation is that the S corporation allows pass-through taxation, the same as an LLC. Remember that pass-through taxation means that the business is taxed only once — at the member/shareholder level, rather than both at the member/shareholder level and

LLC/corporate level. In an S corporation, items of income, gain, loss, deduction, and credit are allocated to the shareholders in proportion to the amount of stock they own.

S corporations sound great. Why form an LLC instead of an S corporation? The reason is that certain limitations are placed on them. For example, an S corporation must be a small business corporation. It must not have more than 75 shareholders. In addition, the shareholders must be individuals, estates, or certain types of trusts. Corporations, partnerships, LLCs, and nonresidents may not be shareholders in an S corporation. All of these entities, however, can be members in an LLC. Another limitation placed on S corporations is that it may have only one class of stock. As a result, the financing options are limited.

S corporations are not good tax shelters because deductions for losses are limited to the shareholder's basis in the corporate stock. In addition, LLCs also have an advantage over S corporations when it comes to foreign investors. The inability of S corporations to take on nonresidents as shareholders prevents them from having much interaction in the fast-growing international business market. Yet another advantage LLCs have over S corporations is that LLCs, unlike S corporations, are not subject to additional partnership tax status qualification requirements. LLCs must simply elect partnership tax status. They need not be continually vigilant in order to retain such status as S corporations must.

4. C corporation versus LLC

At this point, it is helpful to point out some additional similarities between LLCs and corporations. Keep in mind that most of these similarities apply whether the corporation is an S corporation or a C corporation. LLCs and corporations are formed in essentially the same way — through a central filing of articles with the secretary of state. A corporation files Articles of Incorporation, while an LLC typically files Articles of Organization. Unless there is a contractual restriction, corporate stock may be freely transferred to others. When an LLC interest is transferred, however, the financial rights are usually all that may be assigned, and the nontransferring members must agree to the transfer. As well, corporations are managed by a board of directors while LLCs are managed by the members or managers.

Withdrawal is another area of difference. A corporate shareholder withdraws by selling his or her stock. An LLC member usually must give other members written notice of withdrawal, unless the Articles of Organization or Operating Agreement state otherwise. (See chapter 4 for a detailed discussion on the Operating Agreement.)

Dissolution provides yet another area of difference. A corporation is dissolved by the vote of the directors and shareholders followed by the filing of Articles of Dissolution. LLCs dissolve upon death, withdrawal, or consent of a member, but the LLC may continue in existence if the non-dissociating members so agree.

5. Limited partnership versus LLC

LLCs are very similar to limited partnerships. In fact, most LLC dissolution statutes are based on similar provisions found in the Revised Uniform Limited Partnership Act (RULPA). A limited partnership consists of limited partners and at least one general partner. The general partner is personally liable for limited partnership debts and obligations. The limited partners are not personally liable, as long as they do not participate in management of the limited partnership. In other words, if a limited partner becomes too involved in the day-to-day operations of the limited partnership, he or she may lose limited liability status. In an LLC, all members are entitled to limited liability, even if they participate in the management of the business.

Another area in which LLCs differ from limited partnerships is the transfer of interests. In an LLC, a member who obtains an interest by transfer (a transferee) from a prior LLC member typically does not automatically obtain management rights. An LLC member transferee may obtain management rights only if the nontransferring members so agree.

In a limited partnership, nontransferring partners must consent to a transfer, but the partners may agree in advance to admit transferees to the limited partnership. As for dissolution, an LLC usually dissolves when there is a dissolution event for any member. A limited partnership, on the other hand, dissolves only when there is a dissolution event as to a general partner. There are also differences between limited partnerships and LLCs with regard to whether services or services to be performed may be exchanged for ownership interests. In many states, an LLC interest may be obtained in exchange for services or services to be rendered.

3
HOW TO FORM AN LLC

a. FILING THE NECESSARY DOCUMENTS (ULLCA SECTION 202)

Forming an LLC is accomplished by a central filing of Articles of Organization with the appropriate state agency. Once the filing takes place, the LLC springs into existence and very little maintenance filing is needed later. The steps necessary to file the Articles of Organization and create an LLC are quite simple. Of course, the most important part of the process is to include the proper information in the Articles of Organization.

1. Articles of Organization

An LLC's Articles of Organization are similar to the Articles of Incorporation that must be filed by corporations. Keep in mind, though, that some states use different terminology for the Articles of Organization. The corporate division of the secretary of state for each state can provide filers with the correct terminology. Also, the standard forms distributed by the secretary of state always contain the correct terminology. Most states refer to the formation document as the Articles of Organization.

Louisiana calls its LLC Articles of Organization an Initial Report. Other states, such as Iowa, require the filing of a Certificate of Registration as the LLC formation document and require the Articles of Organization to be attached to the Certificate of Registration.

Until the Articles of Organization are filed, an LLC typically may not conduct business or borrow money. Some activities, such as those related to the organizing of the LLC or obtaining capital contributions, may be conducted prior to the filing of the Articles of Organization. Your state's LLC law should be consulted to determine exactly what type of business may be conducted prior to filing.

(a) The purpose of the Articles of Organization

The primary and most obvious purpose of an LLC's Articles of Organization is to officially form the LLC. Formal recognition by the state and attainment of the accompanying benefits of operating as an LLC is, after all, the goal. Beyond this obvious purpose of the Articles of Organization is another purpose: notice. An LLC's Articles of Organization provide notice to third parties that an entity is an LLC. The Articles of Organization also provide notice to third parties of all matters that are statutorily required to be set forth in them. In fact, in some states the Articles of Organization provide notice of all matters contained in them, even if the state's LLC law does not require the information to be included in the Articles of Organization.

You may think that the Articles of Organization do not serve much of a notice purpose and that they simply sit with the secretary of state without ever being examined by others. This is untrue. For example, if your LLC is ever sued, its registered agent, as disclosed in the Articles of Organization, will be served with a summons. In all likelihood, the party suing your LLC got the registered agent's name from your

Articles of Organization. Since the Articles of Organization provide notice of the matters contained in them, it is a good idea to know what information they contain.

Note: Be diligent in preparing the Articles of Organization to ensure that nothing in them may be considered a false statement. In some states, it is a criminal misdemeanor offense to deliver a document to the secretary of state for filing when you know that it contains false information.

(b) Information in the Articles of Organization (ULLCA section 203)

The LLC statutes differ from state to state with regard to the information that must be contained in the Articles of Organization. Perhaps the only universal characteristic of LLC laws related to Articles of Organization is that all states allow the articles to contain whatever provisions the members agree to set forth for the regulation of the LLC's internal affairs.

Certain types of information, though, are required by nearly every LLC statute. Virtually every state requires the articles to include at least the bare bones information, such as the LLC's name, duration, and the name and address of its registered agent. Other states require more detailed information. For example, a state may require that the Articles of Organization include information such as the following:

(a) a statement as to whether the LLC will be managed by its members;

(b) information about the members, such as name, address, membership interest;

(c) a statement of the LLC's business purpose;

(d) disclosure of the extent to which members or managers may bind the LLC in dealings with third parties;

(e) information about the contributions made, or to be made, by members;

(f) whether the LLC may admit additional members;

(g) information about LLC finances;

(h) whether or not the LLC owns, leases, or has an interest in agricultural land, and;

(i) a statement as to the LLC's federal employer's identification number.

Anyone forming an LLC should check his or her formation state's LLC law to determine what information must be included in the Articles of Organization. Failure to include the proper information would likely be pointed out to you by the secretary of state. Nevertheless, it may simply file your incorrect articles without comment and you could run the risk of operating an LLC that fails to give notice of statutorily required information. Your LLC could still defend itself if sued, but the existence of limited liability may be in question. In addition, your LLC may not be able to file its own lawsuit because of the defective formation.

(c) Where to file

In most states, an LLC's Articles of Organization must be filed with the secretary of state. Often, a separate corporate division exits within the secretary of state which handles LLC filings. In some states, such as Arizona and New Mexico, there is a corporate commission which handles LLC filings. Again, when you read the phrase "secretary of state" in this book, remember that it refers to the central filing agency, whether that agency is in fact the secretary of state or not.

In Alabama, an LLC's Articles of Organization must be filed with the probate judge in the county of the LLC's initial registered office. In Michigan, the articles are to be filed with the Department of Commerce, Corporation and Securities Bureau.

These examples are not intended to be an exhaustive list. To determine the proper filing agency, refer to the list of LLC filing agencies for your formation state in Appendix 2 of this book. Save time by calling the necessary office prior to making your trip. Ask for directions.

When the Articles of Organization are ready to be filed, go to the necessary office with your completed Articles of Organization, hand them to the clerk, and ask that they be filed. Some states require copies to be filed along with the original. It is a good idea to ask for a file-stamped copy for your records.

(d) Who may file

No states require that the creator of an LLC have any specific professional credentials, such as a license to practice law. Typically, there is no requirement that the creator of the LLC personally appear to file the Articles of Organization. The filing may be done by anyone.

(e) Postfiling matters

After filing the Articles of Organization, take the file-stamped copy and make several copies of it. Place one copy in your business file containing documents related to your LLC, such as the Operating Agreement, notes, and forms. Consider providing all members of the LLC with a copy of the Articles of Organization so that they are aware of what information has been filed in the public records in order to form the LLC. Finally, if you are the type of person who places little faith in the ability of government employees to complete even the most simple task, you might call the secretary of state to make certain that the Articles of Organization were properly processed.

2. Drafting the Articles of Organization

You do not need to be a lawyer to draft the Articles of Organization. In fact, the LLC concept is so new that you may have difficulty locating a lawyer who has drafted an LLC Articles of Organization. In reality, there is no drafting required in the creation of an LLC Articles of Organization; very little writing needs to be done. In most states, the secretary of state can provide you with a fill-in-the-blanks form. This form tells you what information is required. If your LLC Articles of Organization include more information than is listed on the provided form, you probably need to create a document that lists the required information plus the additional information you want to add. This document is attached to the Articles of Organization.

Appendix 2 shows samples of the forms used in each state.

(a) Format

If you are using a fill-in-the-blanks form for your Articles of Organization, the format has already been decided for you. Keep in mind, though, that some states, such as Georgia, provide a sample form for LLC Articles of Organization, but the form may not be completed and filed. It is simply a sample to use in drafting your own Articles of Organization.

If no form is provided by the secretary of state, check with it to find out whether it requires any specific format.

Some state filing agencies are implementing computer systems that automatically read the information on a typed page, thereby streamlining the filing process by eliminating the need to type in the information contained in filed forms. If this is the case, format is very important. At any rate, determining whether any format idiosyncrasies exist may save you from being turned away at filing time.

Generally, a typewritten page entitled "Articles of Organization," followed by numbered paragraphs containing the necessary information, will suffice. Make certain that you date the document, provide spaces for all necessary signatures, and provide space for a notary public's signature if necessary.

(b) Necessary information

All state LLC laws set forth a listing of the minimum amount of information that must be included in an LLC Articles of Organization in order to officially form the LLC. If your local secretary of state provides a standard form for use in filing an Articles of Organization, rest assured that the form lists all necessary information required.

(c) Optional information (ULLCA section 203)

Your state's LLC law and the form (if any) provided by the secretary of state clearly state the required information that must be included in the Articles of Organization.

You are allowed to include additional information in an LLC's Articles of Organization in all states. Generally, the Articles of Organization may include any additional provisions not inconsistent with law. ULLCA section 203(b)(2) is an example of this type of provision. Maryland allows an LLC's Articles of Organization to include any provision the parties decide is relevant. The standard Articles of Organization form provided by the Connecticut secretary of state makes the fact that the form lists only the required information apparent through the following notice:

> This form constitutes only the minimum statutory requirements for filing with the secretary of state. Should you wish to include additional information, you may attach a plain sheet of 8 ½" X 11" paper to the document.

ULLCA section 203(b)(1) allows the Articles of Organization to include anything permitted to be included in the Operating Agreement. But whether or not you should include optional information is a more difficult question. Since one of the benefits of doing business as an LLC is the confidentiality that stems from not having to make business matters public, you may want to limit your Articles of Organization to the necessary information.

However, including additional information in the Articles of Organization may prove helpful. For example, if your LLC Operating Agreement provides that only LLC managers have the authority to bind the LLC in dealings with third parties, it might be a good idea to include notice of this fact in your Articles of Organization.

The procedures for including additional information in the Articles of Organization are fairly straightforward. The best course is to check with the secretary of state and find out what method it prefers. If you are not using a standard form and are drafting your own Articles of Organization, the additional information may be incorporated anywhere within the document. Include the necessary information at the beginning of the Articles of Organization so that the clerk realizes that the necessary information is present. If you are using a standard form, you probably need only attach additional sheets of paper setting forth the optional information, as suggested by the Connecticut form.

Finally, your state's LLC law may require that certain information be included in the Operating Agreement, but need not be in the Articles of Organization. If so, consider including such information only in the Operating Agreement, because it is not a public record open to inspection.

3. Amendment of the Articles of Organization (ULLCA section 204)

What if your LLC undergoes some sort of change? Perhaps you decide to change your business name or engage in a type of business not listed in your Articles of Organization. Do you need to file any new documents? In all but a few states, the answer is yes.

If you change your LLC's name or begin a new type of business, you probably need to file Amended Articles of Organization.

Fortunately, just as with the original Articles of Organization, the secretary of state usually provides a standard form that may be used to amend your Articles of Organization. Simply fill out the form with the new information and file it with the secretary of state. Be prepared to pay another filing fee. Request a file-stamped copy for your records.

Other changes may occur in your LLC, such as changes in the names and addresses of managers, or a change in the time period before the LLC is to dissolve; you may need to amend your Articles of Organization. Check the LLC law in your LLC's state of formation to learn exactly when an amendment to the Articles of Organization is required.

Besides amending the Articles of Organization from time to time, you may need to file other forms to provide information about changes. For example, if your LLC's registered agent changes or the address of your LLC's registered office changes, you will likely need to file a form with the secretary of state listing the new information. There will probably be a filing fee for updating this information.

At this point, another terminology note is in order. In some states, the LLC law allows Articles of Organization to not only be amended, but to also be restated. Restated Articles of Organization are not the same as Amended Articles of Organization. Articles of Organization are restated if there have been several amendments and, rather than have to refer to the original articles and the later amendments, a new document is created incorporating the amendments into the articles. This new document is called the Restated Articles of Organization. Usually, a filing fee must be paid in order to restate an LLC's Articles of Organization.

4. LLC name and identification (ULLCA sections 105, 106, 107)

Every state LLC law requires that you identify your business as an LLC in the firm name. Use abbreviations like "L.L.C." or the phrase "Limited Liability Company" after the firm name.

Whatever LLC identifier you choose, you must include it whenever and wherever you use your firm name. The LLC identifier must be on items such as signs, stationery, and advertising material. Identify your business as an LLC to provide notice of your business's status to all persons who deal, or may deal, with your business. Presumably, such persons then know that recourse against LLC members is limited. In some states, if you do not properly identify your LLC, managers and members may become liable for damages caused by the failure to properly identify the LLC.

Some states require LLCs to get name approval and register the LLC name. If that is the case in your state of formation, you may be able to obtain forms for name registration purposes from the secretary of state. You may not use an LLC name that is deceptively similar to another business's name. However, in some states you may use an LLC name that is similar to the name of another business if you get the consent of that business.

As a practical matter, you should check on the availability of the name you want to use for your LLC prior to drafting and filing any LLC documents. After all, it would be a big waste of time to draft all of the necessary documents only to be turned away at the time of filing because you have chosen a name that is already in use. It is also a good idea to reserve your LLC's name as soon as you learn that it is available so that no one takes that name during the time period between determining the name's availability and getting the LLC Articles of Organization filed. Usually, there is a fee charged for reserving an LLC name and, in many states, registration of a name and payment of the corresponding fee are required as part of forming an LLC.

b. THE FILING FEES

LLC filing fees vary greatly from state to state. In a few states, the fees are as low as $50. Often, these same states have no annual LLC fee and require minimal fees for later filings, such as amendments to the Articles of Organization.

In other states, the filing fees are quite high, are charged for numerous required forms, and an annual fee must also be paid. For example, in Illinois, the fee for filing an LLC Articles of Organization is $500. Illinois also requires that several other documents be filed with accompanying fees and payment of an annual renewal fee of $300. Most states fall somewhere in between these two extremes. The amount of the filing fee is listed for each state in Appendix 2 at the back of this book.

Some states view LLC filing fees as revenue generators, while other states view them as a way to recover costs associated with processing the paperwork. If you live in a state with low fees, consider yourself lucky. If you live in a state with high fees, try to remember all of the benefits associated with doing business as an LLC when it comes time to pay the fee.

c. OTHER POTENTIAL REQUIREMENTS

Typically, the filing of Articles of Organization and payment of a filing fee is enough to form an LLC. In some states, however, more is required. Usually, the clerk at the secretary of state's office in the state of formation informs you of any additional requirements. Nevertheless, do not rely on the clerk's advice. Find out about additional filing requirements on your own. Hire a lawyer or review your state's LLC law.

The additional filing requirements are many and varied. For example, in New Hampshire, a form must be filed stating that membership interests are either exempt from the securities regulation laws or have been registered in compliance with those laws. In Georgia, those who form LLCs must file a transmittal information form and name reservation certificate. In Arizona, a domestic LLC must publish three consecutive notices of filing within 60 days in a newspaper of general circulation in the county of the LLC's known place of business. In Missouri, the organizers of an LLC must state whether the LLC is to be considered a corporation for tax purposes.

Many other state-specific filing requirements exist. The thing to remember is that a little additional time spent learning the filing requirements prior to creating your LLC may prove invaluable later if its validity is challenged.

d. CHOOSING THE STATE IN WHICH TO FORM AN LLC

You don't have to organize your LLC in your state of residence. You can choose your state of organization based on the LLC law that best serves your needs. Numerous factors are involved in choosing a state of formation. These considerations include the following:

(a) How do you want your LLC to be managed? Some states vest management in the members, unless the Articles of Organization or Operating Agreement provide otherwise. Other states require appointment of managers. Texas, for example, requires that management be vested in elected managers, unless the Articles of Organization provide that management power is reserved to the members.

(b) How does the LLC law address member admission and withdrawal? If you anticipate frequent changes in LLC membership, it may be best to organize in a state that allows for easy member admission and withdrawal.

(c) Who will have power to bind the LLC? The ability of members and managers to act as agents of the LLC varies from state to state.

(d) What standard of care will be imposed on members and managers (i.e., to prevent gross negligence, intentional misconduct, or violations of the law)?

(e) What fiduciary (confidence and trust) standards will be imposed on members and managers?

(f) Will the LLC be required to secure against loss or compensate the members and managers?

(g) Will the LLC have the ability to merge with other entities?

(h) Will LLC members have the right to bring derivative actions on the LLC's behalf?

(i) Is confidentiality important to the LLC and its members?

After you have answered the above questions, review the state-by-state information in Appendix 2. You may locate a state that has more of the features you desire. One state's LLC law probably won't contain all the features you want, but with careful planning and wise, professional advice, you can determine the best state in which to form an LLC for your purposes.

4
THE OPERATING AGREEMENT

An LLC Operating Agreement is similar to a partnership agreement and to corporate bylaws, although the partnership analogy is more accurate. (See Sample #1 at the end of this chapter for a sample Operating Agreement.)

One of the hallmarks of the LLC is that it is based on freedom of contract. That is, the members should be allowed, within reasonable limits set by law, to agree to anything they want related to the nature of the LLC. This concept of freedom of contract flexes its muscle in the LLC Operating Agreement. The beauty of an LLC is that as long as members stay within the framework created by the applicable law, they may agree in the Operating Agreement to anything and everything their hearts desire.

Most LLC statutes do not have a specific section that provides that an LLC must have an Operating Agreement. However, most LLC statutes refer to an Operating Agreement, which makes it clear that its existence is part of an LLC. Your state of formation falls within this category if its LLC statute refers in various places to an Operating Agreement (ULLCA section 103), but there is no separate statute expressly stating that, for example, the members must enter into an Operating Agreement.

In a few states, such as Colorado, an Operating Agreement, either written or oral, is mandatory. Some states, however, require the Operating Agreement to be in writing. The best course is to always have a written Operating Agreement to minimize confusion over LLC operating matters such as designating managers and removing members.

a. CONTENTS OF THE OPERATING AGREEMENT

An LLC Operating Agreement may contain as much or as little as the organizers wish to include in the agreement. Typically, the Operating Agreement addresses the following:

(a) *LLC formation.* For example: the LLC name, effective date, term of existence, registered agent, and registered office.

(b) *LLC accounting and record keeping.* For example: where the records are to be maintained, whether reports will be made to members, and how the accounts will be handled.

(c) *Rights and duties of LLC members.* For example: whether members have management rights, whether a majority or unanimous vote is required to take certain action, the liability of members, and whether members are to be indemnified.

(d) *Managing members.* For example: who the managing members, if any, will be, their term of office, their authority to bind the LLC when dealing with third parties, their compensation, their standard of care, and how they may be removed. (See chapter 8 for more information.)

(e) *Contributions and capital accounts.* For example: member contributions, commitments to make contributions, maintenance of capital accounts, distribution of assets, and the sale or exchange of membership interests.

(f) *Allocations and distributions.* For example: how net profits and losses are allocated, minimum gain chargeback (allocation of income and gain to members when there is a decrease in gain related to debts that the members are not liable for), income offsets (members agree that certain expenses are to be offset against member's income), interim distributions (a member can realize tax savings by taking additional income near the end of a taxable year so income for the coming year is reduced), and limitations on distributions (provisions that can limit distribution amounts).

(g) *Taxes.* For example: who may make tax elections for the LLC, designation of a tax-matters partner, and the LLC method of accounting.

(h) *Disposition of membership interests.* For example: the terms under which a member may dispose of a membership interest and the effect of a noncomplying membership interest disposition.

(i) *Dissociation of a member.* For example: when a member ceases to be a part of the LLC, such as withdrawal, bankruptcy, death, termination of a trust, or dissolution, and the rights of dissociating members.

(j) *Admission of assignees and additional members.* For example: the rights of members who obtain their interests through *assignment*, the terms under which assignee members will gain full membership rights, membership interest transfers that may occur without consent of the other members, and capital contributions of additional members.

(k) *Dissolution.* For example: the events which will cause dissolution of the LLC, such as the end of the term of its existence, the unanimous written consent of members, or dissociation of managing members. This portion may also address the winding up of business affairs, the distribution of assets to members upon dissolution, and the obtaining of a Certificate of Dissolution.

(l) *Changes to the Operating Agreement.* For example: the terms under which the Operating Agreement may be changed, such as by unanimous or majority vote of members or managers.

(m) *Other provisions.* For example: a statement that the Operating Agreement is the *entire agreement* of the members, and that the Operating Agreement is not entered into for the benefit of third parties or creditors.

b. SIGNATURE REQUIREMENTS

Most LLC laws do not require that the Operating Agreement be signed by all members, but they typically recommend that it "should" be signed by all members. All members should sign the Operating Agreement so that privity of contract exists. That is, all members are bound by the same contract.

In some states, the LLC law requires all members to adopt and approve of the Operating Agreement, but does not require that all members sign the agreement. Obviously, difficulties may arise in proving that a member adopted and approved of an Operating Agreement if that member did not sign it. Furthermore, some states require that all members sign the Operating Agreement. Therefore, the best course is for all members to sign the Operating Agreement.

c. CHANGING THE OPERATING AGREEMENT

The Operating Agreement should explain how it may be changed. Several options exist, depending on whether the organizers want members, managers, or both, to decide on changes to the Operating Agreement, and whether the vote is to be unanimous or a majority.

To make changes to the Operating Agreement difficult, insert a provision that requires the members to unanimously agree to the change. At the other end of the spectrum would be a provision allowing a majority of the managers to change the Operating Agreement.

In many states, if the Operating Agreement does not explain how changes can be made, the members must unanimously agree to a change. If changes are contemplated in an LLC Operating Agreement, a qualified tax adviser or lawyer should be consulted to determine whether the change has any tax ramifications.

SAMPLE #1
OPERATING AGREEMENT

OPERATING AGREEMENT

of

_____, a Limited Liability Company

SECTION I

DEFINITIONS

Unless the context clearly indicates otherwise, the terms used in this Operating Agreement shall have the following meanings:

1. Act: The [name of state] Limited Liability Company Act.
2. Additional member: A member other than an initial member or a substitute member.
3. Admission agreement: The agreement between an additional member and the company.
4. Articles: The Articles of Organization of the company.
5. Assignee: A transferee of a membership interest who has not been admitted as a substitute member.
6. Bankrupt member: A member who has become the subject of an Order for Relief under the United States Bankruptcy Code.
7. Business day: A day other than: 1) Saturday; 2) Sunday, or; 3) any legal holiday observed by the state.
8. Capital contribution: A member's contribution of, or obligation to contribute, property or services.
9. Code: The Internal Revenue Code of 1986.
10. Commitment: The capital contributions that a member is obligated to make.
11. Company: The [name of company] limited liability company and any successor limited liability company.
12. Contributing members: Those members making contributions as a result of the failure of a delinquent member to make required contributions.
13. Default interest rate: The legal rate plus 3%.
14. Delinquent member: A member who has failed to meet a commitment.
15. Distribution: A transfer of property to a member on account of a membership interest.

Note: This is a sample Operating Agreement for a manager-managed LLC, and is provided only as a guide. It should not be used "as is" because many of the provisions may affect the tax status, validity, and general rights, duties, and obligations of the LLC and its members. Also, each state's LLC law is different, so no single Operating Agreement may safely be used in all states. A lawyer's advice should be sought before entering into an LLC Operating Agreement.

SAMPLE #1 — Continued

16. Disposition (dispose): Any sale, assignment, transfer, exchange, mortgage, pledge, grant, or other transfer.

17. Dissociation: Any action which causes a person to cease to be a member.

18. Dissolution event: An event which will result in the dissolution of the Company unless the members agree to the contrary.

19. Effective date: _____, 199-.

20. Immediate family: A member's immediate family includes the member's spouse, children (including natural, adopted, and stepchildren), grandchildren, and parents.

21. Initial capital contribution: The capital contribution agreed to be made by the initial members.

22. Initial members: Those persons identified on Exhibit A attached to this Operating Agreement who have executed the Operating Agreement.

23. Management right: A member's right to participate in company management, including the rights to information and to consent to company actions.

24. Member: An initial member, substituted member, or additional member, and, unless the context expressly indicates to the contrary, managing members and assignees.

25. Member nonrecourse liability: Any company liability to the extent the liability is nonrecourse under state law, and on which a member or related person bears the economic risk of loss under §1.752-2 of the code.

26. Membership interest: A member's right to distributions (liquidating or otherwise) and allocations of the profits, losses, gains, deductions, and credits of the company.

27. Net losses: Company losses and deductions determined in accordance with accounting principles consistently applied from year to year and as reported separately or in the aggregate on the company's federal income tax return.

28. Net profits: Company income and gains determined in accordance with accounting principles consistently applied from year to year and as reported on the Company federal income tax return.

29. Nonrecourse liabilities: Company nonrecourse liabilities and member nonrecourse liabilities.

30. Notice: Notice shall be in writing. Notice to the company shall be considered given when mailed by first class mail, postage prepaid, addressed to any managing member in care of the company at the address of principal office. Notice to a member shall be considered given when mailed by first class mail, postage prepaid, addressed to the member at the member's address as reflected in the Operating Agreement unless the member has given the company a notice of a different address.

31. Operating Agreement: This Operating Agreement, including all subsequent agreements and amendments adopted in accordance with the Operating Agreement and the act.

SAMPLE #1 — Continued

32. Organization: A person other than a natural person. Organization includes, without limitation, any type of corporation, any type of partnership, joint ventures, limited liability companies, and unincorporated associations. Organization does not include joint tenancies and tenancies by the entirety.

33. Organization expenses: The expenses incurred in the organization of the company including the costs of preparation of the Operating Agreement and articles.

34. Proceeding: Any judicial or administrative trial, hearing, or other activity, civil, criminal, or investigative, the result of which may result in entry of a judgment, order, decree, or other determination that is binding upon the company or a member.

35. Property: Any property, real or personal, tangible or intangible, including money and any legal or equitable interest in such property. Services and promises to perform services in the future are not property.

36. Permitted transferee: The member's immediate family, or an organization controlled by a member or by the member's immediate family.

37. Person: An individual, trust, estate, or any incorporated or unincorporated organization permitted to be a member of a limited liability company under the laws of the state.

38. Regulations: Except where the context indicates otherwise, the regulations of the department of the treasury under the code.

39. Related person: A person having a relationship to a member that is described in §1.752-4(b) of the regulations.

40. Sharing ratio: The fraction (expressed as a percentage), the numerator of which is the total of the member's capital account and the denominator of which is the total of all capital accounts of all members and assignees.

41. Substitute member: An assignee who has been admitted to all of the rights of membership pursuant to the Operating Agreement.

42. Taxable year: The taxable year of the company as determined pursuant to §706 of the code.

SECTION II
FORMATION

1. Organization: The members hereby organize the company as a limited liability company pursuant to the provisions of the act.

2. Agreement: In consideration of the mutual covenants herein contained, and for other good and valuable consideration, the receipt and sufficiency of which is hereby acknowledged, the members execute this Operating Agreement. The members intend that the Operating Agreement shall be the sole source of agreement of the parties. To the extent any provision of the Operating Agreement is prohibited or ineffective under the act, the Operating Agreement shall be considered amended to the smallest degree possible in

SAMPLE #1 — Continued

order to make the agreement effective under the act. In the event the act is subsequently amended or interpreted in such a way to make invalid any provision of the Operating Agreement, such invalidity shall not affect the remaining valid provisions of the Operating Agreement.

3. Name: The name of the company is _____ Limited Liability Company. All company business shall be conducted under that name.

4. Effective date: The Operating Agreement shall become effective upon its filing with and acceptance by the secretary of state.

5. Term: The company shall be dissolved and its affairs wound up in accordance with the act and the Operating Agreement on _____, 199-, unless the term is extended by amendment to the Operating Agreement and the Articles of Organization, or the company is dissolved and its affairs wound up before that date.

6. Registered agent and office: The registered agent for the service of process and the registered office shall be that person and location reflected in the articles as filed with the secretary of state. The managing members may change the registered agent or office through appropriate filings with the secretary of state. If the registered agent ceases to act as such for any reason or the registered office shall change, the managing members shall promptly designate a replacement registered agent or file a notice of change of address as the case may be. If the managing members shall fail to designate a replacement registered agent or change of address of the registered office, any member may designate a replacement registered agent or file a notice of change of address.

7. Principal office: The principal office of the company shall be located at _____

SECTION III
NATURE OF BUSINESS

The company may engage in any lawful business permitted by the act or the law of any jurisdiction in which the company may do business. The company shall have the authority to do all things necessary or convenient to accomplish its purpose and operate its business. The company exists only for the purpose specified, and may not conduct any other business without the written consent of the members.

SECTION IV
ACCOUNTING AND RECORDS

1. Records to be maintained: The company shall maintain the following records at the principal office:

    a) A current list of the full name and last known business address of each member;

    b) A copy of the Articles of Organization and all amendments thereto, together with executed copies of any powers of attorney pursuant to which any articles have been executed;

SAMPLE #1 — Continued

- c) Copies of the company's federal, foreign, state, and local income tax returns and reports, if any, for the three most recent years;
- d) Copies of the Operating Agreement including all amendments thereto;
- e) Any company financial statements for the three most recent years;
- f) A writing or retrievable computer data setting forth the following:
  - i) the amount of cash and a description and statement of the agreed value of the other property or services contributed by each member and which each member has agreed to contribute;
  - ii) the times at which or events on the happening of which any additional commitments agreed to be made by each member are to be made;
  - iii) a member's right to receive, or of the company to make, distributions, including a return of all or any part of the member's capital contribution; and
  - iv) the company dissolution events.
2. Reports to members: The managing members shall provide all members with the information returns required by the code and the laws of any state.
3. Accounts: The managing members shall maintain a record of capital accounts for each member.

SECTION V
NAMES AND ADDRESSES OF MEMBERS

The names and addresses of the initial members are as reflected on Exhibit A* attached to this Operating Agreement.

SECTION VI
RIGHTS AND DUTIES OF MEMBERS

1. Management rights: All members (other than assignees) who have not dissociated shall be entitled to vote on any matter submitted to a vote of the members. The following actions require the consent of a majority of the members:
   - a) Amendment of the Operating Agreement
   - b) Admission of assignees to management rights
   - c) Continuation of the company after a dissolution event
2. Majority: Whenever any matter is required or allowed to be approved by a majority of the members, such matter shall be considered approved if consented to, either in writing or at a meeting of the members, by members having sharing ratios in excess of one half

---

* **Note:** The list of members and their addresses need not be an elaborate document. Simply type "Exhibit A" at the top of a piece of paper. Underneath, type the names and addresses of the members. Attach Exhibit A as the last page of the Operating Agreement. It need not be signed.

SAMPLE #1 — Continued

of the sharing ratios of all the members entitled to vote. Assignees are not considered to be entitled to vote for purposes of determining a majority. Dissociating members are not considered to be entitled to vote for purposes of determining a majority. If a member has disposed of an entire membership interest to an assignee, but has not been removed, the sharing ratio of the assignee shall be considered in determining a majority and the disposing member's vote or consent shall be determined by such sharing ratio.

3. Liability of members: No Member shall be liable for company liabilities. The failure of the company to observe any formalities or requirements relating to the exercise of its powers or management of its business or affairs under this agreement or the act shall not be grounds for imposing personal liability on the member or managers for company liabilities.

4. Indemnification: The company shall indemnify the members, managing members, and agents for all costs, losses, liabilities, and damages they incur in connection with company business.

5. Representations and warranties: Each member, and in the case of an organization, the person(s) executing the Operating Agreement on behalf of the organization, hereby represents and warrants to the company and each other member that:

    (a) if that member is an organization, that it is duly organized, validly existing, and in good standing under the law of its state of organization and that it has full power to execute and agree to the obligations in this Operating Agreement;

    (b) that the member is acquiring its interest in the company for the member's own account as an investment and without an intent to distribute the interest;

    (c) the member acknowledges that the interests have not been registered under the Securities Act of 1933 or any state securities laws, and may not be resold or transferred by the member without appropriate registration or the availability of an exemption from such requirements.

6. Conflicts of interest

    6.1 Members and managing members shall be entitled to personally enter into transactions that may be considered to be in competition with the company. Members and managing members shall also be entitled to personally enter into a business opportunity that may have benefited the company. Notwithstanding the foregoing, members shall:

    a) Account to the company and hold as trustee for it any property, profit, or benefit derived by the member, without the consent of the other members in the conduct and winding up of the company business.

    b) Account to the company and hold as trustee for it any property, profit, or benefit derived by the member, without the consent of the other members from a use or appropriation by the member of company property, including information developed exclusively for the company and opportunities expressly offered to the company.

    6.2 A member or managing member does not violate a duty or obligation to the company merely because the member's conduct furthers the member's own interest. A member may lend

SAMPLE #1 — Continued

money to and transact other business with the company. The rights and obligations of a member who lends money to or transacts business with the company are the same as those of a person who is not a member. No transaction with the company shall be voidable solely because a member has a direct or indirect interest in the transaction if:

    a) the transaction is fair to the company, or

    b) the disinterested managing members or members know the material facts of the transaction and authorize or ratify it.

SECTION VII
MANAGING MEMBERS

1. Original managing members: The ordinary and usual decisions concerning the business affairs of the company shall be made by the managing members. There shall be three managing members who must be members of the company. The initial managing members shall be the following:

   _____

   _____

   _____

2. Term of office as managing member: No managing member shall have any contractual right to such position. Each managing member shall serve until the earliest of:

       a) the dissociation of such managing member, or

       b) removal of such managing member.

3. Authority of members to bind the company: The members hereby agree that only the managing members and authorized agents of the company shall have the authority to bind the company. No member other than a managing member shall take any action to bind the company, and shall indemnify the company for any costs or damages incurred by the company as a result of the unauthorized action of such member. Each managing member has the power, on behalf of the company, to do all things necessary or convenient to carry out the business and affairs of the company, including, without limitation:

   a) institution, prosecution, and defense of any proceeding in the company's name

   b) purchase, receipt, lease, sale, conveyance, pledge, exchange, disposition, or other transaction dealing with property, wherever located

   c) entering into contracts and guaranties; incurring of liabilities, borrowing money, issuance of notes, bonds, and other obligations and the securing of any of its obligations by mortgage or pledge of any of its property or income

   d) lending money, investment, and reinvestment of the company's funds, and receipt and holding of property as security for repayment, including without limitation, the loaning of money to, and otherwise helping members, officers, employees, and agents

SAMPLE #1 — Continued

      e) conducting the company's business, the establishment of company offices, and the exercise of the powers of the company within or without the state

      f) appointment of employees and agents of the company, the defining of their duties, and the establishment of their compensation

      g) payment of pensions and establishment of pension plans, pension trusts, profit sharing plans, and benefit and incentive plans for all or any of the current or former members, employees, and agents of the company

      h) making donations to the public welfare or for religious, charitable, scientific, literary, or educational purposes

      i) payment of compensation to any members and employees on account of services previously rendered to the company, whether or not an agreement to pay such compensation was made before such services were rendered

      j) purchase of insurance on the life of any member or employee for the benefit of the company

      k) participation in partnership agreements, joint ventures, or other associations of any kind

      l) indemnification of members or any other person

4. Actions of the managing members: Each managing member has the power to bind the company as provided in this section. Any difference arising as to any matter within the authority of the managing members shall be decided by a majority in number (and not a majority as defined in section VI) of the managing members. No act of a member in contravention of such determination shall bind the company to persons having knowledge of such determination. Notwithstanding such determination, the act of a managing member for the purpose of apparently carrying on in the usual way the business or affairs of the company, including the exercise of the authority indicated in this section, shall bind the company and no person dealing with the company shall have any obligation to inquire into the power or authority of the managing member acting on behalf of the company.

5. Compensation of managing member: Each managing member shall be reimbursed for all reasonable expenses incurred in managing the company and shall be entitled to compensation in an amount to be determined by the affirmative vote of a majority of the members.

6. Managing members' standard of care: A managing member's duty of care in the discharge of his or her duties to the company and the other members is limited to refraining from engaging in grossly negligent or reckless conduct, intentional misconduct, or a knowing violation of law. In discharging his or her duties, a managing member shall be fully protected in relying in good faith upon the records required to be maintained by the company and upon such information, opinions, reports, or statements by any of its other managing members, members, or agents, or by any other person, as to matters the managing member reasonably believes are within such other person's professional or expert competence.

SAMPLE #1 — Continued

7. Removal of managing member: A managing member may be removed by the affirmative vote of a majority of the members.

SECTION VIII
CONTRIBUTIONS AND CAPITAL ACCOUNTS

1. Initial contributions: Each initial member shall make the capital contribution described for that member on Exhibit A and shall perform that member's commitment. If no time for contribution is specified, the capital contributions shall be made upon the filing of the Articles of Organization with the secretary of state. The value of the capital contributions shall be as set forth on Exhibit A. No interest shall accrue on any capital contribution except as provided in this Operating Agreement. Each additional member shall make the initial capital contribution described in the Admission Agreement. The value of the additional member's initial capital contribution and the time for making such contribution shall be set forth in the Admission Agreement.

2. Additional contributions: The managing members may determine that additional contributions are needed to enable the company to conduct its business. Upon making such a determination, the managing members shall give notice to all members in writing at least ten business days prior to the date on which such contribution is due. Such notice shall set forth the amount of additional contribution needed, the purpose for which the contribution is needed, and the date by which the members should contribute. Each member shall be entitled to contribute a proportionate share of such additional contribution. Except to the extent of a member's unpaid commitment, no member shall be obligated to make any such additional contributions.

3. Enforcement of commitments: A member who fails to perform a commitment shall be considered a delinquent member. The managing members shall give delinquent members notice of a failure to meet a commitment. If the delinquent member fails to perform the commitment within ten business days of the giving of the notice, the managing members may take such action as authorized by the Operating Agreement, including court action. The managing members may elect to allow the other members to contribute the amount of the commitment in proportion to such other members' sharing ratios. Members who so contribute (contributing members) shall be entitled to treat the amount contributed as a loan from the contributing members bearing interest at the default interest rate secured by the delinquent member's interest in the company. Contributing members shall be entitled to all distributions to which the delinquent member would have been entitled until the loan, with interest, is repaid in full. No commitment or other obligation to make an additional contribution may be enforced by a creditor of the company unless the member expressly consents to such enforcement.

4. Maintenance of capital accounts: The company shall establish and maintain capital accounts for each member. Each member's capital account shall be increased by:

SAMPLE #1 — Continued

>> (1) the amount of any money actually contributed by the member to the capital of the company,
>
>> (2) the fair market value of any property contributed, as determined by the company and the contributing member at arm's length at the time of contribution, and
>
>> (3) the member's share of net profits and of any separately allocated items of income or gain, except adjustments of the code (including any unrealized gain and income from accounts receivable allocated to the member to reflect the difference between the book value and tax basis of assets contributed by the member).
>
> Each member's capital account shall be decreased by:
>
>> (1) the amount of any money distributed to the member,
>
>> (2) the fair market value of any property distributed to the member, and
>
>> (3) the member's share of the losses and of any separately allocated items of deduction or loss (including any loss or deduction allocated to the member to reflect the difference between the book value and the basis of assets contributed by the member).
>
> 5. Distribution of assets: If the company distributes any of its assets in kind to a member, the capital account of each member shall be adjusted to account for that member's allocable share of the net profits or net losses that would have been realized by the company had it sold the distributed assets at their fair market values as of the date of the in-kind distribution.
>
> 6. Sale or exchange of interest: In the event of a sale or exchange of some or all of a member's interest in the company, the capital account of the transferring member shall become the capital account of the assignee, to the extent it relates to the portion of the interest transferred.
>
> 7. Compliance with section 704(b) of the code: The company's maintenance of capital accounts is intended and shall be construed to cause allocations of profits, losses, income, gains, and credit to have substantial economic effect under the regulations promulgated under §704(b) of the code.
>
> ### SECTION IX
> ### ALLOCATIONS AND DISTRIBUTIONS
>
> 1. Allocations of net profits and net losses from operations: Except as may be required by §704(c) of the code, net profits, net losses, and other items of income, gain, loss, deduction, and credit shall be apportioned among the members in proportion to their sharing ratios.
>
> 2. Interim distribution: The managing members shall determine, from time to time in their reasonable judgment, to what extent the company's cash on hand exceeds the current and anticipated needs, including, without limitation, operating expenses, debt service, acquisitions, reserves, and mandatory distributions, if any. The managing members may make distributions from such excess to the members in accordance with their sharing

SAMPLE #1 — Continued

ratios. Such distributions shall be in cash or property (which need not be distributed proportionately) or partly in both.

SECTION X
TAXES

1. Elections: The managing members may make any tax elections for the company allowed under the code or the tax laws of any state.

2. Taxes of taxing jurisdictions: To the extent that the laws of any taxing jurisdiction require, each member requested to do so by the managing members will submit an agreement indicating that the member will make timely income tax payments to the taxing jurisdiction. If the member fails to provide such agreement, the company may withhold and pay over to such taxing jurisdiction the amount of tax, penalty, and interest determined under the laws of the taxing jurisdiction with respect to such income. Any such payments with respect to the income of a member shall be treated as a distribution. The managing members may, where permitted by the rules of any taxing jurisdiction, file a composite, combined, or aggregate tax return reflecting the income of the company and pay the tax, interest, and penalties of some or all of the members on such income to the taxing jurisdiction. The company shall inform the members of the amount of such company tax, interest, and penalties so paid.

3. Tax matters partner: The managing members shall designate one of their number as the company tax matters partner. If there are no managing members eligible to act as tax matters partner, the managing members shall designate any other member as the company tax matters partner. Any member designated as tax matters partner shall take such action as may be necessary to cause each other member to become a notice partner within the meaning of §6223 of the code. Any member who is designated tax matters partner may not take any action contemplated by §§6222 through 6232 of the code without the consent of the managing members.

4. Cash method of accounting: The records of the company shall be maintained on a cash receipts and disbursements method of accounting.

SECTION XI
DISPOSITION OF MEMBERSHIP INTERESTS

1. Disposition: Any member may dispose of all or a portion of his or her membership interest upon compliance with this section. No membership interest shall be disposed of:

    (a) if such disposition, alone or when combined with other transactions, would result in a termination of the company within the meaning of §708 of the code;

    (b) without a legal opinion from a licensed lawyer satisfactory to the managing members that such assignment is subject to an effective registration under, or

SAMPLE #1 — Continued

exempt from the registration requirements of, the applicable state and federal securities laws;

(c) unless and until the company receives from the assignee the information and agreements that the managing members may reasonably require, including, but not limited to, any taxpayer identification number and any agreement that may be required by any taxing jurisdiction.

2. Dispositions not in compliance with this section void: Any attempted disposition of a membership interest, or any part thereof, not in compliance with this section is null and void from the date the attempted disposition occurred.

SECTION XII
DISSOCIATION OF A MEMBER

1. Dissociation: A person shall cease to be a member upon the happening of any of the following events:

    (a) the withdrawal of a member with the consent of a majority of the remaining members prior to _____, 199-;

    (b) the bankruptcy of a member;

    (c) in the case of a member who is a natural person, the death of the member or the entry of an order by a court of competent jurisdiction that the member is incompetent to manage the member's person or estate;

    (d) in the case of a member who is acting as a member by virtue of being a trustee of a trust, the termination of the trust (but not merely the substitution of a new trustee);

    (e) in the case of a member that is a separate organization other than a corporation, the dissolution and commencement of winding up of the separate organization;

    (f) in the case of a member that is a corporation, the filing of a Certificate of Dissolution, or its equivalent, for the corporation or the revocation of its charter, or

    (g) in the case of an estate, the distribution by the fiduciary of the estate's entire interest in the limited liability company.

2. Rights of dissociating member: In the event any member dissociates prior to the expiration of the term:

    (a) if the dissociation causes a dissolution and winding up of the company, the member shall be entitled to participate in the winding up of the company to the same extent as any other member except that any distribution to which the member would have been entitled shall be reduced by the damages sustained by the company as a result of the dissolution and winding up;

    (b) if the dissociation does not cause a dissolution and winding up of the company, the member shall be entitled to an amount equal to the value of the member's membership interest in the company, to be paid within six months of the date of dissociation. If the dissociation is other than as a result of the death or incompetence of the member, the managing members may pay the value of the member's membership interest in the company out over a period not to exceed five years, provided that the dissociating member shall be entitled to participate as an assignee in the company until the value of such interest (plus interest at the default interest rate) is paid in full. The value of the member's membership interest shall include the amount of any distributions to which the member is entitled under the Operating Agreement and the fair value of the member's membership interest as of the date of dissociation based upon the member's right to share in distributions from the company reduced by any damages sustained by the company as a result of the member's dissociation.

SECTION XIII
ADMISSION OF ASSIGNEES AND ADDITIONAL MEMBERS

1. Rights of assignees: The assignee of a membership interest has no right to participate in the management of the business and affairs of the company or to become a member. The assignee is only entitled to receive the distributions and return of capital, and to be allocated the net profits and net losses attributable the membership interest.

2. Admission of substitute members: An assignee of a membership interest shall be admitted as a substitute member and admitted to all the rights of the member who initially assigned the membership interest only with the approval of all the managing members and a majority of the members. The managing members may grant or withhold the approval of such admission. Substitute members have all the rights and powers and are subject to all the restrictions and liabilities of the member originally assigning the membership interest. The admission of a substitute member, without more, shall not release the member originally assigning the membership interest from any liability to company that may have existed prior to the approval.

3. Admission of permitted transferees: The membership interest of any member shall be transferable without the consent of the managing members or any of the members if (i) the transfer occurs by reason of or incident to the death, dissolution, divorce, liquidation, merger, or termination of the transferee member, and (ii) the transferee is a permitted transferee.

4. Admission of additional members: The managing members may permit the admission of additional members and determine the capital contributions of such members.

SECTION XIV
DISSOLUTION AND WINDING UP

1. Dissolution: The company shall be dissolved and its affairs wound up, upon the occurrence of any of the following events:

SAMPLE #1 — Continued

    (a) the expiration of the company term, unless the business of the company is continued with the consent of a majority of the members

    (b) the unanimous written consent of all of the members

2. Effect of dissolution: Upon dissolution, the company shall cease carrying on company business, but the company continues in existence until the winding up of its affairs is completed and a Certificate of Dissolution is issued by the secretary of state.

3. Distribution of assets on dissolution: Upon the winding up of the company, the company property shall be distributed to:

    (a) Creditors, including members who are creditors, to the extent allowed by law, in satisfaction of company liabilities

    (b) Members in accordance with positive capital account balances taking into account all capital account adjustments for the company's taxable year in which the liquidation occurs. Liquidation proceeds shall be paid within 60 days of the end of the company's taxable year or, if later, within 90 days after the date of liquidation. Such distributions shall be in cash or property (which need not be distributed proportionately) or partly in both, as determined by the managing members.

4. Winding up and Certificate of Dissolution: The winding up of the company shall be completed when all debts, liabilities, and obligations of the company have been paid or reasonably adequate provision therefore has been made, and all of the remaining property and assets of the company have been distributed to the members. Upon the completion of winding up of the company, a Certificate of Dissolution shall be delivered to the secretary of state for filing. The Certificate of Dissolution shall set forth the information required by the act.

SECTION XV
AMENDMENT

1. Operating Agreement may be modified: The Operating Agreement may be modified as provided in this section. No member or managing member shall have any vested right in the Operating Agreement.

2. Amendment or modification of Operating Agreement: The Operating Agreement may be amended or modified only by a written instrument adopted by the managing members and executed by a majority of the members.

SECTION XVI
MISCELLANEOUS PROVISIONS

1. Entire agreement: The Operating Agreement represents the entire agreement among all the members and between the members and the company.

2. Rights of creditors and third parties under Operating Agreement: The Operating Agreement is entered into among the company and the members for the exclusive benefit

SAMPLE #1 — Continued

of the company, its members, and their successors and assignees. The Operating Agreement is expressly not intended to be for the benefit of any creditor of the company or any other person. No such creditor or third party shall have any rights under the Operating Agreement or any agreement between the company and any member with respect to any capital contribution or otherwise.

IN WITNESS WHEREOF, we have hereunto set out our signatures on the date set forth beside our names.

_____   _____
Signature   Date

_____   _____
Signature   Date

_____   _____
Signature   Date

_____   _____
Signature   Date

5
CONVERTING AN EXISTING BUSINESS INTO AN LLC

a. CONVERTING A PARTNERSHIP (ULLCA SECTIONS 902, 903)

Do not ignore the LLC form as a way of doing business just because you are presently operating your business as a partnership. It is a simple matter to convert from a partnership into an LLC. Usually, a partnership-to-LLC conversion may take place without tax consequences or the need for out-of-the-ordinary filings.

The IRS has ruled that, in general, limited partnerships and general partnerships may convert to LLC status without being subject to tax on the partnership or the partners. If you are curious about the details of the IRS rulings, you may contact the IRS and request copies of letter rulings 9029019, 9010027, and 9119029.

There are at least four ways that a partnership may convert to an LLC. The four typical ways of converting are as follows:

(a) *Modification of partnership agreement.* With this method, the partners simply modify the partnership agreement and change it into an LLC Operating Agreement. The partners then file the LLC Articles of Organization with the secretary of state. The partnership assigns the partnership assets to the LLC by executing a bill of sale. The LLC takes the assets subject to the partnership liabilities.

(b) *Exchange of interests.* With this method, the partners contribute their partnership interests to the LLC in exchange for all of the LLC's interests. After the exchange, the partnership dissolves and distributes its assets to the LLC. The LLC takes the partnership assets subject to partnership liabilities.

(c) *Dissolution.* With this method, the partnership dissolves by distributing its assets pro rata (proportionately) to the partners. The partners take the assets subject to partnership liabilities. The partners then contribute the formerly partnership assets to the LLC in exchange for the LLC interests. Once again, the LLC takes the assets subject to the partnership liabilities.

(d) *Asset contribution.* With this method, the partnership contributes assets to the LLC. The LLC takes the assets subject to partnership liabilities. In exchange the LLC transfers 99% of LLC interests in capital, profits, and losses to the partnership. The remaining 1% interest is transferred to a *dummy* third party so that the LLC meets the typical two-member requirement. Then, the partnership is dissolved and the 99% interests are distributed pro rata to the partners. The LLC then liquidates the dummy member's interest.

Even though the conversion of a general partnership into an LLC does not typically have tax consequences, scenarios do exist in which a conversion of a partnership may create a tax liability. For example, tax may be due if, in the conversion, a general partner receives a distribution in excess of his or her basis, due to a reduction in the partner's share of liabilities. This is a complicated matter that gets into the area of recourse and nonrecourse debt. When a change in the basis of a partner's interest may result from debt-related changes caused by a conversion, a tax professional should be consulted for assistance.

b. CONVERTING A CORPORATION

There are several ways that a corporation could convert into an LLC. For example, the corporation could make a liquidating distribution of assets to shareholders who would then contribute those assets to an LLC in exchange for membership interests.

Another strategy would be to merge the corporation into the LLC with the LLC surviving and the shareholders receiving LLC interests in exchange for their corporate shares. Unfortunately, converting a corporation into an LLC has tax consequences which differ depending on whether the corporation is an S corporation or a C corporation.

1. S corporation

As you may recall from chapter 2, an S corporation is a pass-through entity for tax purposes. That is, as long as the S corporation is properly formed and operated, there is no tax at the corporate level. A tax is imposed only at the shareholder level. Under both conversion routes — liquidation of assets and merger — an S corporation is required to recognize any gain on the exchange of shares that takes place as part of the conversion. In other words, if the S corporation owned, for example, real estate that had increased in value over the years, that increase in value would be a gain subject to tax. However, the tax would not be imposed at both the corporate and shareholder levels. It would be imposed only at the shareholder level. As a pass-through entity, the gain the S corporation incurred at the corporate level passes through to the shareholders.

There is, however, one exception to the rule that S corporations are taxed only at the shareholder level upon conversion to an LLC. If the corporation began as a C corporation and elected S corporation status after 1986, and its assets had appreciated, then any distribution of those assets within ten years of the election is a taxable event. Gains of this type are commonly known as built-in gains. (This applies in all states.)

2. C corporation

When a C corporation converts to an LLC, the conversion is a taxable event for both the corporation and the shareholders. If the fair market value of the corporate assets exceeds their basis (usually the cost of the property), then this excess is a gain that is subject to a corporate-level tax. Of course, if the fair market value of the property has declined, and is less than the basis, then a loss may exist at the corporate level. Losses may be carried back to offset previously taxed corporate income.

At the shareholder level, if the fair market value of the C corporation's assets exchanged for shareholder stock exceeds the stock's basis, then the shareholders have a taxable gain. If the fair market value is less than the stock's basis, then the shareholder's incur a loss. The loss will be either an ordinary loss or a capital loss, depending on the type of stock.

3. Corporate LLC conversion alternatives

Adverse tax consequences may prevent many corporations from converting to LLCs. For those who are willing to take a risk, however, there are ways to potentially convert a corporation into an LLC without the negative tax effects. One expert has suggested two possible tax-free conversion methods.

The first method is called the mirror LLC method. It is accomplished by first having the corporation's shareholders create an LLC intended to carry on the future business that the corporation would have carried on. The corporation then leases its assets to the LLC. Thereafter, business operations that the corporation would have conducted are instead conducted by the LLC. The corporation simply receives the leasing fees while winding up its remaining business affairs. The problem with such an arrangement is that the IRS could choose to ignore the lease of assets and consider the LLC transactions to be transactions of the corporation.

The second method is called the LLC freeze method. With this method, the corporation and shareholders form an LLC. The corporation provides the assets necessary for the LLC to carry on business, while the shareholders provide cash. In exchange for the assets and cash, the corporation gets preferred-shareholder-type LLC interests, and the shareholders get common-stock-type LLC interests. The purpose of this arrangement is to keep future appreciation away from the corporation and, instead, place it in the LLC.

The above explanations are simplified and do not begin to address the tax matters that are related to converting a corporation into an LLC. Many questions surround both the mirror LLC and the LLC freeze conversion methods, so the advice of professionals should be obtained before attempting either type of conversion.

6
THE BASICS OF LLC MEMBERSHIP

a. LLC MEMBERSHIP IN GENERAL

Forming an LLC is usually as simple as filing the Articles of Organization with the secretary of state and entering into an Operating Agreement with the other members of the LLC. There are two ways to acquire an LLC membership interest. The first way is for the member to be part of the formation of the LLC and enter into the Operating Agreement with the other member or members. The second way is through the transfer of an LLC membership interest from an existing member to a nonmember. When deciding whether to become an LLC member, find out what goes along with being a member.

1. What do I get? — What do I want?

If your state's LLC law is similar to the ULLCA (see Appendix 1), your LLC may be able to create membership certificates that are tangible evidence of your LLC membership interest. Of course, the creation of a piece of paper is probably not your goal in forming an LLC. It is the matters represented by that piece of paper that are important. Therefore, you should become familiar with the rights, duties, privileges, and responsibilities that go along with LLC membership.

The foundation of the LLC is freedom of contract. Within certain limits, the members may agree to the relative rights, duties, responsibilities, and contributions of each member. As a result, LLC members have the flexibility to mold membership interests into countless types of creatures that serve the individual purposes of their creators. For some LLC members, this means a membership interest providing for maximum control, participation, and contribution. For others, it means a membership interest with minimum control, participation, and contribution. Countless varieties of membership interests exist between these two extremes. Therefore, if you are asking yourself, "What do I get with my LLC membership interest?" perhaps you should instead ask yourself, "What do I want from my LLC membership interest?" The answer to this question lies, in part, in the nature of the entity that will own the membership interest. Most states place no restrictions on the type of entity that may own an LLC membership interest.

2. Who may be an LLC member?

LLC members may typically be individuals, corporations, partnerships, or other entities, such as business trusts. As a result, business firms may be able to join forces in creative ways that previously were impractical because of tax, liability, and flexibility concerns. Many creative business ventures are sure to spring up as LLCs over the coming years.

(a) Individuals

Individuals may form LLCs. In fact, individually formed LLCs may be the most common type of LLC. After all, firms that previously would have formed as partnerships will have little reason not to form as LLCs instead. In addition, firms that are already operating as partnerships will have an incentive to convert to LLC status because no tax consequences will arise and the added benefit of liability protection will be gained.

(b) Corporations

Corporations may also be LLC members. This is a significant feature because it allows corporations to join forces with other business firms on flexible terms. As a result, many business ventures that otherwise would never have gotten off the ground will get a crack at success as LLCs. Indeed, some of these ventures may not have any individual LLC members because they may be made up entirely of corporate members.

(c) Partnerships

Partnerships, whether limited or general, may be LLC members. One can imagine many scenarios in which partnerships would join forces as an LLC, or become a member in an LLC made up of individuals, corporations, and other partnerships.

(d) Other entities

Other business entities may also become LLC members. In fact, LLCs may be LLC members. Business trusts, foreign business entities, and any other business entities may become LLC members. The bottom line is that the business structure of a potential member is no impediment to the formation of an LLC.

b. ARE MULTIPLE MEMBERS NECESSARY?

Most LLC laws require or at least contemplate that an LLC be formed by more than one person. Multiple members are usually necessary. However, a few states, including Arkansas, Delaware, Georgia, Idaho, Montana, North Carolina, and Texas, allow one person to form an LLC. One-member LLCs formed under these laws may be taxed as partnerships by electing a partnership tax status on IRS Form 8832 and Form 1065.

c. THE NATURE OF AN LLC MEMBERSHIP INTEREST (ULLCA SECTION 501)

A membership interest in an LLC is personal property. The value of the personal property making up the LLC membership interest is determined by examining the economic rights that accompany the interest. It is generally said that an LLC membership interest consists of the LLC member's share of the LLC's profits and losses, together with the right to receive a distribution of the LLC's assets. This formula for calculating the personal property value of an LLC membership interest is borrowed from partnership law.

As personal property, the economic portion of an LLC membership interest is freely transferable and may be reached by creditors. Of course, LLC members have other rights, such as voting rights and the right to manage the LLC. But these noneconomic rights are not considered part of the membership interest. Furthermore, the noneconomic rights are not freely transferable by the member. The lack of free transferability of noneconomic LLC member rights is one of the features that enables LLCs to attain partnership tax status.

1. Membership contributions (ULLCA sections 401, 402)

Usually, a potential LLC member cannot expect to acquire a membership interest without making some sort of contribution to the LLC. The LLC statutes vary greatly on what may be contributed to the LLC in exchange for a membership interest. Most states allow contributions to be made in any form, typically cash, property, services, or even promises to contribute cash, property, or services. The ULLCA follows this rule.

Other states place limits on what may be contributed. For example, South Dakota's LLC law does not allow contributions to take the form of promissory notes or promises to provide future services. In New Mexico, promissory notes and promises to provide future services may be contributed only if the Operating Agreement or Articles of Organization so provide. In the area of permissible member contributions, it is once again advisable to consult the LLC law in your state of formation to determine what may be contributed in exchange for an LLC membership interest.

Keep in mind that uncertain tax issues may arise if you contribute services, or services to be performed in the future, in exchange for an LLC membership interest. The treasury regulations create the impression that there are no tax consequences when a member receives an interest in LLC profits in exchange for services. In other words, the member is not taxed on the basis of the contribution of services, but will be taxed when a distribution of profits is made. However, the tax court has held that a partner who contributes services for an interest in profits recognized income in the year the interest in profits was received. The advice of an accountant may be helpful if you are considering a contribution of services or future services in exchange for an LLC membership interest.

Be aware that in some states a written record of LLC contributions must be made and disclosed in the Articles of Organization or a separate writing. A few states require contribution disclosures in a record but do not require an additional writing. When written disclosure of member contributions is required, the member usually must sign the document disclosing the contributions. Still other states, and the ULLCA, follow the rule that no writing or record of contributions need be made.

2. Membership transfers (ULLCA section 502)

An LLC member's economic interest may be transferred by assignment. A transfer of an LLC member's economic interest does not transfer the right to manage and participate in the LLC. Usually, the member who receives the transferred LLC interest attains noneconomic rights, such as management and participation, only with the agreement of the nontransferring members. The Articles of Organization and Operating Agreement often dictate the terms under which noneconomic membership interests are acquired. The best course is to specifically address membership transfer terms in the Operating Agreement. This way, there will be no confusion over the rights of new members.

When the nontransferring members do not agree to allow the assignee of the economic membership interest to attain noneconomic rights the assignee simply stands in the shoes of the transferor. That is, the assignee receives distributions from the LLC in the same manner as the original member who assigned the economic membership interest. This type of ownership arrangement is not necessarily bad. Indeed, some assignees of LLC membership interests may prefer to own only the economic portion of the LLC membership interest. When the nontransferring members do agree to allow the assignee of the economic membership interest to attain noneconomic rights, the assignee not only gains the right to manage and control the LLC, but also becomes liable for the transferor's obligations. The transferor remains liable for his or her obligations. However, the nontransferring members and creditors may release the transferor from the obligations.

In some states, LLCs have the option of placing the admission of new members in the hands of the LLC managers. This method may be beneficial for large LLCs that anticipate potential problems if all or most members must consent to membership interest transfers. If membership transfer decisions are to be placed in the hands of the managers, the LLC Articles of Organization and Operating Agreement should specifically address the issue and spell out in detail the manner in which the transfer decisions will be made.

It may be possible for the members to agree in advance that certain persons or entities are immediately entitled to full membership rights upon transfer of an LLC interest to them. In other words, the nontransferring members do not have the power to prevent the new member from attaining full membership rights. This type of advance agreement may be especially useful for family-owned LLCs in which the principal owner of the business wants to ensure that later family members are not locked out of the management of the business.

A transfer of an existing LLC membership interest is not the only way that new members may enter an LLC. The LLC may increase its membership by adding members. There are basically three ways to provide for the admission of new members, depending on which state's statute is involved. Some states allow LLCs to add new members if the Articles of Organization so provide. Other states allow LLCs to add new members upon their compliance with the Operating Agreement or, if the Operating Agreement is silent on additional members, upon the consent of the members. The third category contains states with LLC laws that do not address the terms under which additional members may be added. In these states, it is likely that additional members may be added upon the unanimous consent of the members.

Sometimes members of an LLC do not want additional members to be added. For example, a *closely held* LLC with three members may not want to run the risk that two of the members would agree to additional members over the objection of the third member. In such a case, the Articles of Organization and Operating Agreement should both state that no additional members may be added, or, that additional members will be added only upon the unanimous consent of the original members. However, in most cases, the members will probably want to leave the door open for additional members. If so, both the Articles of Organization and Operating Agreement should spell out, in detail, the terms under which additional members may be admitted. One of the benefits of leaving the door open for additional members is that these members may provide needed capital or services to the LLC.

d. LEAVING AN LLC

It is easy to become an LLC member. One only need be an original LLC member upon formation, obtain an LLC membership interest through transfer, or become an additional member in an existing LLC. As fate may have it, though, circumstances may arise that cause a member to want to leave the LLC. There are many ways out: some easy, some difficult, some voluntary, some involuntary. Leaving an LLC is usually referred to as withdrawal or dissociation.

1. Withdrawal or dissociation (ULLCA sections 601, 602(a))

(a) Voluntary withdrawal

In every state, a member may voluntarily withdraw from the LLC. Usually, the member must give notice of withdrawal (typically six months). The LLC Operating Agreement should explain how a member may withdraw, including factors such as the length of notice required, to whom notice must be given, and the consequences of withdrawal.

(b) Agreed causes of dissociation

The state LLC statutes, like the ULLCA, typically allow members to agree on events that cause a member's dissociation from the LLC. Arranging agreed-upon events of dissociation in the Operating Agreement gives an LLC the ability to create incentives for its members to refrain from, or take, certain types of action. For example, an LLC may rely heavily on creative talent, such as artists or writers. If the quality of this talent is extremely important to the LLC, the members may want to agree that a member's failure to perform artistic or writing services to a certain standard causes dissociation. As a result, the LLC would have the ability to get rid of members who failed to perform to agreed-upon standards.

(c) Expulsion

The ULLCA expressly allows an LLC member to be expelled. Expulsion differs from agreed-upon events of dissociation. The membership can vote for expulsion after the unlawful or inappropriate behavior by the expelled member.

Under the ULLCA, the Operating Agreement may spell out the circumstances under which a member may be expelled. State LLC statutes typically do not address expulsion, although the statutes do contemplate that expulsion of a member may take place by providing that a member's expulsion dissolves an LLC. Expulsion has long been available as a means for partnerships to rid themselves of undesirable partners. Since the courts have enforced partnership expulsion agreements, it is likely that LLC expulsion agreements will also be allowed.

(d) Bankruptcy

A universal provision in LLC statutes is that an LLC member's bankruptcy is an event that causes the dissociation of the bankrupt member.

(e) Death

This one is obvious. If an LLC member dies, he or she is dissociated from the LLC.

(f) Incapacity

Incapacity is a fancy legal term for a person's lack of mental ability to carry on the day-to-day tasks needed to function meaningfully in society. If an LLC member is incapacitated or incompetent, then he or she is dissociated from the LLC.

The LLC statutes often address this condition by making the appointment of a guardian or conservator a dissociating event. This is logical, since a guardian or conservator is appointed when a person has been legally declared incompetent to handle his or her personal or financial affairs.

(g) Entity termination

The ULLCA makes termination of a member who is a business entity an event that causes dissociation. For example, if an LLC member is a corporation, and that corporation is terminated for some reason, such as failure to pay a required fee, then the corporation/member is dissociated from the LLC.

2. Wrongful dissociation (ULLCA section 602)

Under some circumstances, an LLC member acts wrongfully when leaving an LLC. If so, the member is said to have wrongfully dissociated from the LLC. A member who wrongfully withdraws from an LLC may be liable for damages and, in some states, is not entitled to a distribution of the LLC's goodwill.

Under the ULLCA, there are two ways that a member's dissociation may be considered wrongful. First, if the member's dissociation is a breach of an express provision of the Operating Agreement, then it is wrongful. Second, if the LLC is a term company (one that has a stated period of duration), then the member's dissociation is wrongful if it occurs before the LLC termination date, and the member withdraws by express will, is expelled, files bankruptcy, or, in the case of a member that is a business entity, the business entity is terminated. Consequently, an LLC member's withdrawal may be considered wrongful under the ULLCA even if the withdrawal is not a breach of the Operating Agreement.

In most states, an LLC member's withdrawal is not wrongful as long as proper notice is given and it is not a breach of the

Operating Agreement or in violation of the Articles of Organization. In a few states, the LLC Articles of Organization or Operating Agreement may prohibit member withdrawal. As a practical matter, the LLC members may want to create an incentive for members to remain in the LLC. They could do so by placing a liquidated damages clause in the Operating Agreement that applies when a member withdraws. The liquidated damages could be a substantial dollar amount that a wrongfully withdrawing member must pay.

3. What happens when an LLC member dissociates? (ULLCA section 603)

Prior to the passage of the "check the box" regulations, state laws provided for a limited life span for LLCs. This was necessary to minimize the chance that the IRS would consider LLCs formed under a particular state's law to have continuity of life and, therefore, be considered a corporation for tax purposes. This concern no longer exists and most states will likely revise their LLC laws to allow them an unlimited life span.

The LLC continuation terms should be included in the Operating Agreement and, if necessary, in the Articles of Organization. Naturally, the terms should comply with the applicable LLC statute.

Besides causing dissolution of the LLC, a member's dissociation could cause another event to occur — The need to pay the dissociating member the value of his or her interest. The obligation to pay a dissociating LLC member may be controlled by the Operating Agreement and is usually defined by each state's LLC statute. The LLC statutes use several different formulas to determine the amount the dissociating member must be paid. Some states require payment equal to the member's contributions. Other states require payment of the fair market value of the member's interest. Still others base the formula on the fair value of the member's interest.

When the LLC statute uses the term *fair value*, it probably means that the member's LLC interest must be determined by calculating the value of the LLC as an operating business, rather than at its book value (the value of the company's assets). This prevents the dissociating member from being subject to a *minority discount*. Payment of the value of a dissociating member's interest usually must be made within a specified time period. The LLC statutes generally provide six months, 30 days, or a "reasonable" time.

Payment may be in cash or *in kind*, meaning that the dissociating member may receive LLC property instead of cash. In some states, the Operating Agreement may provide that dissociating members are not entitled to in-kind payment. However, the statutes may also provide that dissociating members are not obligated to accept in-kind distributions that are disproportionate to the distributions made to other members.

There is danger in granting a dissociating member the right to refuse an in-kind payment. The danger stems from the possibility that the LLC may be forced to sell assets in order to make a cash payment. If a small LLC anticipates difficulty raising the cash needed to pay a dissociating member, it should consult an LLC lawyer to determine whether there are ways to avoid the sale of assets.

7
LIABILITY OF MEMBERS

a. THE NATURE OF AN LLC'S "LIMITED LIABILITY" (ULLCA SECTIONS 302, 303)

For years, business planners have struggled to come up with the best way to shield business owners from personal liability. A corporation could do the trick, but regular corporations are subject to double taxation. The tax problems were eliminated by S corporations, but those, too, had limitations and flexibility problems. The LLC appears to be the answer.

An LLC member's limited liability should not be considered to be an impenetrable shield against any and all liability. It is, however, a powerful shield that eliminates many of the liability concerns that have stifled business development.

Think of the liability protection provided by an LLC as an umbrella. As long as you stay under the umbrella, you won't get wet. If you step out from underneath the umbrella, you lose its protection and could get soaked. As an LLC member, when are you under the umbrella? In all states, you are protected from personal liability for the debts, obligations, and liabilities of the LLC. This is the case whether you are a member or a manager. Therefore, if your LLC borrows money from the bank and then is unable to pay the money back, the bank cannot collect the unpaid debt from you.

A similar situation exists regarding negligence. If another LLC member negligently damages another person, and you had nothing to do with that negligence, then the victim cannot recover damages from you. This is a major improvement over partnership law, which allows victims to recover from nonnegligent partners. Yet another benefit of limited liability is that the LLC may indemnify members for the costs and expenses of litigation stemming from their membership status.

Unfortunately, as the saying goes, into every life some rain must fall. After all, an umbrella is of no use in a hurricane. Take the example of a bank loan to the LLC. In many situations, a bank will not lend money to an LLC unless some or all of the members personally guarantee that the loan will be repaid. If this is done, the members who make the guarantee are personally liable for the debt. Likewise, an LLC member is not protected from liability for his or her own personal negligence. If your negligence causes damage to another person, that person may recover damages from you notwithstanding the fact that you are an LLC member.

A bank loan with an accompanying personal guarantee is often necessary to start a business, or keep one afloat, and potential liability for personal negligence is an unavoidable fact of life. Take precautions against these and other types of hurricanes to avoid putting your umbrella to the test. The following situations are avoidable with a moderate amount of planning and precaution.

Under most LLC statutes, limited liability does not exist for persons who act as LLC members prior to the actual formation of the LLC or without the LLC's authority. Because of this rule, the LLC should not transact any business before the Articles of Organization are filed. The Operating Agreement also should address what authority members have to transact business for the LLC, and members should not overstep those bounds.

Improper distributions may also result in a member's loss of limited liability. The LLC statutes generally make certain types of payments by an insolvent LLC to its members available to creditors. In other words, if an LLC is unable to pay its debts, it cannot distribute assets to members rather than using those assets to pay its creditors.

Not surprisingly, the IRS may not always bow to an LLC member's limited liability. For example, the Internal Revenue Code may make some members personally liable for unpaid withholding taxes, and an LLC's limited liability does not eliminate this personal liability. Also, members are liable for agreed-upon contributions to the LLC. In some states, if a creditor relies upon a member's agreement to contribute to the LLC, and the contribution is not made, the creditor may be able to enforce the contributions agreement. In other states, the member must have agreed to the third-party enforceability of the contribution agreement.

A contributions agreement is an agreement between the LLC members that each will contribute certain property or services to the LLC. This agreement is usually made prior to the formation of the LLC. The best way to enter into a contributions agreement is to include a section in the Operating Agreement describing each member's obligation to contribute property or services. It does not need to be in writing or witnessed, but an oral contributions agreement is difficult to enforce.

Finally, LLC members may be personally liable if circumstances exist which justify *piercing the LLC veil*. This exception to an LLC's limited liability is significant enough — and uncertain enough — to merit separate consideration.

b. PIERCING THE LLC VEIL

As corporations developed, people began to manipulate and abuse the liability protection provided. Sometimes it was intentional, and other times it was not. For example, if a group of people wanted to start a speculative business enterprise, they could form a corporation, invest little or no money in that corporation, and then convince an investor to loan them money. If the corporation failed, it had no assets for the investor to obtain repayment for the loan. The investor lost money, while the principals of the corporation walked away unscathed.

Because of circumstances like this and other inequities, courts realized that it was not always fair to allow a corporate shareholder the benefit of limited liability merely because the shareholder went through the motions of filing the necessary documents to form a corporation. Courts began to rule that under some circumstances the corporation was just a veil which served to protect a person who should not be entitled to corporate limited liability. If this was the case, the courts pierced the corporate veil, and imposed personal liability on the shareholder.

Whether or not a corporate veil should be pierced is one of the most frequently litigated questions in corporate law. Consequently, veil-piercing issues will likely arise frequently in the context of LLCs. Because LLC laws are still in the infancy stage, courts have not yet had an opportunity to rule on veil piercing questions in the LLC context. This causes some uncertainty.

However, in some states, the question has been answered by the LLC statute. The Colorado LLC statute, for example, expressly recognizes that the LLC veil may be pierced and directs courts to apply

Colorado corporate veil piercing cases to Colorado LLCs.

The legal experts who analyze LLC laws generally agree that LLC members should be subject to veil piercing in the same manner as corporate shareholders. Therefore, when you operate your LLC, avoid conduct that could result in the piercing of your LLC veil.

Protect yourself. Become thoroughly familiar with the situations in which corporate veils have been pierced, and then avoid similar conduct. Generally, there are five areas of concern: inseparability, undercapitalization, illegal purpose, lack of compliance with formalities, and equity and justice.

1. Inseparability

LLCs are formed as an entity that is separate and distinct from its members. In a sense, an LLC is another person. It may be sued. It may sue. It may borrow money. It may lease office space. It won't make you coffee in the morning or tie your shoes, but you get the picture.

If the members take action that causes the LLC's separate identity to disappear, the LLC veil may be pierced and the members subjected to personal liability. What makes an LLC and its members inseparable? If the members form an LLC, and then, rather than use the LLC to conduct business, they carry on business personally as if no LLC existed, the LLC and its members are considered inseparable. Also, a lack of separate bank accounts, no property owned separately by the LLC, and no business transactions conducted separately by the LLC are all examples of things that could cause the LLC and its members to be considered inseparable.

In the corporate veil piercing cases, this type of inseparability is sometimes referred to as a corporate alter ego. In other words, the corporation/LLC has a formal separate existence, but for practical purposes the shareholder/member carries on business the same as if no corporation or LLC existed.

2. Undercapitalization

As a separate and distinct entity, an LLC is expected to own assets and have the financial capacity to adequately carry on the LLC business. It is expected to be adequately capitalized.

If the LLC has little or no assets or cash, it may be considered to be undercapitalized. The corporate veil piercing cases recognize undercapitalization as a reason for piercing the corporate veil. As noted above, the reason for allowing veil piercing based on undercapitalization is that investors may rely on the ability of the LLC to meet its financial obligations. When the LLC is simply a shell without financial means, investors and creditors cannot be repaid, and fairness dictates that the members be personally responsible for payment.

3. Illegal purpose

This one is obvious. If you set up an LLC or corporation to defraud senior citizens of their social security checks, you can expect to be personally liable for repayment when caught. Expect the same for any other LLC or corporation with an illegal purpose.

4. Lack of compliance with formalities

As you may recall from chapter 3, formalities must be complied with in order to create an LLC. Articles of Organization must be filed. An Operating Agreement must be created. A name must be chosen and, in some states, registered. In the same vein, there are other formalities that must be complied with in operating an LLC. Some states require the filing of annual reports and the payment of annual fees. Internal LLC records must be kept. If these formalities are not complied with, the LLC may not be recognized and the members may be subject to personal liability.

Fortunately, because there are fewer formalities that LLCs must comply with compared to corporations, it is less likely that a lack of compliance with formalities will be a ground for piercing the LLC veil.

5. Equity and justice

Occasionally, courts are faced with corporate veil-piercing cases that are pegs that will not fit into any of the above holes. The corporation may lack some separate characteristics, but perhaps it has enough to satisfy the court that it is indeed separate. Similarly, the corporation's capital may be small, but the corporation cannot be characterized as undercapitalized. Perhaps the corporation fails to comply with a few formalities, but there is no glaring reason not to recognize its existence. Yet, despite these facts, the court may believe that the circumstances, nonetheless, justify piercing the corporate veil.

In such cases, some courts simply pierce the corporate veil because doing so is required by equity and justice. Unfortunately, it is difficult to predict when, and for what reason, a court will pierce a veil based on equity and justice. However, if the corporation/LLC conducts business in a proper manner, and the other four reasons for piercing the veil clearly do not apply, the corporate/LLC veil will probably not be pierced.

Only the LLC member or members who cause the veil piercing will be subjected to personal liability. Therefore, members who are simply passive investors run only a slight risk of being subject to personal liability on a veil-piercing theory.

c. HOW TO AVOID HAVING THE LLC VEIL PIERCED

Here are ways to lessen the possibility that your LLC's veil will be pierced. To avoid personal liability, do the following:

(a) *Separate your LLC*: To avoid a claim that you are inseparable from your LLC (that it is your alter ego), trumpet the LLC's separate existence. The LLC should have its own bank account. It should conduct business transactions in its own name. Do not use the LLC for personal dealing or unrelated business. Let people know that they are dealing with an LLC, and not with you personally.

(b) *Adequately capitalize your LLC*: Undercapitalization is one of the most common reasons for piercing a corporate veil. Make certain that your LLC has assets and cash in an amount adequate to carry on its business. Do not mislead any investors or creditors as to the extent of the LLC assets.

(c) *Follow the law*: Obviously, you should not allow your LLC to conduct any illegal business. This includes business that, although not criminal, could be considered fraudulent or otherwise illegal in the civil context.

(d) *Comply with formalities*: It may seem trivial to annually file a report to keep your LLC records current with the secretary of state. However, if you are some day faced with the need to prove that you have complied with all formalities necessary to the proper existence of your LLC, you will be glad you took the time to cross all the t's and dot all the i's.

(e) *Don't slide on any of the above*: Do not think that you may avoid personal liability just because you partially comply with any of the above items. Even though each individual failing may be insufficient to pierce the LLC veil, when taken together, all of your shortcomings could be enough to convince a judge to impose personal liability on you.

8
THE SOURCES OF MANAGEMENT RESPONSIBILITY
(ULLCA SECTION 404)

Generally, LLC management is conducted by the members or by managers. Managers are typically elected according to either the applicable LLC statute or the Operating Agreement. How an LLC is managed is very important. It controls not only the day-to-day functioning of the LLC, but it also controls vital, power-related details, such as admission of new members, distributions, merger, and dissolution. The source of management power in an LLC may be traced to either the Articles of Organization or the Operating Agreement. Be aware, though, that what may be included in these two documents is often dictated by statute.

a. MANAGEMENT PROVISIONS IN THE ARTICLES OF ORGANIZATION

The Articles of Organization can include any provision the members desire, as long as it is not inconsistent with law. Consequently, the Articles of Organization may contain management-related details. The Articles of Organization are filed with the secretary of state and are a matter of public record. Do you want the whole world to have the right to analyze the power structure of your company? Most people probably do not. For these people, include only the statutorily required matters in the Articles of Organization. Everything else may be addressed in the Operating Agreement, which is a confidential document.

Of course, if privacy is of no concern, you may want to include management-related matters in the Articles of Organization. There could be advantages in this. Take, for example, an LLC that wants to limit the agency power of certain members; the LLC does not want certain members to borrow money, purchase items, or otherwise act on behalf of the LLC.

When a third person deals with an agent, that third person may rely on the agent's authority to bind the principal (the LLC), unless the third person knows that the agent does not have authority to do so. Therefore, if the LLC Articles of Organization, which are available for public inspection, state that a certain person has no agency power for the LLC, then anyone who deals with that person should know of his or her lack of power.

Certainly, information in a public document is not the same as knowing what the document contains. However, when all of the circumstances are considered, if the Articles of Organization limit the member's agency power, it may be enough to avoid LLC liability for the member's unauthorized actions. Indeed, in some cases, third parties may have an obligation to inquire into an agent's power, which may include reviewing the Articles of Organization.

Including management-related matters in the Articles of Organization is an option. You should not, however, consider management-related matters an optional part of the Operating Agreement. The Operating Agreement should provide detailed information regarding management of the LLC.

b. MANAGEMENT PROVISIONS IN THE OPERATING AGREEMENT

The Operating Agreement is the most important document addressing how an LLC is to be managed. Many of the early LLC statutes made little or no mention of how an LLC was to be managed. The obvious intent was to allow members to address management questions in the Operating Agreement. As a result, an LLC is very similar to a partnership, which sets forth management provisions in a partnership agreement.

Some LLC statutes do not require members to enter into an Operating Agreement, although doing so is clearly contemplated by the statute. If you form an LLC in a state that does not expressly require an Operating Agreement, do not look at this omission as an opportunity to avoid having to reach an agreement with the other members. A written Operating Agreement should always be entered into among the LLC members.

How should the Operating Agreement address LLC management? There is no single right way to set forth management responsibilities in an LLC Operating Agreement. The members should decide, before entering into the Operating Agreement, what rights, duties, and responsibilities related to management each member will have. Then, these matters may be put into writing. Do not be afraid to be flexible and creative when drafting management provisions in the Operating Agreement. If, for example, the LLC will have ten members, and the consensus is that only two of those members will play an active role in managing the LLC, then, by all means, set forth this understanding in the Operating Agreement.

The Operating Agreement should also address additional management-related provisions such as how to change the LLC management structure, the consequences of failing to perform management duties, and the consequences of exercising management duties when no such power has been granted.

Initially, the Operating Agreement should define what is meant by the word manage. One standard Operating Agreement form defines *management right* as "[the] right of a Member to participate in the management of the Company, including the rights to information and to consent or approve actions of the Company."

The Operating Agreement should also define who is to be considered a managing member. Again, the standard Operating Agreement form provides an example. It defines a managing member as "[a] Member selected to manage the affairs of the Company under Article VII hereof." Article VII is the portion of the standard Operating Agreement form addressing managing members. In other words, if you have been formally selected to be a managing member, then you are a managing member. If you have not been so selected, then you are not a managing member. This may seem obvious, but given the fact that most LLC statutes indicate that all members have management rights, some confusion could exist over which members in fact are to be considered the formal managing members of the LLC. To avoid this confusion, make certain that the Operating Agreement is clear regarding who is a managing member and how managing members are selected and dismissed.

If the LLC will have managing members, the Operating Agreement should state this. In addition, the Operating Agreement should specifically address matters related to the managing members. For example, the Operating Agreement should address the term of office of managing members, the authority of managing members to bind the LLC in its relations with third parties, and the number of managers required to reach a decision.

The Operating Agreement may also address whether, and in what amount, managers are to be paid. The typical provision states that managing members are entitled to reimbursement for their expenses and are to be paid in the amount that the managing members determine, from time to time, to be appropriate.

The Operating Agreement should also state how a managing member may be removed. Usually, the Operating Agreement will provide that a managing member may be removed by a majority vote of the members. However, the Operating Agreement could require a unanimous vote of the members, or either a majority or unanimous vote of the managing members. If the managers retain the right to remove other managers, it is advisable to limit removal to circumstances where the manager being removed is guilty of some wrongdoing. That way, there is less of a chance that the LLC will be considered to have centralized management for tax purposes.

Finally, the Operating Agreement should address the standard of care expected of managing members. For example, it could contain an admonition that the managing members are not to engage in gross negligence, intentional misconduct, or violations of the law.

Include a *self-dealing* clause in the management portion of the Operating Agreement. This clause would prohibit members and managers from using LLC opportunities to their own advantage and provide the penalties for doing so. Therefore, a member is liable if, for example, he or she personally acquired property that was supposed to be purchased for the LLC.

When drafting the Operating Agreement, keep the following points in mind related to management for both manager-managed and member-managed LLCs.

Manager-managed LLCs

(a) What are the necessary qualifications, if any, of the managers?

(b) How many managers will there be?

(c) How long will the managers serve?

(d) Will any of the managers have more, or less, authority than the others?

(e) Who may vote to elect the managers?

(f) What percentage vote is necessary to elect the managers?

(g) May the managers be removed before the end of their term? If so, on what basis? By whom? By what percentage vote?

(h) What decisions are left to the managers, and what decisions are left to the members? What decisions may be made by either the members or the managers?

(i) What is the voting power of managers?

(j) What voting percentage is necessary in order for managers to take action? Do some decisions require a greater or lesser percentage?

(k) Must a vote of the managers take place at a meeting? If not, when may managers act without meeting?

(l) May members vote outside of meetings? If so, in what context?

(m) Do members, managers, or both, have a duty of loyalty? If so, what is the nature of that duty?

(n) May members, managers, or both, be indemnified if, for example, they are sued?

Note: Some of the above provisions related to manager-managed LLCs may also apply to member-managed LLCs.

Member-managed LLCs

(a) Are there any restrictions or enlargements of member powers?

(b) What is the voting power of members?

(c) What percentage vote is necessary for member decisions? Will some decisions require a greater or lesser vote?

(d) May members vote outside of meetings? If so, in what context?

(e) Do members have a duty of loyalty? If so, what is the nature of that duty?

(f) May members be secured against loss?

9
CONDUCTING THE BUSINESS OF AN LLC
(ULLCA SECTION 301(a))

a. GENERAL MANAGEMENT CONSIDERATIONS

The Operating Agreement is the primary source of LLC management power. When properly drafted, it should provide the answer to nearly every management-related question. But the Operating Agreement does not conduct the LLC business: the members and managers do. The LLC statutes typically do not require any type of membership meetings, nor do the statutes dictate how the LLC's day-to-day operations should take place. Those matters are left to the discretion of the members and managers. They must decide, for example, which members can act as agents of the LLC, who should be managers, when distributions should be made and in what amount, and whether property should be transferred. These matters are best resolved with good, old-fashioned common sense. A little business acumen also goes a long way. In addition, there are some prevailing themes that run throughout LLC management, and business management in general, that are worth covering.

1. Member agents

The authority to act as the agent of a business firm is a great privilege and responsibility that should not be granted to just any Tom, Dick, or Harriet. Scores of businesses have suffered severe financial losses because of unscrupulous or incompetent agents. Indeed, many businesses have failed because of the mistakes and misdeeds of their agents. Do not let your LLC fall victim to the agent-gone-awry syndrome.

The LLC Operating Agreement should clearly set forth who has authority to act as an agent of the LLC and the extent of those agency powers. Take some time, prior to drafting the Operating Agreement, to consider who should be granted agency authority and the extent of that authority. Keep the number of authorized agents to a minimum. The fewer people who have authority to act for the LLC, the less chance an unauthorized transaction will take place.

Also, consider the character and history of those who are potential LLC agents. Tom may seem like a nice guy, and he may have asked to be named an LLC agent, but if Tom has had a problem keeping his personal finances in order and has a couple of misdemeanor larceny convictions, he probably should not be granted authority to act as an agent for your LLC. To avoid stepping on any toes, keep the agency decision as businesslike as possible.

At this point, a brief lesson on agency law is in order. First of all, do not confuse business affairs-type agency with employment-type agency. That is, the type of agency authority you may consider granting to LLC members or managers will not be the same type of agency authority granted to, for example, real estate agents and insurance agents. An insurance agent is an employee-type agent who has authority to sell a certain insurer's product. An insurance agent, though, usually does not have the power to borrow money for his or her company or sell its assets.

The type of agent we are discussing, on the other hand, is an agent who can act for the LLC in specified business transactions. An agent has the power to bind the principal (the LLC) in any transaction for which the agent has authorization. A third party who knows that an agent has the power to act for an LLC is justified in relying on that power. Therefore, if your LLC agent has the authority to purchase products from a certain supplier, and that supplier knows of that authority, you cannot later avoid having to pay for the agent's purchase of that product on grounds that the agent did not have authority to make the purchase. This is known as a case of *actual authority*.

More important, though, is an understanding of the consequences of creating apparent authority in your agent. In the above example, if the LLC agent did not have actual authority to purchase the products, yet the agent reasonably appeared to have authority, you again cannot avoid responsibility to pay for the products, even though the agent's actions were unauthorized. This example, of course, assumes that the third party with whom the agent was dealing had no reason to doubt the agent's authority. Consequently, one of the most important things an LLC can do, after settling on the identity of its agents and the scope of their powers, is to contact all third parties with whom the LLC deals and identify the agents and the scope of their powers.

The third parties should know that the specified agents, and only the specified agents, have authority to conduct business for the LLC. Likewise, when an agent's authority no longer exists, third parties should be notified.

Unfortunately, there may be unknown third parties with whom an unauthorized agent will deal. Your LLC's liability to unknown third parties would probably boil down to whether the third party was justified in believing the unauthorized agent had authority to act for the LLC. That means that if, for example, your LLC is in the tree trimming business, and an unauthorized agent attempts to purchase 200 computers, the seller of the computers should be suspicious about making a sale of that number of computers to a tree trimming business. In other words, the seller would not be justified in carrying out the sale.

The importance of addressing agency issues in the Operating Agreement is underscored because, generally, the LLC statutes provide that each member of an LLC has the agency power to bind the LLC in its business dealings. So in the absence of an Operating Agreement provision concerning agency matters, each member has, for example, the authority to borrow money, purchase property, and sell property for the LLC.

Again, including agency matters in the Operating Agreement may not help when unauthorized transactions take place with a third party who does not know the agent lacks authority. However, addressing these matters in the Operating Agreement may be enough of an incentive to prevent unauthorized transactions from taking place. This is especially true if penalties are imposed on members who take unauthorized agency actions. For example, the Operating Agreement could contain an indemnification clause stating that the LLC has the right to recover any losses caused by the unauthorized acts of its members or managers from the member or manager who took the unauthorized action.

2. Selecting managers

Most LLC statutes state that the members have the ability to select managers who will manage the LLC, but some do not. However, even in these states, it is clear that managers may be selected to manage an LLC. The Operating Agreement should address the manner in which managers are to be selected and their management powers once selected. Check your state's LLC law regarding managers.

In a few states, such as Colorado and Texas, there are rules addressing the number of managers, how they are to be elected and classified, and how management positions are to be filled and eliminated. Generally, the Operating Agreement should set forth whether all, or a specified percentage, of the members are entitled to select managers. It should also address the percentage vote required to select a manager, the term of managers, and the removal method.

Are managers necessary? In a small LLC, the selection of managers may cause more problems than it solves. After all, if there are three members in the LLC, all of them may want to perform some management functions. Since members inherently have the power to manage the LLC, there would be no reason to elect managers if all members agreed to have management rights. That is not to say, however, that all small LLCs should be solely member-managed. Some members of small LLCs prefer to be passive investors with no management rights. In such a case, it may be worthwhile to designate managers.

Most large LLCs may want to designate managers along traditional business management lines. For example, each department, such as purchasing, accounting, research and development, and shipping, may have its own manager. Remember, though, that the LLC form of doing business provides an opportunity to exercise some creativity. If one department, such as research and development, is the key department in the firm, it may be wise to designate more managers in that department and provide those managers with expanded powers. After all, you would not want the managers from shipping and maintenance to block a key decision related to the direction and development of the company.

3. Manager agents

Selection of managers is crucial, but just as crucial is the decision of whether, and to what extent, the managers will have agency power. Like members, managers are LLC agents unless there is a specific provision in the Articles of Organization or Operating Agreement disclaiming the agency authority. In a few states, if the Articles of Organization explain the limits of a manager's agency powers, it may be enough to avoid LLC liability to third parties for a manager's unauthorized acts. However, notice of management agency limitations in the Articles of Organization is no guarantee of insulation from third-party claims. Make all third parties who may possibly deal with the LLC aware of the agency powers of members and managers.

The Operating Agreement should address the agency authority of each manager. Naturally, the LLC may want to limit each manager's agency authority within the agent's area of management. In some companies, the members want only the managers, not the members, to have the authority to bind the company in transactions with third parties. For example, the managers could have the right to bring lawsuits on the LLC's behalf, defend lawsuits brought against the LLC, purchase and sell property, and borrow money. This makes good sense in a large LLC because it is difficult to keep track of member actions. Remember, though, that the Operating Agreement must state that only managers have agency authority. Otherwise, under most LLC statutes, both members and managers have agency authority.

b. SPECIAL RESPONSIBILITIES OF MEMBERS AND MANAGERS (ULLCA SECTION 409)

LLC members and managers have a special relationship with their LLC. In legal jargon, this relationship is often referred to as a *fiduciary* relationship. To understand a fiduciary relationship, consider some hypothetical situations on a more personal basis.

Assume that your best friend asks you to be the guardian of her only child if anything should ever happen to her and her husband. You agree. One week later, your friend and her husband die. You become guardian of their child and take control of all of their assets in trust. One of your responsibilities is to invest these assets on behalf of the child. You own a rundown rental house that you have been trying for years to sell for $50,000. Everyone thinks it's overpriced. Should you sell the rental property to the trust for $50,000? The answer is no because to do so would be *self-dealing*. If you did, you would breach a duty to your friend's child on both a moral and legal level.

Next, you discover that your friend's child is a genius. The child has invented an efficient way to turn seawater into fresh water. Should you patent the process and go into business for yourself? Again, the answer is no because you would be taking an opportunity from the child. You would breach a fundamental moral and legal duty to your friend's child by taking an opportunity that justifiably belongs to the child.

Finally, imagine that the child's business advisers set up a thriving business converting seawater to fresh water. Should you set up the same type of business? The answer is no, because you would be competing against the child you were obligated to watch over, protect, and guide. Once again, by competing against the child you would breach a fundamental moral and legal duty to your friend's child.

These are situations in which, before acting, you must ask yourself what your friend would do if she were in your shoes. As a good parent, your friend would most certainly do the right thing for the child's sake. This is the essence of a fiduciary duty.

If you are subject to a fiduciary duty, you have an obligation to take the high road and not do anything that would harm the person to whom the duty is owed. Think of your LLC as your friend's child. Think of yourself as the guardian of that child. In a nutshell, LLC members and managers may have a fiduciary duty not to engage in self-dealing, take personal advantage of LLC opportunities, and compete with the LLC. These duties are commonly referred to as duties of loyalty.

The other type of duty is known as a duty of care. A typical statement of the duty of care is found in the ULLCA, which provides that a member's duty of care "is limited to refraining from engaging in grossly negligent or reckless conduct, intentional misconduct, or a knowing violation of law." Under statutes of this type, an LLC member is not liable to other members or the LLC if, for example, the member's *ordinary* negligence causes damage to the LLC. In other words, if a member is driving down the street in the LLC car, and negligently runs into another vehicle, the member is not liable to the LLC or its members unless the operation of the car could be considered "grossly negligent or reckless conduct, intentional misconduct, or a knowing violation of law." In the typical automobile accident, the level of negligence does not rise to these standards.

Yet another fiduciary duty is the "obligation of good faith and fair dealing." This is a broad duty that is difficult to define. Good faith and fair dealing is the opposite of fraud. Ask yourself: Would an ordinary and sensible person in my shoes take the type of action I am about to take? If your answer is no, then you are probably not acting in good faith.

LLC statutes do not always state that a member or manager has a duty of good faith and fair dealing. For example, the Delaware, Florida, and Nevada statutes allow the members and managers to set the standard of care in the Operating Agreement. Of course, the ability to agree to standards of care may be subject to oversight by a judge. If a standard of care is particularly onerous, a judge may find it invalid. Also, some of the states that allow members and managers to agree to a standard of care impose standards of conduct in other portions of the LLC law. Florida allows involuntary dissolution of an LLC if the LLC acts fraudulently or illegally or abuses its power. Nevada allows members and managers to be indemnified as long as their actions were taken in good faith.

In some states, the LLC statutes impose duties on managers and do not address member duties. In other states, and under the ULLCA, members and managers are held to identical standards of conduct.

Become familiar with the standard of care you owe to your LLC, whether that standard is set forth in the Operating Agreement or by statute. That way, you know what actions you can take and what actions of other members are objectionable.

c. DISTRIBUTIONS (ULLCA SECTIONS 405, 406, 407)

If your LLC is successful, you will encounter a very pleasing problem: how to pay the profits to the members. Payments are generally referred to as distributions. There are two things to keep in mind when making distributions. First, distributions must be properly allocated among the members. Second, distributions must not be made at the expense of creditors. In the discussion below, these concepts are referred to as *member allocations* and *wrongful distributions*.

Member allocations are undoubtedly the greatest source of dissension in LLCs. People want to be paid their fair share, and if they don't feel properly compensated, trouble usually follows. When forming any LLC, clearly delineate member allocations and make sure these allocations conform with the applicable law.

Under most LLC statutes, member allocations are based on the amount of capital the member has contributed to the LLC. Therefore, if Member A, Member B, and Member C each contribute capital of equal value, each member is entitled to a one-third distribution. Of course, the Articles of Organization and Operating Agreement may vary this formula. For example, the members may want to vary the formula if some members are passive investors who take no active part in the operation of the company. In this scenario, the members may agree in the Operating Agreement that the passive members are entitled to a lesser distribution.

Naturally, one of the key questions related to distributions is how each member's contributions will be valued. Imagine a bitter dispute developing over whether the business equipment contributed by Member A is worth $10,000 or $5,000. After all, if the business equipment is Member A's only capital contribution, then the valuation would have a substantial impact on the amount of his or her distributions.

To avoid valuation disputes, the members should always agree on the value of that contribution at the time it is made. Furthermore, the Operating Agreement should contain a listing of the agreed-upon value of each member's capital contributions. In addition, whenever new capital is contributed, its value should be determined and listed in the Operating Agreement. Consider including a provision in the Operating Agreement setting forth the method to be used when valuing member contributions.

For example, the Operating Agreement could state that if no agreement is made on the value of a contribution, a licensed appraiser, selected by a majority of the members, and a licensed appraiser selected by the contributing member, would each value the property. Then, the actual value placed on the property would be the midpoint between the two appraisers' values. This is just one example. Countless other valuation formulas could be used. Keep in mind, however, that in some cases a member may be contributing services, which may be difficult to value. Agree on the value of those services when it is agreed that they constitute the member's contribution. Allocating distributions properly among the members helps prevent internal disputes in the LLC.

But no matter how fairly the members themselves think they have been treated when distributions are made, third parties may feel cheated because of the timing or nature of a distribution. These third parties, typically creditors, may believe that your LLC has made a wrongful distribution. Usually, a wrongful distribution occurs if an LLC makes a distribution to members while the LLC is insolvent. A distribution may also be wrongful if it renders the LLC insolvent.

To understand wrongful distribution, you must first understand what is meant by insolvent. The LLC statutes vary in the definitions of insolvency. Generally, though, a person or entity is insolvent if it is unable to pay its debts as they become due in the ordinary course of business. Therefore, if your LLC is unable to pay its debts, yet it makes a distribution to members of money or assets that could be applied to those debts, then the distribution will likely be considered wrongful.

The penalties for making a wrongful distribution vary greatly from state to state. In some states, if a member takes a distribution with knowledge that it is wrongful, that member is personally liable both to the third party and to the other members in the amount of the wrongful distribution. In other states, the members or managers who voted in favor of, or agreed to, the wrongful distribution are personally liable in the amount of the wrongful distribution, as are members who knowingly receive a wrongful distribution. In still other states, a member is personally liable in the amount of a wrongful distribution even if the member did not know that the distribution was wrongful.

Some states use a limited partnership-type rule. Under this rule, a trust is imposed in the amount of the wrongful distribution on the member who received the wrongful distribution. Check your state's law to determine your potential personal liability. To avoid problems related to wrongful distributions, don't make any distributions when, in fact, the money or assets should go to pay creditors.

Under some circumstances, the members of an LLC may want to make a distribution in the form of noncash property, such as business equipment, real estate, or other tangible assets. This type of distribution is known as an in-kind distribution. An in-kind distribution may be particularly attractive when a member of a small LLC withdraws and seeks payment for his or her membership interest. It avoids the need to raise the necessary cash by other methods. Members may also want to make an in-kind distribution when the LLC winds up its affairs upon dissolution.

The LLC statutes generally state that a member cannot be forced to accept an in-kind distribution that is disproportionate to other members. By the same token, a member does not have the right to force the LLC to make an in-kind distribution. Both of these rules, though, like many other LLC statutory rules, may be varied by the Operating Agreement. If you want your LLC to have the ability to make in-kind distributions, then the Operating Agreement should expressly allow them. Likewise, if you want members to be able to force the LLC to make an in-kind distribution, the Operating Agreement should expressly grant this right. This latter type of provision may be useful if a member has contributed property that he or she wants to be returned upon the member's withdrawal or upon dissolution of the LLC.

Consider whether the members want distributions to be made on occasions other than member withdrawal and LLC dissolution. This issue should be addressed because there usually is no requirement that the LLC make distributions other than upon member withdrawal or LLC dissolution. Therefore, the Operating Agreement should grant the members or managers the right to make interim distributions on a schedule, and under circumstances, that the members deem appropriate.

Finally, consider the importance members will place on access to information about the LLC finances. After all, a member may need to know details about the financial status of the LLC in order to determine whether a distribution is fair. Some LLC statutes, and the ULLCA, address this issue by providing members and their agents with the right to inspect LLC books and records. Once again, this may be a matter to include in the Operating Agreement. If the LLC refuses to disclose information to a member, the member may resort to a court action to force the LLC to provide a detailed statement about its finances. This type of action is known as an action for an accounting.

10
"CHECK THE BOX" TAX STATUS

a. A SIMPLIFIED PROCESS

In December 1996, the IRS approved regulations that allow a business entity that is not a corporation to "elect" not to be taxed as a corporation. The election is made by merely checking a box on IRS Form 1065 (see Sample #3 in the next chapter) indicating what type of entity is filing the return. An LLC simply checks the LLC box on the return and need not worry about whether it will qualify for pass-through tax status.

This new "check the box" regulation has greatly simplified the process of determining whether an LLC was entitled to pass-through tax status rather than double taxation as a corporation. State law and previous tax law addressing whether a business entity would be taxed as a corporation or partnership is now irrelevant.

1. Elimination of flexible/bulletproof characterization

Now that a noncorporate entity may elect partnership tax status by checking a box on a tax return, it is no longer necessary for state LLC laws to include corporate-type characteristics. Before "check the box" was approved, states were often concerned about whether their LLC laws would satisfy the IRS that LLCs formed under their laws could be taxed as partnerships. For example, one of the methods that states used to ensure that LLCs formed under their laws would be entitled to partnership tax status was to require LLCs to state a dissolution date (usually 30 years) in the Articles of Organization. That way, the corporate characteristic of "continuity of life" was not present.

States that tailored their laws to virtually guarantee that LLCs would not be taxed as corporations were said to have "bulletproof" LLC laws. Those that played fast and loose with their LLC laws in order to allow LLCs to closely resemble corporations were said to have "flexible" LLC laws. This flexible/bulletproof distinction is no longer of much importance.

During the next few years, state legislatures will fine tune their LLC laws to remove some of the provisions that initially were included to increase the likelihood that an LLC would be taxed as a partnership. The most likely area of change is in the period of duration. Again, the "bulletproof" laws always contained a 30-year limitation on the lifespan of an LLC. Since this is no longer necessary, states should eliminate this limitation and allow LLCs to have a perpetual duration. The same is true for laws that required LLCs to dissolve upon the death or withdrawal of a member. If you formed an LLC in a state that limited its LLCs to a 30-year life span or to the death or withdrawal of a member, it may be a good idea to amend or restate the Articles of Organization to provide for perpetual duration.

Allowing perpetual duration for LLCs will make them more attractive for family business planning because no fancy legal maneuvering will be necessary to pass the business along to children. States may also eliminate the requirement that members vote to approve the transfer of a membership interest in order to make the transfer effective. Finally, the states may grant LLCs the right to do business with a more centralized system of management, rather than requiring management to be placed with all members.

2. Single-member LLCs

Only a handful of states allow a single person to form an LLC. That, too, may change because of the "check the box" regulations. Single-person firms are "disregarded entities" under the check the box regulations, which means that they may elect partnership tax status no matter what type of noncorporate form they operate within.

If you are operating as a sole proprietor, you should look into the possibility of forming a single-person LLC in order to get the liability protection it affords. Keep in mind that single-person entities that elect partnership tax status may not be taxed as partnerships under state law.

3. Firms ineligible for "check the box" status

Some businesses cannot take advantage of the "check the box" regulations. They include the following:

(a) Entities incorporated under specific federal and state statutes

(b) Associations treated as corporations under state law

(c) Wholly owned state organizations

(d) Joint stock companies

(e) Insurance companies

(f) Banks

(g) Publicly traded partnerships

(h) Taxable mortgage pools

(i) Specified foreign organizations

b. MAKING THE ELECTION

The election to be treated as an entity taxable as a partnership or as a single-owner entity to be disregarded as a separate entity is made by filing IRS Form 8832 (see Sample #2). Simply check the box that applies to your situation and send the form in to the IRS. If you do not file Form 8832, your business will be classified under default rules, which provide that a domestic eligible entity will be classified as a partnership if it has two or more members and will be disregarded as a separate entity if it has a single owner.

Form 8832 must be filed by any domestic entity that is electing to change its current classification, even if it currently classified under the default rule. The form must be filed with the Internal Revenue Service Center, Philadelphia, PA 19255. You must attach a copy of Form 8832 to your company's federal income tax or information return for the year of the election. If your company is not required to file a return for that year, a copy of its Form 8832 must be attached to the federal income tax or information returns of all direct or indirect owners of the company for the tax year of the owner that includes that date on which the election took effect.

A penalty may be assessed for failing to attach Form 8832 to a return. Form 8832 must be signed by each member of the electing entity who is an owner at the time the election is filed or by an officer, manager, or member who is authorized to make the election.

c. TAXATION OF MEMBER CONTRIBUTIONS

Contributing property to an LLC, whether at formation or during the LLC's existence, may have tax consequences. Generally, the Internal Revenue Code allows an LLC member to contribute property to an LLC in exchange for a membership interest without recognizing a gain or loss on the transaction. This is called a nonrecognition rule. The member's basis in the LLC membership interest and the LLC's basis in the contributed property are equal to the member's adjusted basis in the property at the time it was contributed. In other words, the member's basis and the LLC's basis are generally equal to what the member originally paid for the property.

Under some circumstances, the nonrecognition rule does not apply. For example, if a member contributes property to an LLC, and then receives money or assets from the LLC, the transaction may, in reality, be a sale. If so, the contribution is taxable.

A taxable event may also occur if a member receives a membership interest in exchange for services rendered, or to be rendered, to the LLC. The nonrecognition rule requires an exchange of property, and services are not considered property. Therefore, when a member contributes services, the money or assets paid to the member in exchange for those services must be included in the member's gross income.

Yet another exception to the nonrecognition rule involves contributions of property which is subject to debt. If the debt exceeds the member's basis in the property, a gain is recognized. Gain may also be recognized if part of the exchange involves relieving a member of liability on debts related to the contributed property.

Finally, keep in mind that contributions of property in exchange for an LLC membership interest may require allocation of a built-in gain or loss to the contributing member. The Internal Revenue Code requires such an allocation so that members may not shift built-in gains or losses among the members. If you will be contributing property to an LLC and believe that the contribution may have tax consequences, seek the advice of a professional tax adviser.

d. POSSIBLE TAXATION AT THE STATE LEVEL

The states do not have to treat LLCs as partnerships simply because the IRS has chosen to do so. Fortunately, most states have decided to allow LLCs to be taxed at the state level as partnerships. However, a few states have viewed the increasing popularity of LLCs as an opportunity to generate revenue by imposing LLC income taxes and other taxes. For example, Michigan subjects LLCs to a single business tax and members are subject to tax on LLC income. Other states have imposed an annual LLC fee. For example, Tennessee requires each member to pay a $50 annual fee, but the maximum total of these fees per LLC cannot exceed $3,000. Most LLCs will probably consider fees of this type to be insignificant when compared to the benefits of limited liability, federal partnership tax status, and flexibility.

SAMPLE #2
FORM 8832

Form 8832
(December 1996)
Department of the Treasury
Internal Revenue Service

Entity Classification Election

OMB No. 1545-1516

Please Type or Print

Name of entity

Employer identification number (EIN)

Number, street, and room or suite no. If a P.O. box, see instructions.

City or town, state, and ZIP code. If a foreign address, enter city, province or state, postal code and country.

1 Type of election (see instructions):

a ☐ Initial classification by a newly-formed entity (or change in current classification of an existing entity to take effect on January 1, 1997)

b ☐ Change in current classification (to take effect later than January 1, 1997)

2 Form of entity (see instructions):

a ☐ A domestic eligible entity electing to be classified as an association taxable as a corporation.

b ☐ A domestic eligible entity electing to be classified as a partnership.

c ☐ A domestic eligible entity with a single owner electing to be disregarded as a separate entity.

d ☐ A foreign eligible entity electing to be classified as an association taxable as a corporation.

e ☐ A foreign eligible entity electing to be classified as a partnership.

f ☐ A foreign eligible entity with a single owner electing to be disregarded as a separate entity.

3 Election is to be effective beginning (month, day, year) (see instructions) ▶ ___/___/___

4 Name and title of person whom the IRS may call for more information

5 That person's telephone number

Consent Statement and Signature(s) (see instructions)

Under penalties of perjury, I (we) declare that I (we) consent to the election of the above-named entity to be classified as indicated above, and that I (we) have examined this consent statement, and to the best of my (our) knowledge and belief, it is true, correct, and complete. If I am an officer, manager, or member signing for all members of the entity, I further declare that I am authorized to execute this consent statement on their behalf.

Signature(s)	Date	Title

For Paperwork Reduction Act Notice, see page 2.

Cat. No. 22598R

Form **8832** (12-96)

11
GENERAL LLC TAX CONSIDERATIONS

a. WHAT TAX FORMS MUST BE FILED?

Since an LLC is taxed as a partnership, it files the same tax forms as a partnership. A partnership must file a Form 1065 (see Sample #3). Form 1065 is not used to pay taxes because an LLC pays no taxes. Instead, it is an informational form which provides the IRS with information about your LLC. The form may be obtained from the IRS; call its toll-free number (1-800-829-1040) to request this tax form. The form is the same for all states.

LLC income and losses pass through the LLC and are taxed when they reach the members. Form 1065 contains a box in Schedule B that is to be checked if the form is being filed by an LLC. If you need more space than is provided on Form 1065, you may attach additional sheets. Simply follow the same format as the form and make sure that you include the LLC name and employer identification number on the attached sheets.

Before getting into the details of Form 1065, a review of some of the general issues related to filing is helpful.

1. Due date for Form 1065

The due date for filing a Form 1065 is not always April 15. LLCs that use a calendar year accounting method must file Form 1065 on a specified date. For example, the 1997 Form 1065 for calendar-year LLCs was required to be filed on or before April 17, 1998. An LLC that uses a fiscal-year accounting method must file Form 1065 on or before the 15th day of the fourth month following the end of its fiscal year. A three-month extension of the due date may be obtained by filing Form 8736. If reasonable cause exists, an additional extension of up to three months may be obtained by filing Form 8800. These forms are available from the IRS. The extension does not, however, extend a partner's due date for filing a return or paying taxes.

2. Where to file

Form 1065 must be filed with the designated service center in the state in which the LLC has its principal place of business or principal office. Your Form 1065 will explain where to file it in your state.

3. Failure to file Form 1065

If your LLC fails to file its Form 1065, and the failure is not excused by reasonable cause, a penalty may be imposed. The penalty is equal to $50 times the total number of members in the LLC. Even if the LLC files a Form 1065, the penalty may be imposed if the form is incomplete. The LLC may also have to pay a penalty if it does not provide copies of Schedule K-1 to its members. A Schedule K-1 lists the distributions made by showing the money that is paid out (see Sample #4). Therefore, the IRS knows what a person earned through an LLC. Form 1065 is an informational return; Schedule K-1 is the financial situation of particular members. Other penalties are also possible. Therefore, LLCs should always file a complete and correctly filled out Form 1065 on or before its due date.

4. Taxable year

An LLC has its own taxable year. However, the members may not select the LLC's taxable year. Instead, the taxable year is determined by examining the taxable year of the members owning a majority interest in the profits and capital of the LLC. All taxpayers have a taxable year. For individuals, the taxable year is typically January 1 to December 31, a calendar taxable year.

Business entities often have noncalendar taxable years and may be taxed based on a year starting June 1 and ending May 31. If several business entities, such as corporations or partnerships, are members of an LLC, and those entities have noncalendar taxable years, the LLC may have a noncalendar taxable year.

The taxable year of members must be used as the taxable year for the LLC. The taxable year is the same as that of the principal members. If this second formula fails, then the LLC uses a calendar year method.

An LLC is not necessarily bound by these taxable year formulas. It may use a different taxable year if it shows a satisfactory business purpose for doing so. Generally, an LLC uses a calendar tax year. A fiscal tax year is likely used when a corporation owns a majority of the LLC.

5. Tax matters member

If the IRS needs to send a notice to your LLC, it sends it to the tax matters member. An LLC may designate a tax matters member on Schedule B of Form 1065. If an LLC does not designate a tax matters member, the member with the largest interest in LLC profits at the end of the tax year is considered the tax matters member. If several members have the largest interest in LLC profits, the tax matters member is the one whose name comes first alphabetically. In tax court litigation, a member may be appointed by the court as the tax matters member.

The tax matters member should have management power. Since he or she is responsible for notifying other members of tax matters, you should address the responsibilities of the tax matters member in the Operating Agreement.

6. Signing the return

Form 1065 must be signed by one LLC member. If a person is paid to prepare the return, this person must also sign the return and the "Paid Preparer's Use Only" section must be completed.

7. Audits

If an LLC has more than ten members, has a nonindividual member, or a nonresident member, it is subject to the unified audit procedures, which makes the auditing of large LLCs a manageable task. A unified audit is an audit of an LLC or partnership at the entity level; the individual partners or members are not audited. The LLC or partnership is audited as a single entity.

8. Accounting method

There are two methods of accounting: cash and accrual. Under the cash method, the LLC realizes income when cash or property are actually received. Under the accrual method, the LLC realizes income when it has the right to receive cash or property. As a general rule, smaller firms use the cash method of accounting.

Under the Internal Revenue Code, the accrual method of accounting is required in two sets of circumstances. First, accrual accounting is required if a C corporation is a member and it has average annual gross receipts exceeding $5 million. Second, accrual accounting is required if the LLC falls within the code's definition of a tax shelter.

There are three tests used to determine whether an LLC is a tax shelter. There is the *registered offering* test and the *tax avoidance or evasion* test. The registered offering test is met if the enterprise (other than a C corporation) offers ownership interests for sale and the offering is required to be registered with a state or federal agency. The tax avoidance or evasion test is met if the principal purpose of the LLC is to avoid or evade taxes.

The test most likely to apply to an LLC is the *syndicate* test. An LLC is considered a syndicate (tax shelter) if more than 35% of its losses are allocable to limited partners or limited entrepreneurs. Determining whether an LLC is a tax shelter is a complicated matter, and professional tax advice may be necessary.

b. DETAILS OF FORM 1065

Form 1065 (Sample #3) contains more than general information about an LLC. It also contains schedules setting forth the cost of goods sold, "other information," partners' shares of income, balance sheets, a reconciliation of income, an analysis of partners' capital accounts, and capital gains and losses.

1. Cost of goods sold

Form 1065, Schedule A, contains a calculation of the LLC's cost of goods sold. This calculation is necessary so that the LLC may compute its income. Even though an LLC does not pay taxes on its income, it still must report its income. Schedule A is used to report the value of the LLC inventory and the method that was used in reaching the inventory valuation.

2. Other information

Form 1065, Schedule B, contains general information about the LLC. This is also where a firm designates whether it is a general partnership, limited partnership, or LLC. Schedule B also lists the three criteria for determining whether the LLC will be required to file additional schedules. The additional schedule is not required if the LLC had total receipts of less than $250,000, total assets of less than $600,000, and filed a Schedule K-1 (and furnished it to members) on or before the due date. The tax matters member is also designated in Schedule B.

3. Partners' share of income

Form 1065, the Schedule K section, is used to report all members' shares of income, credits, deductions, earnings from self-employment, foreign taxes, and investment matters. If the LLC has income or loss from real estate activities, it must report the income or loss on Schedule K and attach a Form 8825, which is available from the IRS.

Other types of income, such as dividend and royalty income, are also reported on Schedule K. If a section 179 expense deduction is taken, it must be reported on Schedule K and a Form 4562 must be attached. A section 179 expense deduction is a deduction of up to $17,500 that is allowed for investments in tangible depreciable property in the year the property is placed in service. The Schedule K and Form 4562 may be obtained from the IRS. These forms are filed with the IRS at the same time as the member's personal tax forms are filed.

4. Balance sheets

Form 1065, Schedule L, reports the LLC balance sheets. This schedule need not be filed if the LLC meets the three criteria described above in the discussion of "other information." Schedule L merely shows the beginning and ending balances in various asset, liability, and capital accounts.

5. Reconciliation of income

Form 1065, Schedule M-1, is a reconciliation of income or loss (per books) with income or loss (per return). Schedule M-1 also need not be filed if the LLC meets the three criteria described in the above discussion of "other information." Schedule M-1 reconciles the income or loss reported in the LLC's books with the income or loss reported on Form 1065, Schedule K.

6. Analysis of partners' capital accounts

Form 1065, Schedule M-2, is an analysis of the members' capital accounts. Schedule M-2 also does not need to be filed if the

LLC meets the three criteria described in the above discussion of "other information." Schedule M-2 lists the balance in the members' capital accounts at the beginning of the year, and then adjusts the balance based on items such as contributions, income, and distributions in order to reach a year-end capital accounts balance.

7. Capital gains and losses

Form 1065, Schedule D, is a report of the LLC's short-term and long-term capital gains and losses. It is not included in Form 1065. It must be separately obtained and filed if the LLC is reporting capital gains or losses. Short-term capital gains and losses are those related to assets held one year or less. Long-term capital gains and losses are related to assets held more than one year.

c. SELF-EMPLOYMENT TAXES

In a general partnership, the distributions received by a partner are considered self-employment income subject to self-employment taxes. Often, in an LLC, distributions made to members bear a direct relation to work the member performed through the LLC and, therefore, should be subject to self-employment tax. But what about a member who is simply an investor and takes no active part in the management or control of the LLC? Isn't this type of member more like a limited partner?

Limited partners are not subject to the self-employment tax, so it would stand to reason that an LLC member who has the characteristics of a limited partner also should not be subject to self-employment tax. The IRS has amended Treasury Regulations so that it is clear that an LLC member who is essentially a limited partner is not obligated to pay self-employment taxes. Under the regulation, an LLC member will not be liable for self-employment taxes if the member is not a manager, and if the LLC could have been formed as a limited partnership in the same jurisdiction and the member could have qualified as a limited partner in that limited partnership.

d. THE LLC ACCOUNTANT

Hiring an accountant to advise your LLC on tax matters and to prepare tax documents is a wise investment. LLC tax law is in its infancy, causing many uncertain tax questions to arise. A good accountant who is familiar with LLCs stays abreast of developments related to LLC taxation.

LLC members may not only realize tax savings from an accountant's expertise, but may also avoid getting into trouble with the IRS. If your LLC hires an accountant, choose one with experience in LLC tax matters. Ask other business owners operating as LLCs who they use for accounting work. Call several accountants and ask them how much of their work is devoted to handling LLC tax matters. Ask them about their fees. When you locate two or three good prospects, set up interviews. Often, an accountant is willing to meet with you at no charge in hopes of landing your business.

When you meet with a prospective LLC accountant, ask for the names of other LLCs for whom the accountant has provided services. You may not get a response because of client confidentiality. However, a good LLC accountant may have several clients who are so happy with his or her work that they have offered to put in a good word with the accountant's prospective clients.

When hiring an LLC accountant, make the terms of the working arrangement clear from the beginning. Get an accurate fee estimate and an explanation of exactly what type of work the accountant will be doing. After hiring an LLC accountant, make sure that he or she is kept informed about all matters affecting LLC tax issues.

Finally, keep thorough and organized LLC records. There is no greater waste of an accountant's time, and LLC money, than when the accountant is forced to wade through a messy, incomplete, and unorganized stack of receipts, documents, and account books.

SAMPLE #3
FORM 1065

Form **1065**		**U.S. Partnership Return of Income**		OMB No. 1545-0099
Department of the Treasury Internal Revenue Service		For calendar year 1996, or tax year beginning .... , 1996, and ending .... , 19 ..... . ▶ See separate instructions.		**1996**

A Principal business activity	Use the IRS label. Otherwise, please print or type.	Name of partnership	**D** Employer identification number
B Principal product or service		Number, street, and room or suite no. If a P.O. box, see page 10 of the instructions.	**E** Date business started
C Business code number		City or town, state, and ZIP code	**F** Total assets (see page 10 of the instructions) $

G Check applicable boxes: (1) ☐ Initial return (2) ☐ Final return (3) ☐ Change in address (4) ☐ Amended return
H Check accounting method: (1) ☐ Cash (2) ☐ Accrual (3) ☐ Other (specify) ▶ ....
I Number of Schedules K-1. Attach one for each person who was a partner at any time during the tax year ▶ ....

Caution: *Include **only** trade or business income and expenses on lines 1a through 22 below. See the instructions for more information.*

Income
- **1a** Gross receipts or sales **1a**
- **b** Less returns and allowances . . . . **1b** . . . **1c**
- **2** Cost of goods sold (Schedule A, line 8) **2**
- **3** Gross profit. Subtract line 2 from line 1c **3**
- **4** Ordinary income (loss) from other partnerships, estates, and trusts *(attach schedule)* . . . **4**
- **5** Net farm profit (loss) *(attach Schedule F (Form 1040))* **5**
- **6** Net gain (loss) from Form 4797, Part II, line 20 . . . . **6**
- **7** Other income (loss) *(attach schedule)* **7**
- **8** **Total income (loss).** Combine lines 3 through 7 . . . . **8**

Deductions (see page 11 of the instructions for limitations)
- **9** Salaries and wages (other than to partners) (less employment credits) **9**
- **10** Guaranteed payments to partners **10**
- **11** Repairs and maintenance **11**
- **12** Bad debts **12**
- **13** Rent **13**
- **14** Taxes and licenses **14**
- **15** Interest **15**
- **16a** Depreciation (if required, attach Form 4562) **16a**
- **b** Less depreciation reported on Schedule A and elsewhere on return **16b** . . . **16c**
- **17** Depletion **(Do not deduct oil and gas depletion.)** **17**
- **18** Retirement plans, etc **18**
- **19** Employee benefit programs **19**
- **20** Other deductions *(attach schedule)* **20**
- **21** **Total deductions.** Add the amounts shown in the far right column for lines 9 through 20 . **21**

- **22** Ordinary income (loss) from trade or business activities. Subtract line 21 from line 8 . . **22**

Please Sign Here
Under penalties of perjury, I declare that I have examined this return, including accompanying schedules and statements, and to the best of my knowledge and belief, it is true, correct, and complete. Declaration of preparer (other than general partner or limited liability company member) is based on all information of which preparer has any knowledge.

▶ Signature of general partner or limited liability company member   ▶ Date

Paid Preparer's Use Only
Preparer's signature ▶	Date	Check if self-employed ▶ ☐	Preparer's social security no.
Firm's name (or yours if self-employed) and address ▶		EIN ▶	
		ZIP code ▶	

For Paperwork Reduction Act Notice, see page 1 of separate instructions.   Cat. No. 11390Z   Form **1065** (1996)

SAMPLE #3 — Continued

Form 1065 (1996) Page **2**

Schedule A — Cost of Goods Sold (see page 13 of the instructions)

1	Inventory at beginning of year	1
2	Purchases less cost of items withdrawn for personal use	2
3	Cost of labor	3
4	Additional section 263A costs *(attach schedule)*	4
5	Other costs *(attach schedule)*	5
6	**Total.** Add lines 1 through 5	6
7	Inventory at end of year	7
8	**Cost of goods sold.** Subtract line 7 from line 6. Enter here and on page 1, line 2	8

9a Check all methods used for valuing closing inventory:
  (i) ☐ Cost as described in Regulations section 1.471-3
  (ii) ☐ Lower of cost or market as described in Regulations section 1.471-4
  (iii) ☐ Other (specify method used and attach explanation) ▶ ....
 b Check this box if there was a writedown of "subnormal" goods as described in Regulations section 1.471-2(c) . . . ▶ ☐
 c Check this box if the LIFO inventory method was adopted this tax year for any goods *(if checked, attach Form 970)* . ▶ ☐
 d Do the rules of section 263A (for property produced or acquired for resale) apply to the partnership? . . ☐ Yes ☐ No
 e Was there any change in determining quantities, cost, or valuations between opening and closing inventory? ☐ Yes ☐ No
   If "Yes," attach explanation.

Schedule B — Other Information

		Yes	No
1	What type of entity is filing this return? Check the applicable box:		
	a ☐ General partnership b ☐ Limited partnership c ☐ Limited liability company		
	d ☐ Other (see page 14 of the instructions) ▶		
2	Are any partners in this partnership also partnerships?		
3	Is this partnership a partner in another partnership?		
4	Is this partnership subject to the consolidated audit procedures of sections 6221 through 6233? If "Yes," see **Designation of Tax Matters Partner** below		
5	Does this partnership meet **ALL THREE** of the following requirements?		
	a The partnership's total receipts for the tax year were less than $250,000;		
	b The partnership's total assets at the end of the tax year were less than $600,000; **AND**		
	c Schedules K-1 are filed with the return and furnished to the partners on or before the due date (including extensions) for the partnership return.		
	If "Yes," the partnership is not required to complete Schedules L, M-1, and M-2; Item F on page 1 of Form 1065; or Item J on Schedule K-1		
6	Does this partnership have any foreign partners?		
7	Is this partnership a publicly traded partnership as defined in section 469(k)(2)?		
8	Has this partnership filed, or is it required to file, **Form 8264**, Application for Registration of a Tax Shelter?		
9	At any time during calendar year 1996, did the partnership have an interest in or a signature or other authority over a financial account in a foreign country (such as a bank account, securities account, or other financial account)? See page 14 of the instructions for exceptions and filing requirements for Form TD F 90-22.1. If "Yes," enter the name of the foreign country. ▶		
10	During the tax year, did the partnership receive a distribution from, or was it the grantor of, or transferor to, a foreign trust? If "Yes," see page 14 of the instructions for other forms the partnership may have to file		
11	Was there a distribution of property or a transfer (e.g., by sale or death) of a partnership interest during the tax year? If "Yes," you may elect to adjust the basis of the partnership's assets under section 754 by attaching the statement described under **Elections Made By the Partnership** on page 5 of the instructions		

Designation of Tax Matters Partner (see page 15 of the instructions)
Enter below the general partner designated as the tax matters partner (TMP) for the tax year of this return:

Name of designated TMP ▶ ....   Identifying number of TMP ▶ ....

Address of designated TMP ▶ ....

SAMPLE #3 — Continued

Form 1065 (1996) Page **3**

Schedule K — Partners' Shares of Income, Credits, Deductions, etc.

	(a) Distributive share items		(b) Total amount
Income (Loss)	1 Ordinary income (loss) from trade or business activities (page 1, line 22)	1	
	2 Net income (loss) from rental real estate activities (attach Form 8825)	2	
	3a Gross income from other rental activities 3a		
	b Expenses from other rental activities (attach schedule) . . . 3b		
	c Net income (loss) from other rental activities. Subtract line 3b from line 3a	3c	
	4 Portfolio income (loss): a Interest income	4a	
	b Dividend income	4b	
	c Royalty income	4c	
	d Net short-term capital gain (loss) (attach Schedule D (Form 1065))	4d	
	e Net long-term capital gain (loss) (attach Schedule D (Form 1065))	4e	
	f Other portfolio income (loss) (attach schedule)	4f	
	5 Guaranteed payments to partners	5	
	6 Net gain (loss) under section 1231 (other than due to casualty or theft) (attach Form 4797)	6	
	7 Other income (loss) (attach schedule)	7	
Deductions	8 Charitable contributions (attach schedule)	8	
	9 Section 179 expense deduction (attach Form 4562)	9	
	10 Deductions related to portfolio income (itemize)	10	
	11 Other deductions (attach schedule)	11	
Investment Interest	12a Interest expense on investment debts	12a	
	b (1) Investment income included on lines 4a, 4b, 4c, and 4f above	12b(1)	
	(2) Investment expenses included on line 10 above	12b(2)	
Credits	13a Low-income housing credit:		
	(1) From partnerships to which section 42(j)(5) applies for property placed in service before 1990	13a(1)	
	(2) Other than on line 13a(1) for property placed in service before 1990	13a(2)	
	(3) From partnerships to which section 42(j)(5) applies for property placed in service after 1989	13a(3)	
	(4) Other than on line 13a(3) for property placed in service after 1989	13a(4)	
	b Qualified rehabilitation expenditures related to rental real estate activities (attach Form 3468)	13b	
	c Credits (other than credits shown on lines 13a and 13b) related to rental real estate activities	13c	
	d Credits related to other rental activities	13d	
	14 Other credits	14	
Self-Employment	15a Net earnings (loss) from self-employment	15a	
	b Gross farming or fishing income	15b	
	c Gross nonfarm income	15c	
Adjustments and Tax Preference Items	16a Depreciation adjustment on property placed in service after 1986	16a	
	b Adjusted gain or loss	16b	
	c Depletion (other than oil and gas)	16c	
	d (1) Gross income from oil, gas, and geothermal properties	16d(1)	
	(2) Deductions allocable to oil, gas, and geothermal properties	16d(2)	
	e Other adjustments and tax preference items (attach schedule)	16e	
Foreign Taxes	17a Type of income ▶ .... b Foreign country or U.S. possession ▶		
	c Total gross income from sources outside the United States (attach schedule)	17c	
	d Total applicable deductions and losses (attach schedule)	17d	
	e Total foreign taxes (check one): ▶ ☐ Paid ☐ Accrued	17e	
	f Reduction in taxes available for credit (attach schedule)	17f	
	g Other foreign tax information (attach schedule)	17g	
Other	18 Section 59(e)(2) expenditures: a Type ▶ .... b Amount ▶	18b	
	19 Tax-exempt interest income	19	
	20 Other tax-exempt income	20	
	21 Nondeductible expenses	21	
	22 Distributions of money (cash and marketable securities)	22	
	23 Distributions of property other than money	23	
	24 Other items and amounts required to be reported separately to partners (attach schedule)		
Analysis	25a Income (loss). Combine lines 1 through 7 in column (b). From the result, subtract the sum of lines 8 through 12a, 17e, and 18b	25a	

b Analysis by type of partner:	(a) Corporate	(b) Individual		(c) Partnership	(d) Exempt organization	(e) Nominee/Other
		i. Active	ii. Passive			
(1) General partners						
(2) Limited partners						

73

SAMPLE #3 — Continued

Form 1065 (1996) Page **4**

Note: *If Question 5 of Schedule B is answered "Yes," the partnership is not required to complete Schedules L, M-1, and M-2.*

Schedule L — Balance Sheets per Books

Assets	Beginning of tax year (a)	(b)	End of tax year (c)	(d)
1 Cash				
2a Trade notes and accounts receivable				
b Less allowance for bad debts				
3 Inventories				
4 U.S. government obligations				
5 Tax-exempt securities				
6 Other current assets (attach schedule)				
7 Mortgage and real estate loans				
8 Other investments (attach schedule)				
9a Buildings and other depreciable assets				
b Less accumulated depreciation				
10a Depletable assets				
b Less accumulated depletion				
11 Land (net of any amortization)				
12a Intangible assets (amortizable only)				
b Less accumulated amortization				
13 Other assets (attach schedule)				
14 **Total** assets				
Liabilities and Capital				
15 Accounts payable				
16 Mortgages, notes, bonds payable in less than 1 year				
17 Other current liabilities (attach schedule)				
18 All nonrecourse loans				
19 Mortgages, notes, bonds payable in 1 year or more				
20 Other liabilities (attach schedule)				
21 Partners' capital accounts				
22 **Total** liabilities and capital				

Schedule M-1 — Reconciliation of Income (Loss) per Books With Income (Loss) per Return
(see page 23 of the instructions)

1 Net income (loss) per books
2 Income included on Schedule K, lines 1 through 4, 6, and 7, not recorded on books this year (itemize): ....
3 Guaranteed payments (other than health insurance)
4 Expenses recorded on books this year not included on Schedule K, lines 1 through 12a, 17e, and 18b (itemize):
   a Depreciation $ ....
   b Travel and entertainment $ ....
5 Add lines 1 through 4

6 Income recorded on books this year not included on Schedule K, lines 1 through 7 (itemize):
   a Tax-exempt interest $ ....
7 Deductions included on Schedule K, lines 1 through 12a, 17e, and 18b, not charged against book income this year (itemize):
   a Depreciation $ ....
8 Add lines 6 and 7
9 Income (loss) (Schedule K, line 25a). Subtract line 8 from line 5

Schedule M-2 — Analysis of Partners' Capital Accounts

1 Balance at beginning of year
2 Capital contributed during year
3 Net income (loss) per books
4 Other increases (itemize): ....
5 Add lines 1 through 4

6 Distributions: a Cash
              b Property
7 Other decreases (itemize): ....
8 Add lines 6 and 7
9 Balance at end of year. Subtract line 8 from line 5

SAMPLE #4
SCHEDULE K-1

SCHEDULE K-1 (Form 1065) Department of the Treasury Internal Revenue Service	Partner's Share of Income, Credits, Deductions, etc. ▶ See separate instructions. For calendar year 1996 or tax year beginning , 1996, and ending , 19	OMB No. 1545-0099 **1996**
Partner's identifying number ▶	Partnership's identifying number ▶	
Partner's name, address, and ZIP code	Partnership's name, address, and ZIP code	

A This partner is a ☐ general partner ☐ limited partner
☐ limited liability company member
B What type of entity is this partner? ▶ ....
C Is this partner a ☐ domestic or a ☐ foreign partner?
D Enter partner's percentage of: (i) Before change or termination (ii) End of year
Profit sharing . . . .% ....%
Loss sharing . . . .% ....%
Ownership of capital . . . .% ....%
E IRS Center where partnership filed return:

F Partner's share of liabilities (see instructions):
Nonrecourse . . . . $ ....
Qualified nonrecourse financing . $ ....
Other . . . . $ ....
G Tax shelter registration number . ▶ ....
H Check here if this partnership is a publicly traded partnership as defined in section 469(k)(2) . . . . ☐
I Check applicable boxes: (1) ☐ Final K-1 (2) ☐ Amended K-1

J Analysis of partner's capital account:

(a) Capital account at beginning of year	(b) Capital contributed during year	(c) Partner's share of lines 3, 4, and 7, Form 1065, Schedule M-2	(d) Withdrawals and distributions	(e) Capital account at end of year (combine columns (a) through (d))
			( )	

	(a) Distributive share item		(b) Amount	(c) 1040 filers enter the amount in column (b) on:
Income (Loss)	1 Ordinary income (loss) from trade or business activities . . .	1		See pages 5 and 6 of Partner's Instructions for Schedule K-1 (Form 1065).
	2 Net income (loss) from rental real estate activities	2		
	3 Net income (loss) from other rental activities	3		
	4 Portfolio income (loss):			
	a Interest	4a		Sch. B, Part I, line 1
	b Dividends	4b		Sch. B, Part II, line 5
	c Royalties	4c		Sch. E, Part I, line 4
	d Net short-term capital gain (loss)	4d		Sch. D, line 5, col. (f) or (g)
	e Net long-term capital gain (loss)	4e		Sch. D, line 13, col. (f) or (g)
	f Other portfolio income (loss) (attach schedule)	4f		Enter on applicable line of your return.
	5 Guaranteed payments to partner	5		See page 6 of Partner's Instructions for Schedule K-1 (Form 1065).
	6 Net gain (loss) under section 1231 (other than due to casualty or theft)	6		
	7 Other income (loss) (attach schedule)	7		Enter on applicable line of your return.
Deductions	8 Charitable contributions (see instructions) (attach schedule) . .	8		Sch. A, line 15 or 16
	9 Section 179 expense deduction	9		See page 7 of Partner's Instructions for Schedule K-1 (Form 1065).
	10 Deductions related to portfolio income (attach schedule) . . .	10		
	11 Other deductions (attach schedule)	11		
Investment Interest	12a Interest expense on investment debts	12a		Form 4952, line 1
	b (1) Investment income included on lines 4a, 4b, 4c, and 4f above	b(1)		See page 7 of Partner's Instructions for Schedule K-1 (Form 1065).
	(2) Investment expenses included on line 10 above . . .	b(2)		
Credits	13a Low-income housing credit:			
	(1) From section 42(j)(5) partnerships for property placed in service before 1990	a(1)		Form 8586, line 5
	(2) Other than on line 13a(1) for property placed in service before 1990	a(2)		
	(3) From section 42(j)(5) partnerships for property placed in service after 1989	a(3)		
	(4) Other than on line 13a(3) for property placed in service after 1989	a(4)		
	b Qualified rehabilitation expenditures related to rental real estate activities	13b		See page 8 of Partner's Instructions for Schedule K-1 (Form 1065).
	c Credits (other than credits shown on lines 13a and 13b) related to rental real estate activities	13c		
	d Credits related to other rental activities	13d		
	14 Other credits	14		

For Paperwork Reduction Act Notice, see Instructions for Form 1065. Cat. No. 11394R Schedule K-1 (Form 1065) 1996

SAMPLE #4 — Continued

Schedule K-1 (Form 1065) 1996 — Page 2

		(a) Distributive share item		(b) Amount	(c) 1040 filers enter the amount in column (b) on:
Self-employment	15a	Net earnings (loss) from self-employment	15a		Sch. SE, Section A or B
	b	Gross farming or fishing income	15b		See page 8 of Partner's Instructions for Schedule K-1 (Form 1065).
	c	Gross nonfarm income	15c		
Adjustments and Tax Preference Items	16a	Depreciation adjustment on property placed in service after 1986	16a		See pages 8 and 9 of Partner's Instructions for Schedule K-1 (Form 1065) and Instructions for Form 6251.
	b	Adjusted gain or loss	16b		
	c	Depletion (other than oil and gas)	16c		
	d	(1) Gross income from oil, gas, and geothermal properties	d(1)		
		(2) Deductions allocable to oil, gas, and geothermal properties	d(2)		
	e	Other adjustments and tax preference items (attach schedule)	16e		
Foreign Taxes	17a	Type of income ▶			Form 1116, check boxes
	b	Name of foreign country or U.S. possession ▶			
	c	Total gross income from sources outside the United States (attach schedule)	17c		Form 1116, Part I
	d	Total applicable deductions and losses (attach schedule)	17d		
	e	Total foreign taxes (check one): ▶ ☐ Paid ☐ Accrued	17e		Form 1116, Part II
	f	Reduction in taxes available for credit (attach schedule)	17f		Form 1116, Part III
	g	Other foreign tax information (attach schedule)	17g		See Instructions for Form 1116.
Other	18	Section 59(e)(2) expenditures: a Type ▶			See page 9 of Partner's Instructions for Schedule K-1 (Form 1065).
	b	Amount	18b		
	19	Tax-exempt interest income	19		Form 1040, line 8b
	20	Other tax-exempt income	20		See page 9 of Partner's Instructions for Schedule K-1 (Form 1065).
	21	Nondeductible expenses	21		
	22	Distributions of money (cash and marketable securities)	22		
	23	Distributions of property other than money	23		
	24	Recapture of low-income housing credit:			
	a	From section 42(j)(5) partnerships	24a		Form 8611, line 8
	b	Other than on line 24a	24b		

25 Supplemental information required to be reported separately to each partner (attach additional schedules if more space is needed):

Supplemental Information

12
WILL MY LLC BE RECOGNIZED IN OTHER STATES?

a. INTERSTATE RECOGNITION OF LLCs — IN GENERAL

Assume that you form and operate an LLC in Wyoming. Your business takes you into Colorado, where you negligently perform company work. Will the Colorado courts recognize the limited liability intended by the Wyoming LLC law? In all likelihood, they will, because Colorado also has an LLC law.

Now that every state has enacted an LLC law, concerns about whether members in an LLC formed and operating in one state will have limited liability in another state have lessened. Once again, though, this is an untested area. The courts have not had an opportunity to address the interstate application of LLC limited liability. And while most legal scholars agree that LLC limited liability in one state will be recognized in another, uneasiness will prevail until a few courts take this position. A short lesson in conflict of laws, the legal phrase for this problem, may help avoid problems in interstate commerce.

The general rule is that the law of the state in which a lawsuit is filed applies to procedural issues. Procedural issues include the number of days one party has to respond to a motion by the other party or the types of pretrial motions available.

However, a different rule applies to substantive issues. Substantive issues are the ultimate issues in the case, such as the legal definition of what constitutes negligence. Courts have more difficulty deciding which state's law applies to substantive issues. The general rule is that the law of the state with the most significant relationship to the parties and transaction applies to substantive issues. In the example above, a lawsuit filed in Colorado would likely be controlled by both the substantive and procedural law of Colorado because the lawsuit would be on file in Colorado and the incident at issue took place in Colorado.

What if Colorado's substantive law grants less protection to LLC members than Wyoming's? A Wyoming LLC member, despite having greater protection in Wyoming, may be subject to the lesser protection afforded by Colorado law. And if Colorado did not have an LLC law, an LLC member may have no protection at all.

This discussion about conflict of laws does not answer every question that may arise regarding the interstate viability of an LLC. Answers to conflict of laws often elude even the most competent lawyers. Instead, this discussion makes you aware that a different law may apply to determine the scope of an LLC member's limited liability if the LLC does business outside of its home state. Given this possibility, take some precautions.

b. HOW TO AVOID INTERSTATE PROBLEMS

You can lessen the possibility that another state will not recognize the limited liability granted to LLC members by the law of your state. The most obvious way, of course, is to not form an LLC and, instead, do business as a corporation or limited partnership. This method is for people who want absolutely no risk. These people can wait until the interstate recognition issue is resolved before deciding whether to form an LLC.

1. Form a manager-managed LLC

Most people, though, are willing to risk interstate nonrecognition because of the many benefits flowing from LLCs. If your LLC will be operating in another state or its products may reach another state through the stream of commerce, you should take steps to ensure that the other state recognizes the members' limited liability. Increase the probability of interstate LLC recognition by structuring the LLC so it is managed by managers. That way, the LLC may be viewed as having corporate-type characteristics entitling the members to limited liability, just as corporate shareholders are entitled to limited liability. But the LLC should not be structured too much like a corporation because it needs to avoid corporate characteristics in order to be classified as a partnership for tax purposes.

2. Include a choice of law statement in documents

Another precaution is to include a provision in all LLC contracts, invoices, and relation-establishing documents stating that all dealings and transactions with the LLC are to be governed by the law of the state in which the LLC was formed.

Provisions of this type are commonly referred to as *choice of law* provisions. Most states allow the parties to a contract to choose the law that applies to the contract. Take advantage of this right by making your state's law applicable whenever possible.

3. Properly identify the LLC

The LLC should be properly identified on all correspondence, advertising, and other material that may reach clients and customers outside of the state in which the LLC was formed.

Proper identification means using the term "limited liability company" or the abbreviation "LLC" behind the firm name. This identification makes it more difficult for people seeking damages (whether in or out of state) to claim that they did not know the entity's members had limited liability. You may want to notify customers and clients about the limited liability of LLC members so that they cannot later claim that they thought the members were personally liable for LLC obligations.

4. Educate members and employees

Regularly remind all members and employees that limited liability may not exist in other states. Members and employees should be educated about the methods the LLC is using to increase the members' chances of interstate limited liability. This way, the members and employees can follow the precautionary steps and be more diligent when dealing with interstate matters.

5. Form other entities and make them members

Some commentators have suggested creative methods of ensuring interstate limited liability such as forming S corporations or limited partnerships as LLC members. These methods appear to be too cumbersome for the typical LLC. Nevertheless, they may be the best option for firms with genuine concerns about interstate recognition.

6. Obtain adequate insurance coverage

Perhaps the best way to avoid problems with interstate recognition of LLC member limited liability is to obtain adequate insurance coverage. If general liability and product liability insurance in the proper coverage amounts are obtained, the issue of individual member liability is less likely to arise. Any person who has a legitimate claim against the LLC would be compensated by the insurance coverage and would have no need to impose personal liability on an LLC member.

7. Register in other states

Some states know that an LLC formed in that state may not be recognized in another state. These states attempted to eliminate this possibility by including a section in their LLC laws stating that LLCs formed under these laws were entitled to recognition in other states. These provisions may be comforting to some LLC operators, but in reality they may be more bark than bite.

The courts in other states have no legal obligation to honor such directives. While provisions of this type may not be effective, many states also included a procedure in their LLC laws whereby an LLC from another state (a "foreign" LLC) may register to do business in that state. Under these provisions, an LLC in Wyoming may, for example, register to do business as a foreign LLC in Colorado. If the Wyoming LLC is properly registered in Colorado, there will be no question about the existence of limited liability for members when the LLC does business in Colorado.

Usually a fee, ranging from $20 to several hundred dollars, is charged for registering an LLC in another state. Sometimes, this fee must be paid annually. Consequently, if your LLC does business across the United States, and will be registering in many states, the total annual fees could be quite substantial.

13
IS MY LLC MEMBERSHIP INTEREST A SECURITY?

a. WHAT IS A SECURITY?

Under federal law, a security includes an investment contract. The U.S. Supreme Court has defined an investment contract as a contract, transaction, or scheme whereby a person invests his or her money in a common enterprise and is led to expect profits solely from the efforts of the promoter or a third party. This definition appears to include some types of limited liability company membership interests. After all, an LLC may easily be characterized as a common enterprise in which the members seek profits.

Yet it is unclear whether an LLC member expects profits solely from the efforts of a third party or promoter. At this point, it is difficult to determine whether an LLC membership interest will be considered a security. It seems clear, however, that there are some types of LLC membership interests that are considered securities.

b. LLCs AND THE FEDERAL SECURITIES LAWS

Securities are subject to the Securities Act of 1933. This act requires the registration of securities unless the securities fall within a registration exemption. Exemptions exist for *limited offerings*. One example of a limited offering is an issuance of securities with a value of up to $2 million that is sold within six months to no more than 35 investors. Also exempt are nonissuer transactions, which are sales of certain securities by someone other than the issuer of the security, an underwriter, or a dealer. Some types of private resales, and some types of intrastate transactions (sale of securities exclusively to residents of a single state) also have exemptions.

Also, under the Securities Exchange Act of 1934, firms that are listed on an exchange or have total assets exceeding $1 million, and equity securities held by more than 750 people, must register their securities. The 1934 act also imposes report filing requirements on firms that are required to register.

In addition to the registration and reporting requirements, securities are subject to the antifraud provisions of both the 1933 and 1934 acts. The antifraud provisions apply even if the securities are not subject to the registration and reporting requirements. State laws also regulate securities. All states have blue sky laws, which require all securities sold within the state to be registered, unless a registration exemption applies. The state laws also usually contain antifraud provisions similar to the federal laws.

State and federal securities laws protect investors from fraudulent schemes. Some people use LLCs in fraudulent ways. The Securities and Exchange Commission has already taken action. In one case, the SEC alleged that an LLC violated securities laws by falsely depicting first-year investment returns. In another case, the SEC alleged that an LLC violated securities laws by using high-pressure sales techniques and making false statements. On the state level, the Kansas Securities Commissioner took action against a Nevada LLC by issuing a cease and desist order after finding that the company had violated Kansas securities laws by fraudulently offering membership interests for sale.

Other states have helped to define when an LLC may be subject to securities laws. For example, the Michigan Corporations and Securities Bureau determined that the offer and sale of a professional LLC membership interest was exempt from the registration requirements.

c. AVOIDING APPLICATION OF THE SECURITIES LAWS

If an LLC is closely held or managed by all members, and all members participate in the LLC, the securities laws don't apply. On the other hand, the securities laws probably apply to an LLC that is large, managed by nonmembers, and engaged in the sale of membership interests to nonparticipating members. In other words, if an LLC is similar to a general partnership, the securities laws will probably not apply. But if an LLC is similar to a limited partnership, the securities laws will probably apply.

If you do not want federal and state securities laws applying to your LLC, make it member managed with all members taking an active part in its management, control, and operation. If some members do not want to participate in the management and control of the LLC, at least give the members the power to control and manage the LLC. This may be difficult in some large LLCs and could create managerial problems. If so, perhaps you should simply concede that membership interests are securities and comply with the securities laws.

Eventually, the states may impose a formation requirement similar to New Hampshire's. There, LLC organizers must state in the Certificate of Formation whether the membership interests will be sold or offered for sale within the meaning of the New Hampshire Securities Act. In other words, the organizers must state that they will comply with the New Hampshire Securities Act. The Certificate of Formation must also be accompanied by a form which the state filing agency provides. On the form, state that the company's membership interests have either been registered, or are exempt from registration under the New Hampshire Securities Act. Formation statements of this type will likely be required only if LLCs become a breeding ground for widespread securities fraud.

14
WHAT TYPES OF BUSINESSES ARE FORMING AS LLCs?

a. LLCs ARE SUITABLE FOR NEARLY ANY TYPE OF BUSINESS

LLCs are appropriate for many different types of businesses. Although it is still too early to tell exactly what types of businesses are most likely to form as LLCs, many firms have already embraced the LLC concept. Initial filings disclose that LLCs are being used for real estate ventures, natural resource development, accounting firms, high technology firms, law firms, medical practices, agricultural holdings, and estate planning. Many other entities will also use the LLC form. An in-depth look at the operation of some of these firms can help those who want to establish identical LLCs by illustrating the flexibility of LLCs.

1. Real estate ventures

Real estate ventures pose many types of risks and raise complex tax issues. The risks include liability based on mortgages, contracts, and leases, as well as potential title problems and negligence concerns. The tax issues include the possibility that appreciated assets will be taxed upon distribution when the venture does business as a corporation. Doing business as an LLC may eliminate many liability concerns and provide tax benefits.

Limited partnerships and S corporations have traditionally been used for real estate investment ventures. A limited partnership offers limited liability for the limited partners, but at least one general partner must be personally liable for the limited partnership's debts and obligations. Also, if a limited partner participates in the management and control of the limited partnership, the limited partner becomes a general partner, and, as a result, is also personally liable for limited partnership debts and obligations.

In an LLC, however, all members may participate in and carry out decisions related to the management and operation of the real estate venture. All responsibility for the day-to-day operation and management of the real estate venture is not in the hands of a general partner. Limited partners also do not qualify for the annual loss deduction available to real estate investors. LLC members who actively participate in the venture may, however, qualify for the annual loss deduction. An LLC member actively participates in the real estate venture by, for example, arranging for the maintenance and repair of the property, screening tenants, or setting rental rates and terms. In order to qualify for the annual loss deduction, the member must also have adjusted gross income of less than $150,000, own at least 10% of the firm, and the firm must not be publicly traded.

S corporations suffer other types of drawbacks when used as real estate investment entities. For example, they are limited to 75 shareholders, and none of the shareholders may be foreign investors. Further, a shareholder's basis is limited to his or her capital contribution.

An LLC member's basis, however, consists of both capital contributions and the member's share of LLC debts. Therefore, an LLC member may have a higher basis and, as a result, avoid taxes on transactions related to appreciated property. This same concept could also allow an LLC member to realize a tax loss in excess of the member's cash investment.

An S corporation may have only one class of stock. This limitation prevents shareholders from flexibly allocating gains and losses among them. An LLC, on the other hand, may allocate gains and losses among the members in any way it sees fit.

Some real estate investors desire confidentiality. LLCs allow title to be held by the LLC, thereby keeping the investor's identity out of the public records. This, of course, assumes that the investor's identity is not otherwise disclosed in the LLC's public records, such as the Articles of Organization. However, if an LLC holds title to real estate, it may cause some confusion about which members have the authority to convey the real estate.

Until clear standards are worked out for determining authority to transfer real estate titles, those who purchase real estate from an LLC should exercise extreme caution and make certain that the member they are dealing with has the power to convey the LLC's property.

Finally, LLC members in a real estate venture should keep in mind that title insurance problems could arise. Title insurance protects buyers from the possibility that the seller of the real estate does not have a good title, or that somebody else has ownership. This is a potential problem with an LLC, because it contains several members, which can make ownership issues uncertain.

Several years ago, a court ruled that a partnership was no longer insured under a title insurance policy because the partnership membership had changed, thereby dissolving the partnership. This same problem could occur in an LLC if a membership change occurs. Some title insurers are issuing policy endorsements to make clear that coverage exists notwithstanding a dissolution of the partnership. An LLC purchasing real estate should make certain that title insurance coverage will exist even if a dissolution event occurs. One way to do this is to request a title insurance policy endorsement like those being issued to partnerships.

2. Natural resource development

One of the best uses of an LLC is in natural resources development such as oil, gas, and mineral exploration and production. You may recall that the nation's first LLC law was enacted in Wyoming in the seventies as special interest legislation for an oil and gas development company.

Historically, limited partnerships were considered the best form of business for natural resource development by small investors. Corporations were considered unattractive because of the negative tax consequences. Partnerships were not used because of the potential personal liability of the partners.

Another entity used in natural resource development is called *concurrent ownership*. This arrangement is based on the parties' joint ownership and operation of the property, with each owning separate parts of the property for tax purposes. The result is that the parties are taxed as if they were active partners. However, concurrent ownership does not guarantee limited liability, nor is there a guarantee of partnership-type taxation.

Even though limited partnerships have been widely used in natural resource development, they were not considered an ideal form of doing business. The primary drawback of limited partnerships is the inability of limited partners to get involved in the management and operation of the business venture. LLCs eliminate this drawback. Just as important, though, is the retention of limited liability.

Natural resource development is a high-risk business. Finding oil is not easy. A substantial amount of time, money, and effort may go into a venture, only to result in little or no production of the desired resource. Large losses of money are possible. More investors would invest in natural resource development if their personal assets were not at stake if the venture failed. Furthermore, those who invest in natural resource development often want to take an active part in the management and operation of the venture. When the high risk and resulting liability concerns are combined with the desire for partnership tax status and operational control, it is easy to see that LLCs are well suited for natural resource development.

3. Accounting firms

Accountants jumped on the LLC bandwagon early and have stayed on for the ride. A combination of factors have caused accountants to embrace LLCs. Naturally, accountants are keenly aware of the tax benefits flowing from LLCs. Accountants are also familiar with the drawbacks of partnerships because they were forced for years to do business as partnerships and often suffered the consequences of unlimited personal liability. It is not surprising, then, that in 1991 the American Institute of Certified Public Accountants amended its rule specifying the permissible forms of practice for certified accounting to include LLCs. Some states have enacted not only LLC laws, but have also enacted "professional" LLC laws applicable to professionals such as accountants, lawyers, and doctors. If you are a professional in a state with such a law, you will need to form a professional LLC, rather than a regular LLC.

4. High technology firms

Like natural resource development, investment in high technology firms involves greater than average risk. The market for high technology items is subject to extreme fluctuations, and the brain power necessary to operate such firms may suddenly disappear if there are wholesale defections from the firm. Limited liability is important to investors, as is flexibility and favorable tax treatment. Therefore, high technology firms are good candidates for LLC usage.

5. Law firms

Law firms tend to fall in to the same category as accounting firms. Law firms are traditionally partnerships or professional corporations. However, the unlimited personal liability makes a partnership arrangement very risky. For policy reasons, many state regulatory bodies oppose efforts by professionals such as lawyers to limit their liability, reasoning that to do so is a disservice to clients harmed by the professional's negligence. Therefore, in some states, the LLC may not be available to lawyers and other professionals. In other states, lawyers can form professional LLCs. At any rate, lawyers, like accountants, are forming LLCs and will likely be prime users of the LLC form.

6. Medical practices

Operating a medical practice can also be a high-risk venture. Medical malpractice lawsuits and investments in expensive medical equipment create liability concerns. LLCs may someday provide a convenient way for medical professionals to consolidate several types of services and possibly engage in interstate practice.

Neither the American Medical Association Principles of Medical Ethics nor the American Dental Association Principles of Ethics prohibit LLC use by doctors and dentists. However, at least one state (Illinois) prohibits the practice of dentistry through an LLC.

7. Agricultural holdings

Many states have laws that prohibit corporate farming. LLCs might be prohibited from being vehicles for farm-related business activities. Anyone seeking to form a farming or ranching business as an LLC should determine whether doing so would violate a law prohibiting corporate farming. Seek an official attorney general's legal opinion.

8. Family businesses: estate planning

Before LLCs came into existence, estate planning was often handled through various types of corporations or partnerships. The most popular types were S corporations and limited partnerships. Tax professionals and estate planning lawyers are now beginning to realize that LLCs are often a better entity for estate planning. The goals of estate planning are to reduce taxes upon death yet retain control over those assets before death. LLCs are flexible and may be classified as partnerships, which helps to meet the above goals.

Unlike S corporations, LLCs may have complex trusts as members. S corporations also cannot have more than one class of stock. Therefore, S corporations cannot be used to distribute income among various classes of people. When an S corporation shareholder dies, that person's stock may be transferred only to an S corporation stockholder. LLCs have no such restriction. Also, an LLC may provide advantages over S corporations when it comes time to determine if an asset transfer results in a *stepped-up basis*, thereby reducing taxes. If the asset is transferred into a family LLC, and your child becomes a member of the LLC, the asset is essentially transferred to the child with a stepped-up basis. This is true because the basis of the asset will be its value at the time it is transferred to the LLC, rather than its value at the time you originally acquired it.

(a) Business succession planning

If an LLC is used as part of a business succession plan, it allows distribution of appreciated property to members without triggering LLC gain or member income. LLCs also have advantages over S corporations by allowing flexibility of allocations, the creation of different classes of ownership, and loss deduction flexibility.

Limited partnerships provide many of the same tax advantages of LLCs when used in estate planning, but suffer from a lack of control by the limited partners and the personal liability of the general partners. In a family business, an LLC allows all family members to participate in the management and control of the business, while allowing some family members more power in the decision-making and operational process. For example, assume that mom and dad started the family business, and now have three grown children who will work in the business and will ultimately own it. Mom and dad could create an LLC with the children as members, and enter into an Operating Agreement placing the ultimate decision-making powers in mom and dad. The Operating Agreement would grant the children limited decision-making power. Under this arrangement, the children could play a part in the business, yet mom and dad would retain control.

(b) Insurance planning

Insurance planning is one of the best uses of LLCs in the estate planning context. Many people create irrevocable life insurance trusts as part of their state plan. Unfortunately, these trusts are inflexible and are exactly as described — irrevocable. Consequently, there may be serious side effects if things do not go as planned. For example, if an irrevocable life insurance trust is set up with a husband as beneficiary and the wife contributing the assets to the trust, a divorce gives the wife two options. She must either leave the trust as is and let the husband eventually receive the proceeds, or let the policy lapse and lose everything that has been contributed.

Using an LLC can avoid this result. The member could contribute cash to the LLC, which would in turn purchase life insurance. The member would own 1% of the LLC but retain complete management control. The other members of the family would own the remaining interest in the LLC. They would obtain their interest in the LLC though gifts. The LLC Operating Agreement could contain an expulsion clause stating that the occurrence of certain events, such as a divorce, would be grounds for a member's expulsion from the LLC. Then, when a divorce occurred, the members could vote on whether the member should be expelled. Or perhaps the Operating Agreement could even contain a provision that certain members are automatically expelled upon divorce. In this sense, the LLC is similar to a premarital agreement.

Another option during a change of family circumstances is dissolving the LLC. By using an LLC instead of an irrevocable life insurance trust, the member retains control of the insurance policy but has only a fraction of it included in his or her estate. The member also has access to cash in the LLC for making investments. Finally, an LLC may also provide lower tax rates when compared to the tax rates imposed on an irrevocable life insurance trust.

(c) Gift taxes

A gift tax is imposed on property that is given away. However, taxpayers are entitled to an annual gift tax exclusion of $10,000 for property given to children. Therefore, a person with three children may give away $30,000 annually without paying gift taxes. Gift taxes may be reduced or eliminated by using an LLC. After all, a parent's transfer of property to an LLC in which his or her children own an interest is essentially the same as giving a gift. However, transferring property to an LLC will not typically be considered a gift for gift tax purposes.

(d) Trusts

Some trusts have provisions granting beneficiaries the power to demand immediate possession of trust principal and interest. A provision of this type is considered a *present interest* even if the trust also provides for accumulation of trust income and deferred principal distribution.

A person with a present interest in a trust can demand immediate possession of the trust principal and income. (Trust principal is the asset or assets that make up the trust and the income, of course, is the income earned off those assets.) If a beneficiary of a trust has a present interest in trust property, he or she has a right to a *Crummey* notice. This notice tells the beneficiary that he or she has a right to demand immediate possession of trust principal and income. ("Crummey" is not used in a negative sense. The court case that imposed a notice requirement on gifts to certain trusts involved a party whose last name was Crummey. Legal concepts are often named after one of the parties in a landmark case.)

This discussion points out one advantage of an LLC over a trust. Transferring property into an LLC, rather than into a trust, may avoid the need for Crummey notices because there is no IRS rule (as there is with trusts) that a person who has a right to demand immediate possession of property in an LLC must be given notice of that fact.

People often make gifts to Crummey trusts for estate planning purposes so that property may be transferred without the gift tax. (Remember the $10,000 gift tax exclusion for gifts by a parent to a child.) Consider also the practical difference between making a gift of assets and making a gift of an interest in an LLC. If all of the family assets are combined in an LLC, rather than spread out among family members, administrative costs related to the assets may be lessened and the assets may have more investment potential as a group than when splintered.

(e) Premarital agreements

Finally, the LLC may, as mentioned above, serve the family by acting as a type of premarital agreement. The LLC takes on such characteristics when family-related transfer restrictions are placed on LLC interests. This avoids the possibility that a spouse who divorces a family member could transfer a court-awarded interest to a nonfamily member.

Members of family-owned businesses often worry about having the spouse of one of the family members claim an interest in the business during a divorce. A provision can be inserted in the LLC Operating Agreement to restrict transfers of membership interest. For instance, the Operating Agreement could provide that if a family member wants to sell his or her membership interest in the family LLC, the sale may take place only if the buyer is another family member. This prevents an ex-spouse of a family member from obtaining an ownership interest in the family LLC. Even if the ex-spouse is awarded an ownership interest in the LLC, that interest may be of little value because it can be transferred only to other family members.

Estate planning is complicated. The tax and business implications are usually significant enough to warrant obtaining advice from professionals. If you plan on using an LLC as an estate planning device, you should consult a lawyer or an accountant with expertise in this area.

b. SOME BUSINESSES MAY NOT OPERATE AS LLCs

Many state LLC laws prohibit certain types of businesses from operating as LLCs. For example, in Nevada and Illinois, LLCs may not be formed for banking or insurance. Illinois also prohibits dentists from doing business as LLCs. Even if your state LLC law does not specifically prohibit the use of an LLC as a form of doing business in your profession, a professional regulatory agency, such as a bar association or medical regulatory agency, may prohibit practice as an LLC.

Usually, the type of business you want can be carried on by an LLC. Nevertheless, before investing time and money, find out whether your business may operate as an LLC.

15
THE LLC LAWYER

a. IS AN LLC LAWYER NECESSARY?

An LLC does not have to be formed and created by a lawyer or any other type of professionally licensed person. Anyone who is willing to pay the filing fee and draft the necessary documents may create an LLC. Your particular circumstances dictate whether an LLC lawyer is necessary. If you are forming a small LLC to operate a closely held family business with few assets, you may not need much, if any, assistance from a lawyer. On the other hand, if you are forming an LLC to operate a large business with hundreds of employees and substantial assets, you should seek the assistance of a lawyer.

Use common sense. If you do not understand what is required to form an LLC or cannot draft the necessary documents, obtain a lawyer's advice. However, if you are a do-it-yourselfer with plenty of business experience and a grasp of the legal points related to the formation and operation of an LLC, you may be able to handle things on your own. As a rule of thumb, if you have any doubt about the implications of what you are doing, find a lawyer.

b. HOW TO SELECT AN LLC LAWYER

Finding a lawyer is not difficult. There are thousands to choose from. It is difficult, however, to find a lawyer with LLC experience. LLCs have been on the scene for just a short period of time and, in fact, when this book is published, there may still be a few states with LLC laws not yet in effect. Consequently, many lawyers have no experience with LLCs. They will learn with you.

If you happen to be forming an LLC in a state with brand-new LLC laws and no experienced LLC lawyers are available, find one with experience in closely related fields, such as partnership and corporation law. Lawyers with this type of experience will be most likely to understand the issues surrounding LLCs and will be most eager to learn.

Talk to other people who have formed LLCs and ask about their lawyer. Ask questions. Were they satisfied with the lawyer's services? Were they charged an appropriate fee? Has the lawyer followed up with additional advice and services? Did the lawyer seem to understand LLC law? If all of your questions are satisfactorily answered, you need look no more. Call this lawyer.

If you are unable to locate a good lawyer through word-of-mouth, use lawyer referral services, directories, and advertisements. Many state and local bar associations provide free lawyer referral services. Often, these referral services provide the names of lawyers who specialize in a particular area of law, such as LLC law.

If you call a referral service and are provided the names of LLC lawyers, do not automatically assume that the names you are given are lawyers with appropriate experience. Sometimes, these referral services simply ask lawyers to identify the areas in which they accept referrals without investigating to determine whether the lawyer actually has experience in that area. Ask the referral service whether the lawyers on its list are required to have experience and, if so, the amount of experience required.

Directories are also a good source of information about lawyers. One of the best is the *Martindale-Hubbell Directory*, which most public libraries carry. It is a multi-volume directory that is divided into state-by-state sections. The lawyers listing in this directory often include a detailed description of their work and the clients they represent. You may be able to find the names and phone numbers of area LLC lawyers.

Also, do not ignore the Yellow Pages in telephone directories as a source for information about LLC lawyers. If a lawyer has invested money in an advertisement stating that he or she specializes in LLC law, chances are that the lawyer has experience. Beware of Yellow Pages advertisements that indicate that a lawyer has experience in nearly every field of law. Try to find an advertisement in which the lawyer lists LLC law as an exclusive or primary area of practice.

If you are computer literate, or know someone who is, you may also want to consider searching computer databases for an LLC lawyer. West Publishing Company provides an on-line directory of lawyers through its computer legal research service, and this service is available through the Internet and various other commercial on-line services. Using this on-line directory, you could conduct a search by area of expertise and geographic location to find an LLC lawyer in your area. The commercial on-line services, such as CompuServe, Prodigy, and America Online also may be a source for information about LLC lawyers. Most of these services have areas in which messages about legal services may be posted for review by other subscribers, including lawyer subscribers.

If you simply posted a message that you were searching for an LLC lawyer, you may be surprised at the number of responses you receive. Posting messages to other subscribers inquiring about their experiences with LLC lawyers may also be a good way to find out what questions to ask, what services to expect, and the fees charged.

Be persistent and try to find a lawyer with LLC experience. In many communities, this may be impossible. If it is, use what you have learned about LLCs to assist your lawyer and do not be afraid to question your lawyer's decisions.

c. SERVICES AND FEES

Usually, an LLC lawyer provides services in one of three ways. Those three types of services may be described as peace-of-mind service, start-up service, and full service.

1. Peace-of-mind service

If you are forming a small, closely held, simple LLC, you may want to create all the documents necessary to form and operate the LLC yourself. Nevertheless, you may also want the peace of mind that comes from receiving a lawyer's opinion that your LLC is indeed properly formed. If you have drafted all of the documents and will be filing them yourself, a lawyer's fee for simply reviewing the documents and telling you whether they accomplish your intended purpose should not be more than a few hundred dollars — perhaps even less than one hundred dollars. If you are the type who would stay awake at night worrying about whether your LLC will indeed be taxed as a partnership rather than as a corporation, the fee you pay for a lawyer's opinion is money well spent.

If you want peace-of-mind service from an LLC lawyer, make this desire clear from the very start. You should also get a fee estimate at the time of your first meeting with the lawyer. Otherwise, you may later find that, because of a misunderstanding, the lawyer not only reviewed the documents, but totally revised them and created new documents at a fee substantially exceeding what you wanted to pay.

2. Start-up service

Many people require more than just peace-of-mind service from an LLC lawyer. Perhaps their LLC is somewhat complex. Perhaps they are not do-it-yourselfers. Perhaps they simply do not have the time or expertise to create and file the necessary documents. Perhaps they feel more comfortable with professional assistance. For these people, start-up service from an LLC lawyer may be appropriate. Start-up service is exactly what the name implies: service necessary to start the LLC. This would involve the lawyer's drafting of the Articles of Organization and Operating Agreement, together with any other necessary documents, and filing them with the appropriate offices.

After the LLC is created, the lawyer's participation ends. The fee for start-up service will likely be around $1,000, although it could be much higher for a large and complicated LLC. When obtaining a fee estimate, find out whether the filing fees and other costs are included in the estimate. After all, if the estimated fee is $1,000, and the filing fees and other costs amount to $500, the total amount you will pay to start the LLC will be $1,500 instead of $1,000.

3. Full service

For large and/or complex LLCs, get a full-service LLC lawyer. Under this type of arrangement, the LLC lawyer is involved in all aspects of the LLC, including the initial planning stages, formation, and follow-up work. Often, the LLC lawyer will be used in conjunction with other professionals, such as accountants and financial planners. Some people may want their LLC lawyer to provide full service even when the LLC is relatively small and simple. For these people, keeping legal fees low is not as important as making certain that all aspects of the LLC are professionally organized and managed.

Naturally, it is difficult to estimate the amount of legal fees to be paid when a lawyer provides a full range of services to the LLC. Even so, when hiring a full-service LLC lawyer, find out the following:

(a) The lawyer's hourly rate

(b) Whether any other lawyers will be providing assistance, and if so, their hourly rates

(c) Whether any services will be provided on a fixed-fee basis

(d) Whether any support staff such as paralegals, law clerks, or legal assistants will be providing services and, if so, their hourly rates

(e) Whether the lawyer will bill for routine matters such as brief telephone conversations and short, informational letters

(f) What costs will be billed as part of the fee, rather than considered part of the lawyer's overhead (e.g., will there be a charge for photocopies, long-distance telephone charges, office supplies, or on-line legal research?)

Any fee agreements should be in writing. If a billing question arises, express your concerns to the lawyer. Occasionally, billing mistakes are made, and even if no mistake is made, the lawyer may write off the billed item in order to retain good relations with a client.

Finally, as you read any legal fee estimates in this book, keep in mind that lawyers' fees vary greatly from one area of the country to another. Clients in rural areas can expect hourly legal fee rates of about $75. On the other hand, clients in some urban areas may find that hourly legal rates hover around the $250 mark for lawyers in high-profile law firms. Wherever your location, it pays to shop around and negotiate for the lowest rate possible.

16
TERMINATING AN LLC

a. THE BASICS OF DISSOLUTION (ULLCA SECTIONS 801, 802)

When an LLC ends, it *dissolves*. The process of ending the business of an LLC, then, is called dissolution. As previously noted, the passage of "check the box" regulations by the IRS will likely cause many states to change their LLC laws to allow for perpetual duration. Nevertheless, it is worthwhile to cover the various ways LLCs are currently dissolved.

Generally, the LLC statutes set forth three events that may cause an LLC to dissolve. The first event is the expiration of the LLC's period of duration stated in its Articles of Organization. Many states require such a statement in the articles. If, for example, the duration is stated as 30 years, the LLC will dissolve 30 years from the date of its formation.

The second event is the dissociation of a member (see chapter 6). A member is dissociated upon voluntary withdrawal, death, bankruptcy, expulsion, or other agreed-upon events.

The third event is the agreement of the members that the LLC should be dissolved. The agreement to dissolve should be in writing because dissolution triggers the winding up of the company business and the resulting need to distribute assets to members and creditors.

Some states, and the ULLCA, define additional events that may cause dissolution of the LLC. Several states allow dissolution upon entry of a judicial decree. Usually, the court must find that it is not reasonably practicable to carry on the LLC business in conformity with the Operating Agreement and Articles of Organization. This would occur if, for example, one member's misconduct prevents the LLC from being able to carry out its business. Judicial dissolution may also occur if a member is forced to seek court assistance in order to withdraw and be paid for his or her membership interest.

Yet another additional dissolution event sometimes provided for in the statutes is dissolution upon failure of an LLC to return a contribution to a member.

While the first three dissolution events listed above are fairly universal, the additional dissolution events are many and varied. Therefore, you should check your state's LLC statute to determine what events cause dissolution. If you desire dissolution events that are not listed in your state's LLC statute, you should include those events in the Operating Agreement.

LLCs must dissolve due to certain events in order to avoid the corporate characteristic of continuity of life. If it did not, it may be similar enough to a corporation to lose partnership tax status. However, if a member dissociation is the event that causes the LLC to dissolve, the members may agree to continue the LLC, rather than to dissolve it. This feature preserves the ability of the LLC to continue in business, despite the above events. Often, the vote to continue must be a majority of the remaining members, although this rule may sometimes be modified by agreement so the LLC may continue with less than the majority vote of remaining members.

1. Winding up

When an LLC dissolves, it does not immediately cease to exist. It must continue in order to sell its assets, pay its debts, and make final distributions to members. This process is called the winding up of the LLC. Winding up does not occur only upon dissolution. It may also occur if the LLC is sold and will continue with new ownership.

Because of the valuation issues that may arise, you should insert a provision in the Operating Agreement requiring a final accounting to set forth the firm's assets and liabilities. All work in progress during dissolution should be finished prior to completion of the winding up so that members are not responsible for customer claims or clients left hanging after the termination of the LLC.

2. Filing matters

The secretary of state plays a vital role in the creation and termination of an LLC. The secretary of state is to an LLC what a doctor is to a patient. It plays a part in both the beginning and the end.

'The LLC statutes uniformly require some sort of public filing when an LLC dissolves. The documents to be filed are usually called Articles of Dissolution or Articles of Cancellation. The statutes vary as to the timing of the filing. Some statutes require that the filing be made after the LLC has wound up its affairs. Upon filing of the Articles of Dissolution, the LLC ceases to exist.

Other statutes require the filing to be made when the LLC dissolves. These statutes typically describe the document to be filed as a *notice of intent to dissolve* or a *notice of winding up*. Finally, some statutes require the filing of documents both at the time of dissolution and after the LLC business is wound up. These filings give creditors notice that the LLC is dissolving so that they may make claims for payment. The filings also provide notice to third parties that any further actions by the members and managers is conducted as part of the winding up of the company business.

3. Agency considerations (ULLCA section 804)

Members and managers have the agency power to properly wind up the LLC. They can collect accounts receivables, pay company liabilities, defend claims against the LLC, sell LLC property, and complete LLC contracts. These matters are considered appropriate for members and managers to handle during the winding up of the LLC's business and, therefore, are permissible.

To find out what is inappropriate requires a little common sense and some good business judgment to guide the way. If your LLC is winding up to close in a month, don't purchase a two-year supply of material or upgrade the company computer system. Under some LLC statutes, and the ULLCA, a member whose inappropriate acts damage the LLC is personally liable to the LLC for that damage.

4. Distributions

When an LLC dissolves, creditors stand first in line when it comes time to distribute LLC assets. This rule applies to both creditors who are LLC members and third party creditors with nonequity claims. Nonequity claims do not arise from a member's right to distributions or from a member's right to capital returns. If a bankruptcy court becomes involved in the proper allocation of distributions upon dissolution, it may decide that it would be equitable, that is, more fair, to place a third party's claim ahead of a member's claim. This is known as equitable subordination.

Priority among creditors regarding equity claims (distribution rights and capital returns) depends on the specific terms of the applicable state LLC statute. There are at least five different formulas used by the various LLC statutes and all are somewhat complicated. Given the variation and complexity, the best course is to carefully check your state's LLC statute regarding equity distributions upon dissolution.

b. CREDITORS' RIGHTS UPON DISSOLUTION (ULLCA SECTIONS 807, 808)

Naturally, the members and managers are interested in how an LLC winds up its affairs upon dissolution. Another group that may be even more interested in the LLC dissolution is the people and entities to whom the LLC owes money — its creditors. Creditors want to know the details of the dissolution and how to collect on their claims. Most LLC statutes do not go into as much detail as the ULLCA does in addressing creditors' rights upon dissolution.

The ULLCA requires the mailing of a detailed notice of dissolution to known creditors, the publishing of notice of dissolution for the benefit of all creditors, and the setting of deadlines for the filing of claims.

An LLC debt does not terminate simply because the LLC is dissolved. The winding-up period is for the LLC to pay off the debts remaining upon dissolution. The LLC may have to perform contracts it agreed to perform prior to the dissolution. In many cases, though, legal remedies exist to avoid enforcement of such contracts. For example, assume that Member A is a talented computer programmer. She has more knowledge about computer programming than anyone else in the company. Prior to dissolution, the company enters into a contract with a software publisher to create a new applications program. The software company knows that Member A will be doing most of the programming work. If Member A then dissociates from the company, and the company dissolves, the company may be relieved of its burden of performing the contract because the contract implied that Member A would conduct the work.

Of course, not all contracts fall within this category. Therefore, an LLC should avoid the possibility that a pre-dissolution contract will require full performance upon dissolution. The LLC must make certain that every long-term contract is in writing and contains a clause stating that the LLC's duty to perform under the contract is extinguished upon its dissolution. A third party may not agree to this contract term. If it does not, you must decide whether a post-dissolution performance requirement is a risk the LLC should take.

An LLC can dissolve and continue in existence as another firm. For example, the LLC may merge with another company. When this happens, the dissolving LLC may be able to convince existing creditors to give up their claims against the dissolving LLC and seek payment only from the continuing firm. If a creditor does not agree that the continuing firm may assume sole responsibility for the original obligations, the creditor may be able to obtain payment from either the dissolved LLC or the continuing firm.

c. TERMINATING AN LLC THROUGH MERGER

An LLC can be dissolved if it merges with another business firm. Some LLC statutes specifically state that an LLC may merge with other LLCs or business entities. The ULLCA specifically addresses LLC mergers. It requires the creation and approval of a *plan of merger* in order for the merger to take place. The plan of merger basically sets forth information about the entities that are merging, such as names, addresses, and terms of the merger.

After the plan of merger is approved, the LLC must file *articles of merger* with the secretary of state. The articles of merger set forth details about the merging entities and the effective date of the merger. This filing requirement is not unique. Many of the state LLC statutes contain a similar filing requirement. If an LLC does not survive the merger, it may have to file articles of dissolution. In some cases, this filing must take place before the effective date of the merger.

If you are a member of an LLC that is merging, and you are opposed to the merger, you may have dissenter's rights. Dissenter's rights give you a right to oppose, and possibly prevent, the merger. Members who are concerned about the consequences of a merger may want to include a provision in the Operating Agreement requiring their consent to a merger.

However, this may be a difficult term to obtain if the majority of members are in favor of unrestricted merger.

17
MISCELLANEOUS ISSUES

a. LLC RECORDS

Keeping records is a necessary part of business. Unfortunately, record keeping often interferes with the business's main goal — making money. Yet record keeping is not always a bad thing. If a company is able to track its customer base and make better marketing decisions because of its record keeping, then the time spent keeping records is time well spent.

There is no single, right way to keep records, and each business must establish its own method. Nevertheless, a few types of records must be kept when doing business as an LLC. Do not consider this list to be all-inclusive, though, because the recent creation of LLC laws means that no clear record keeping rules have yet been created.

In some states, the LLC statute addresses record keeping requirements. Check your state's law to find out whether there are certain records that must, by statute, be kept. Generally, the following records should be kept in order to avoid problems with the IRS, creditors, or among LLC members:

(a) *Membership lists*: Keep all membership lists, current and past, along with the names and mailing addresses of each member. The list should be reviewed occasionally to make certain that the information remains correct.

(b) *Articles of Organization*: Keep copies of the Articles of Organization, including copies of all amendments to the Articles of Organization. If a member executed a power of attorney in connection with the execution of the Articles of Organization or amendments, keep a copy of the power of attorney.

(c) *Tax returns*: Keep copies of all tax returns. If you do not want to keep copies of older tax returns, contact a lawyer or accountant to determine the number of prior-year returns the IRS requires to be kept.

(d) *Financial statements*: If the LLC or its members created any financial statements in connection with operation of the LLC, copies of those statements should be kept.

(e) *Operating Agreement*: Perhaps the most important document to keep on file is the LLC Operating Agreement and any amendments to it. Copies of Operating Agreements that are no longer in effect should also be kept, but should be identified as superseded.

(f) *Statement of cash, property, or service contributed*: Keep a copy of any written statement setting forth the cash, property, or services contributed by each member. These statements should be kept both for initial and subsequent contributions, and should include any agreements for future contributions. The failure to keep adequate records of contributions could lead to a nasty dispute over who contributed what, and in what amount.

(g) *Voting records*: Any vote by the LLC related to such things as dissolution, admission of new members, and general operation of the LLC should be reduced to a writing and kept in the LLC records.

LLC records should be kept in a secure, fireproof location at the LLC's business offices, and key members should keep copies of the records in a safe and secure nonbusiness location.

b. KEEPING UP WITH LLC CHANGES

Review the Articles of Organization and Operating Agreement from time to time for any necessary changes. In some states, you must file amended Articles of Organization if there are changes in the LLC, such as the addition of new members.

Keep abreast of any changes in your state's LLC law. LLC laws will change over the next few years as the states fine tune the laws to correct any perceived problems. If you have a full-service LLC lawyer, any necessary changes will be explained to you and made in the Articles of Organization and Operating Agreements. If you do not have a full-service lawyer to keep you informed about changes, review the law yourself at least annually and read all local news and journal articles related to LLCs.

There is at least one newsletter dedicated solely to LLCs. It is called *LLC Reporter*, and is published by Philip Whynott & William Bagley. Subscription information may be obtained by sending inquiries to:

LLC Reporter
P.O. Box 1436
Cheyenne, WY 82003

Subscribing to a newsletter such as *LLC Reporter* may help you keep track of important changes in LLC laws and provide you with helpful hints on management issues.

Seminars are another good source of LLC information. Your local and state bar associations probably sponsor periodic seminars on LLCs. Often, a book or some other informational material is provided as a source for continuing reference. You can meet other LLC owners at these seminars and learn from their experiences.

If some sort of LLC networking group does not exist in your area, consider starting one yourself. A group of this type provides not only a forum for discussions about LLC issues but it may also provide valuable business contacts.

Finally, if you are an Internet "surfer," you should be able to access a wealth of information on the World Wide Web related to LLCs. You will also find sources for obtaining answers to your LLC questions.

c. ANNUAL FEES AND REPORTS

Keep track of any annual fees or annual reports. For example, in Arkansas, an LLC is required to pay an annual franchise tax, similar to the franchise tax paid by corporations. In Illinois, LLCs must pay a $300 annual renewal fee. Indiana and Montana require the filing of an annual report listing the LLC name, its registered agent, and principal address. No financial information is required in the report. In Rhode Island, LLCs must file an annual report and pay an annual fee of $50. Call your secretary of state. Its staff should be able to explain any annual report and fee requirements.

Failure to pay an annual fee or file an annual report could have negative consequences. In the corporate context, the failure to file a report or pay a fee often results in being labelled "not in good standing." LLCs will probably be treated the same way. Therefore, all fees should be paid and reports filed on a timely basis so that the members continue to enjoy limited liability.

d. WORKERS' AND UNEMPLOYMENT COMPENSATION

It is unclear how regulatory agencies will treat LLC members concerning workers' compensation and unemployment compensation laws. The question is whether members will be considered employees and, therefore, entitled to compensation and benefits. If members are entitled to these benefits, the LLC must then pay the corresponding insurance premiums and payroll taxes.

Generally, the officers and directors of a corporation are considered employees and, therefore, are subject to the workers' compensation and unemployment compensation laws. Partners who are active in a partnership, however, are usually not considered employees and are excluded from those laws. Often, partnerships and sole proprietors may elect to be treated as employees and receive coverage under the workers' compensation law. Corporate officers may be able to make the reverse election and choose not to be treated as employees for purposes of the workers' compensation law.

One commentator on the issue of workers' and unemployment compensation laws believes that their application should depend on whether the LLC is member managed or manager managed. His proposal is to treat member-managed LLCs as partnerships for purposes of the workers' and unemployment compensation laws. Manager-managed LLCs, however, would be treated as corporations. In other words, members of a member-managed LLC would not fall within the workers' and unemployment compensation laws. However, they may be able to elect employee status and fall within the workers' compensation law. Members of manager-managed LLCs would fall within the workers' and unemployment compensation laws, but members may be able to elect nonemployee status and fall outside the workers' compensation law.

Certainly, the regulatory agencies responsible for implementing the workers' and unemployment compensation laws will provide some guidance. Contact the appropriate agency if you have any concerns about your LLC's status under these laws. State legislatures will also probably take some action in the next few years to clarify the application of many laws to LLCs.

e. IS AN LLP MORE APPROPRIATE?

For some businesses, such as professional firms that are not allowed to operate as LLCs, a limited liability partnership (LLP) may be more appropriate than an LLC. At least 35 states have enacted LLP laws. LLP laws have also enjoyed the enormous growth experienced by LLC laws. But there are important differences between an LLP and an LLC.

An LLP is a partnership that has filed a document with the secretary of state in order to provide the partners with limited liability. An LLP, like an LLC, must identify itself by either using the phrase "limited liability partnership" or the abbreviation "LLP" after the firm's name. Members of an LLC, however, are able to agree on many things, such as voting rights and continuation after member dissociation, that may not be agreed on by a partnership. Perhaps the most important difference, though, is the nature of the liability limitation. An LLP partner remains liable for his or her share of the partnership debts, liabilities, and obligations. An LLC member, on the other hand, is not liable for the LLC's debts, liabilities, and obligations.

f. A FINAL NOTE

We are living through the birth and infancy of a new business entity. Adolescence and adulthood come later. LLCs are designed to provide the best mixture of limited liability, tax classification, flexibility, and freedom of contract. The exciting thing about LLCs is that the creators have the power to mold their businesses to serve a variety of purposes. LLCs have the ability also to make operation of the businesses easier, more efficient, and, hopefully, more profitable.

As with most infants, an LLC initially needs a lot of attention. However, infants grow up and become adults in the blink of an eye. Most people will probably find that their LLC requires less attention after awhile.

If this book makes the initial LLC learning period easier for the reader, it will have served its purpose. Don't think that the learning period will someday magically end. It won't. LLC law and the ways in which they are formed and operated will continue to evolve for many years to come. You are riding the crest of a wave that could fundamentally change the way in which business is conducted in the United States for years to come. Enjoy the ride!

APPENDIX 1
UNIFORM LIMITED LIABILITY COMPANY ACT

COPYRIGHT 1995
BY
NATIONAL CONFERENCE OF COMMISSIONERS
ON UNIFORM STATE LAW

[ARTICLE] 1
GENERAL PROVISIONS

Section 101. Definitions.
Section 102. Knowledge and Notice.
Section 103. Effect of Operating Agreement; Nonwaivable Provisions.
Section 104. Supplemental Principles of Law.
Section 105. Name.
Section 106. Reserved Name.
Section 107. Registered Name.
Section 108. Designated Office and Agent for Service of Process.
Section 109. Change of Designated Office or Agent for Service of Process.
Section 110. Resignation of Agent for Service of Process.
Section 111. Service of Process.
Section 112. Nature of Business and Powers.

SECTION 101. DEFINITIONS. In this [Act]:

(1) "Articles of organization" means initial, amended, and restated articles of organization and articles of merger. In the case of a foreign limited liability company, the term includes all records serving a similar function required to be filed in the office of the [secretary of state] or comparable office of the company's jurisdiction of organization.

(2) "Business" includes every trade, occupation, profession, and other lawful purpose, whether or not carried on for profit.

(3) "Debtor in bankruptcy" means a person who is the subject of an order for relief under Title 11 of the United States Code or a comparable order under federal, state, or foreign law governing insolvency.

(4) "Distribution" means a transfer of money, property, or other benefit from a limited liability company to a member in the member's capacity as a member or to a transferee of the member's distributional interest.

(5) "Distributional interest" means all of a member's interest in distributions by the limited liability company.

Note: The ULLCA is not a state or federal statute. It is a "model" law created by a panel of lawyers and law professors with LLC expertise. This model will likely serve as the basis for any fine tuning of state LLC laws or may replace current LLC laws in effect. Reprinted with permission from the National Conference of Commissioners on Uniform State Laws.

(6) "Entity" means a person other than an individual.

(7) "Foreign limited liability company" means an unincorporated entity organized under laws other than the laws of this State which afford limited liability to its owners comparable to the liability under Section 303 and is not required to obtain a certificate of authority to transact business under any law of this State other than this [Act].

(8) "Limited liability company" means a limited liability company organized under this [Act].

(9) "Manager" means a person, whether or not a member of a manager-managed limited liability company, who is vested with authority under Section 301.

(10) "Manager-managed limited liability company" means a limited liability company which is so designated in its articles of organization.

(11) "Member-managed limited liability company" means a limited liability company other than a manager-managed company.

(12) "Operating agreement" means the agreement under Section 103 concerning the relations among the members, manager, and limited liability company. The term includes amendments to the agreement.

(13) "Person" means an individual, corporation, business trust, estate, trust, partnership, limited liability company, association, joint venture, government, governmental subdivision, agency, or instrumentality, or any other legal or commercial entity.

(14) "Principal office" means the office, whether or not in this State, where the principal executive office of a domestic or foreign limited liability company is located.

(15) "Record" means information that is inscribed on a tangible medium or that is stored in an electronic or other medium and is retrievable in perceivable form.

(16) "Signed" includes any symbol executed or adopted by a person with the present intention to authenticate a record.

(17) "State" means a State of the United States, the District of Columbia, the Commonwealth or Puerto Rico, or any territory or insular possession subject to the jurisdiction of the United States.

(18) "Transfer" includes an assignment, conveyance, deed, bill of sale, lease, mortgage, security interest, encumbrance, and gift.

SECTION 102. KNOWLEDGE AND NOTICE.

(a) A person knows a fact if the person has actual knowledge of it.

(b) A person has notice of a fact if the person:

(1) knows the fact;

(2) has received a notification of the fact; or

(3) has reason to know the fact exists from all of the facts known to the person at the time in question.

(c) A person notifies or gives a notification of a fact to another by taking steps reasonably required to inform the other person in ordinary course, whether or not the other person knows the fact.

(d) A person receives a notification when the notification:

(1) comes to the person's attention; or

(2) is duly delivered at the person's place of business or at any other place held out by the person as a place for receiving communications.

(e) An entity knows, has notice, or receives a notification of a fact for purposes of a particular transaction when the individual conducting the transaction for the entity knows, has notice, or receives a notification of the fact, or in any event when the fact would have been brought to the individual's attention had the entity exercised reasonable diligence. An entity exercises reasonable diligence if it maintains reasonable routines for communicating significant information to the individual conducting the transaction for the entity and there is reasonable compliance with the routines. Reasonable diligence does not require an individual acting for the entity to communicate information unless the communication is part of the individual's regular duties or the individual has reason to know of the transaction and that the transaction would be materially affected by the information.

SECTION 103. EFFECT OF OPERATING AGREEMENT; NONWAIVABLE PROVISIONS.

(a) Except as otherwise provided in subsection (b), all members of a limited liability company may enter into an operating agreement, which need not be in writing, to regulate the affairs of the company and the conduct of its business, and to govern relations among the members, managers, and company. To the extent the operating agreement does not otherwise provide, this [Act] governs relations among the members, managers, and company.

(b) The operating agreement may not:

(1) unreasonably restrict a right to information or access to records under Section 408;

(2) eliminate the duty of loyalty under Section 409(b) or 603(b)(3), but the agreement may:

(i) identify specific types or categories of activities that do not violate the duty of loyalty, if not manifestly unreasonable; and

(ii) specify the number or percentage of members or disinterested managers that may authorize or ratify, after full disclosure of all material facts, a specific act or transaction that otherwise would violate the duty of loyalty;

(3) unreasonably reduce the duty of care under Section 409(c) or 603(b)(3);

(4) eliminate the obligation of good faith and fair dealing under Section 409(d), but the operating agreement may determine the standards by which the performance of the obligation is to be measured, if the standards are not manifestly unreasonable;

(5) vary the right to expel a member in an event specified in Section 601(5);

(6) vary the requirement to wind up the limited liability company's business in a case specified in Sections 801(4) or (5); or

(7) restrict rights of third parties under this [Act], other than managers, members or their transferees.

SECTION 104. SUPPLEMENTAL PRINCIPLES OF LAW.

(a) Unless displaced by particular provisions of this [Act], the principles of law and equity supplement this [Act].

(b) If an obligation to pay interest arises under this [Act] and the rate is not specified, the rate is that specified in [applicable statute].

SECTION 105. NAME.

(a) The name of a limited liability company must contain "limited liability company" or "limited company" or the abbreviation "L.L.C.", "LLC", "L.C.", or "LC". "Limited" may be abbreviated as "Ltd.", and "company" may be abbreviated as "Co.".

(b) Except as authorized by subsections (c) and (d), the name of a limited liability company must be distinguishable upon the records of the [Secretary of State] from:

(1) the name of any corporation, limited partnership, or company incorporated, organized or authorized to transact business, in this State;

(2) a company name reserved or registered under Section 106 or 107;

(3) a fictitious name approved under Section 1005 for a foreign company authorized to transact business in this State because its real name is unavailable.

(c) A limited liability company may apply to the [Secretary of State] for authorization to use a name that is not distinguishable upon the records of the [Secretary of State] from one or more of the names described in subsection (b). The [Secretary of State] shall authorize use of the name applied for if:

(1) the present use, registrant, or owner of a reserved name consents to the use in a record and submits an undertaking in form satisfactory to the [Secretary of State] to change the name to a name that is distinguishable upon the records of the [Secretary of State] from the name applied for; or

(2) the applicant delivers to the [Secretary of State] a certified copy of the final judgment of a court of competent jurisdiction establishing the applicant's right to use the name applied for in this State.

(d) A limited liability company may use the name, including a fictitious name, of another domestic or foreign company which is used in this State if the other company is organized or authorized to transact business in this State and the company proposing to use the name has:

(1) merged with the other company;

(2) been formed by reorganization with the other company; or

(3) acquired substantially all of the assets, including the company name, of the other company.

SECTION 106. RESERVED NAME.

(a) A person may reserve the exclusive use of the name of a limited liability company, including a fictitious name for a foreign company whose company name is not available, by delivering an application to the [Secretary of State] for filing. The application must set forth the name and address of the applicant and the name proposed to be reserved. If the [Secretary of State] finds that the name applied for is available, it must be reserved for the applicant's exclusive use for a nonrenewable 120-day period.

(b) The owner of a name reserved for a limited liability company may transfer the reservation to another person by delivering to the [Secretary of State] a signed notice of the transfer which states the name and address of the transferee.

SECTION 107. REGISTERED NAME.

(a) A foreign limited liability company may register its company name subject to the requirements of Section 1005, if the name is distinguishable upon the records of the [Secretary of State] from company names that are not available under Section 105(b).

(b) A foreign limited liability company registers its company name, or its company name with any addition required by Section 1005, by delivering to the [Secretary of State] for filing an application:

(1) setting forth its company names, or its company name with any addition required by Section 1005, the State or country and date of its organization, and a brief description of the nature of the business in which it is engaged; and

(2) accompanied by a certificate of existence, or a record of similar import, from the State or country of organization.

(c) A foreign limited liability company whose registration is effective may renew it for successive years by delivering for filing in the office of the [Secretary of State] a renewal application complying with subsection (b) between October 1 and December 31 of the preceding year. The renewal application renews the registration for the following calendar year.

(d) A foreign limited liability company whose registration is effective may qualify as a foreign company under its company name or consent in writing to the use of its name by a limited liability company later organized under this [Act] or by another foreign company later authorized to transact business in this State. The registered name terminates when the limited liability company is organized or the foreign company qualifies or consents to the qualification of another foreign company under the registered name.

SECTION 108. DESIGNATED OFFICE AND AGENT FOR SERVICE OF PROCESS.

(a) A limited liability company and a foreign limited liability company authorized to do business in this State shall designate and continuously maintain in this State:

(1) an office, which need not be a place of its business in this State; and

(2) an agent and street address of the agent for service of process on the company.

(b) An agent must be an individual resident of this State, a domestic corporation, another limited liability company, or a foreign corporation or foreign company authorized to do business in this State.

SECTION 109. CHANGE OF DESIGNATED OFFICE OR AGENT FOR SERVICE OF PROCESS.
A limited liability company may change its designated office or agent for service of process by delivering to the [Secretary of State] for filing a statement of change which sets forth:

(1) the name of the company;

(2) the street address of its current designated office;

(3) if the current designated office is to be changed, the street address of the new designated office;

(4) the name and address of its current agent for service of process; and

(5) if the current agent for service of process or street address of that agent is to be changed, the new address or the name and street address of the new agent for service of process.

SECTION 110. RESIGNATION OF AGENT FOR SERVICE OF PROCESS.

(a) An agent for service of process of a limited liability company may resign by delivering to the [Secretary of State] for filing a record of the statement of resignation.

(b) After filing a statement of resignation, the [Secretary of State] shall mail a copy to the designated office and another copy to the limited liability company at its principal office.

(c) An agency is terminated on the 31st day after the statement is filed in the office of the [Secretary of State].

SECTION 111. SERVICE OF PROCESS.

(a) An agent for service of process appointed by a limited liability company or a foreign limited liability company is an agent of the company for service of any process, notice, or demand required or permitted by law to be served upon the company.

(b) If a limited liability company or foreign limited liability company fails to appoint or maintain an agent for service of process in this State or the agent for service of process cannot with reasonable diligence be found at the agent's address, the [Secretary of State] is an agent of the company upon whom process, notice, or demand may be served.

(c) Service of any process, notice, or demand on the [Secretary of State] may be made by delivering to and leaving with the [Secretary of State], the [Assistant Secretary of State], or clerk having charge of the limited liability company department of the [Secretary of State's] office duplicate copies of the process, notice, or demand. If the process, notice, or demand is served on the [Secretary of State], the [Secretary of State] shall forward one of the copies by registered or certified mail, return receipt requested, to the company at its designated office. Service is effected under this subsection at the earliest of:

(1) the date the company receives the process, notice, or demand;

(2) the date shown on the return receipt, if signed on behalf of the company; or

(3) five days after its deposit in the mail, if mailed postpaid and correctly addressed.

(d) The [Secretary of State] shall keep a record of all processes, notices, and demands served pursuant to this section and record the time of and the action taken regarding the service.

(e) This section does not affect the right to serve process, notice, or demand in any manner otherwise provided by law.

SECTION 112. NATURE OF BUSINESS AND POWERS.

(a) A limited liability company may be organized under this [Act] for any lawful purpose, subject to any law of this State governing or regulating business.

(b) Unless its articles of organization provide otherwise, a limited liability company has the same powers as an individual to do all things necessary or convenient to carry on its business or affairs, including power to:

(1) sue and be sued, and defend in its company name;

(2) purchase, receive, lease, or otherwise acquire, and own, hold, improve, use, and otherwise deal with real or personal property, or any legal or equitable interest in property, wherever located;

(3) sell, convey, mortgage, grant a security interest in, lease, exchange, and otherwise encumber or dispose of all or any part of its property;

(4) purchase, receive, subscribe for, or otherwise acquire, own, hold, vote, use, sell, mortgage, lend, grant a security interest in, or otherwise dispose of and deal in and with, share, or other interests in or obligations of any other entity;

(5) make contracts and guarantees, incur liabilities, borrow money, issue its notes, bonds, and other obligations, which may be convertible into or include the option to purchase other securities of the limited liability company, and secure any of its obligations by a mortgage on or a security interest in any of its property, franchises, or income;

(6) lend money, invest and reinvest its funds, and receive and hold real and personal property as security for repayment;

(7) be a promoter, partner, member, associate, or manager of any partnership, joint venture, trust, or other entity;

(8) conduct its business, locate offices, and exercise the powers granted by this [Act] within or without this State;

(9) elect managers and appoint officers, employees, and agents of the limited liability company, define their duties, fix their compensation, and lend them money and credit;

(10) pay pensions and establish pension plans, pension trusts, profit sharing plans, share bonus plans, share option plans and benefit or incentive plans for any or all of its current or former members, managers, officers, employees, and agents;

(11) make donations for the public welfare or for charitable, scientific, or educational purposes; and

(12) make payments or donations, or do any other act, not inconsistent with law, that furthers the business of the limited liability company.

[ARTICLE] 2
ORGANIZATION

Section 201. Limited Liability Company as Legal Entity.
Section 202. Organization.
Section 203. Articles of Organization.
Section 204. Amendment or Restatement of Articles of Organization.
Section 205. Signing of Records.
Section 206. Filing in Office of [Secretary of State].
Section 207. Correcting Filed Record.
Section 208. Certificate of Existence or Authorization.
Section 209. Liability for False Statement in Filed Record.
Section 210. Filing by Judicial Act.
Section 211. Annual Report for [Secretary of State].

SECTION 201. LIMITED LIABILITY COMPANY AS LEGAL ENTITY. A limited liability company is a legal entity distinct from its members.

SECTION 202. ORGANIZATION.

(a) One or more persons may organize a limited liability company, consisting of one or more members, by delivering articles of organization to the office of the [Secretary of State] for filing.

(b) Unless a delayed effective date is specified, the existence of a limited liability company begins when the articles of organization are filed.

(c) The filing of the articles of organization by the [Secretary of State] is conclusive proof that the organizers satisfied all conditions precedent to the creation of the organization.

SECTION 203. ARTICLES OF ORGANIZATION.

(a) Articles of organization of a limited liability company must set forth:

(1) the name of the company;

(2) the address of the initial designated office;

(3) the name and street address of the initial agent for service of process;

(4) the name and address of each organizer;

(5) whether the duration of the company is for a specified term and, if so, the period specified;

(6) whether the company is to be manager-managed, and, if so, the name and address of each initial manager; and

(7) whether the members of the company are to be liable for its debts and obligations under Section 303(c).

(b) Articles of organization of a limited liability company may set forth:

(1) provisions permitted to be set forth in an operating agreement; or

(2) other matters not inconsistent with law.

(c) Articles of organization of a limited liability company may not vary the nonwaivable provisions of Section 103(b). As to all other matters, if any provision of an operating agreement is inconsistent with the articles of organization:

(1) the operating agreement controls as to managers, members, and members' transferees; and

(2) the articles of organization control as to persons other than managers, members, and their transferees who rely on the articles to their detriment.

(d) The duration of a limited liability company is at-will unless a term for its duration is specified in its articles of organization.

SECTION 204. AMENDMENT OR RESTATEMENT OF ARTICLES OF ORGANIZATION.

(a) Articles of organization of a limited liability company may be amended at any time by delivering articles of amendment to the [Secretary of State] for filing. The articles of amendment must set forth the:

(1) name of the limited liability company;

(2) date of filing of the articles of organization; and

(3) amendment to the articles.

(b) A limited liability company may restate its articles of organization at any time. Restated articles of organization must be signed and filed in the same manner as articles of amendment. Restated articles of organization must be designated as such in the heading and state in the heading or in an introductory paragraph the limited liability company's present name and, if it has been changed, all of its former names and the date of the filing of its initial articles of organization.

SECTION 205. SIGNING OF RECORDS.

(a) Except as otherwise provided in this [Act], a record to be filed by or on behalf of a limited liability company in the office of the [Secretary of State] must be signed in the name of the company by a:

(1) manager of a manager-managed company;

(2) member of a member-managed company;

(3) person organizing the company, if the company has not been formed; or

(4) fiduciary, if the company is in the hands of a receiver, trustee, or other court-appointed fiduciary.

(b) A record signed under subsection (a) must state adjacent to the signature the name and capacity of the signer.

(c) A person signing a record to be filed under subsection (a) may do so as an attorney-in-fact without any formality. An authorization, including a power of attorney, to sign a record need not be in writing, sworn to, verified, or acknowledged or filed in the office of the [Secretary of State].

SECTION 206. FILING IN OFFICE OF [SECRETARY OF STATE].

(a) Articles of organization or any other record authorized to be filed under this [Act] must be in a medium permitted by the [Secretary of State] and must be delivered to the office of the [Secretary of State]. Unless the [Secretary of State] determines that a record fails to comply as to form with the filing requirements of this [Act], and if all filing fees have been paid, the [Secretary of State] shall file the record and send a receipt for the record and the fees to the limited liability company or its representative.

(b) Upon request and payment of a fee, the [Secretary of State] shall send to the requester a certified copy of the requested record.

(c) A record accepted for filing by the [Secretary of State] is effective:

(1) on the date it is filed, as evidenced by the [Secretary of State] maintaining a record of the date and time of the filing;

(2) at the time specified in the record as its effective time; or

(3) on the date and at the time specified in the record if the record specifies a delayed effective date and time.

(d) If a delayed effective date for a record is specified but no time is specified, the record is effective at 12:01 a.m. on that date. A delayed effective date that is later than the 90th day after the record is filed makes the record effective as of the 90th day.

SECTION 207. CORRECTING FILED RECORD.

(a) A limited liability company or foreign limited liability company may correct a record filed by the [Secretary of State] if the record contains a false or erroneous statement or was defectively signed.

(b) A record is corrected:

(1) by preparing articles of correction that:

(i) describe the record, including its filing date, or attach a copy of it to the articles of correction;

(ii) specify the incorrect statement and the reason it is incorrect or the manner in which the signing was defective; and

(iii) correct the incorrect statement or defective signing; and

(2) by delivering the corrected record to the [Secretary of State] for filing.

(c) Articles of correction are effective retroactively to the effective date of the record they correct. However, a person who has relied on the uncorrected record and was adversely affected by the correction is not bound by the correction until the articles are filed.

SECTION 208. CERTIFICATE OF EXISTENCE OR AUTHORIZATION.

(a) A person may request the [Secretary of State] to furnish a certificate of existence for a limited liability company or a certificate of authorization for a foreign limited liability company.

(b) A certificate of existence for a limited liability company must set forth:

(1) the company's name;

(2) that it is duly organized under the laws of this State, the date of organization, whether its duration is at-will or for a specified term, and, if the latter, the period specified;

(3) if payment is reflected in the records of the [Secretary of State] and nonpayment affects the existence of the company, that all fees, taxes, and penalties owed to this State have been paid;

(4) whether its most recent annual report required by Section 211 has been filed with the [Secretary of State];

(5) that articles of termination have not been filed; and

(6) other facts of record in the office of the [Secretary of State] which may be requested by the applicant.

(c) A certificate of authorization for a foreign limited liability company must set forth:

(1) the company's name used in this State;

(2) that it is authorized to transact business in this State;

(3) if payment is reflected in the records of the [Secretary of State] and nonpayment affects the authorization of the company, that all fees, taxes, and penalties owed to this State have been paid;

(4) whether its most recent annual report required by Section 211 has been filed with the [Secretary of State];

(5) that a certificate of cancellation has not been filed; and

(6) other facts of record in the office of the [Secretary of State] which may be requested by the applicant.

(d) Subject to any qualification stated in the certificate, a certificate of existence or authorization issued by the [Secretary of State] may be relied upon as conclusive evidence that the domestic or foreign limited liability company is in existence or is authorized to transact business in this State.

SECTION 209. LIABILITY FOR FALSE STATEMENT IN FILED RECORD. If a record authorized or required to be filed under this [Act] contains a false statement, one who suffers loss by reliance on the statement may recover damages for the loss from a person who signed the record or caused another to sign it on the person's behalf and knew the statement to be false at the time the record was signed.

SECTION 210. FILING BY JUDICIAL ACT. If a person required by Section 205 to sign any record fails or refuses to do so, any other person who is adversely affected by the failure or refusal may petition the [designate the appropriate court] to direct the signing of the record. If the court finds that it is proper for the record to be signed and that a person so designated has failed or refused to sign the record, it shall order the [Secretary of State] to sign and file an appropriate record.

SECTION 211. ANNUAL REPORT FOR [SECRETARY OF STATE].

(a) A limited liability company, and a foreign limited liability company authorized to transact business in this State, shall deliver to the [Secretary of State] for filing an annual report that sets forth:

(1) the name of the company and the State or country under whose law it is organized.

(2) the address of its designated office and the name and address of its agent for service of process in this State;

(3) the address of its principal office; and

(4) the names and business addresses of any managers.

(b) Information in an annual report must be current as of the date the annual report is signed on behalf of the limited liability company.

(c) The first annual report must be delivered to the [Secretary of State] between [January 1 and April 1] of the year following the calendar year in which a limited liability company was organized or a foreign company was authorized to transact business. Subsequent annual reports must be delivered to the [Secretary of State] between [January 1 and April 1] of the following calendar years.

(d) If an annual report does not contain the information required in subsection (a), the [Secretary of State] shall promptly notify the reporting limited liability company or foreign limited liability company and return the report to it for correction. If the report is corrected to contain the information required in subsection (a) and delivered to the [Secretary of State] within 30 days after the effective date of the notice, it is timely filed.

[ARTICLE] 3
RELATIONS OF MEMBERS AND MANAGERS TO PERSONS DEALING WITH
LIMITED LIABILITY COMPANY

Section 301. Agency of Members and Managers.
Section 302. Limited Liability Company Liable for Member's or Manager's Actionable Conduct.
Section 303. Liability of Members and Managers.

SECTION 301. AGENCY OF MEMBERS AND MANAGERS.

(a) Subject to subsections (b) and (c):

(1) each member is an agent of the limited liability company for the purpose of its business;

(2) an act of a member, including the signing of an instrument in the company name, for apparently carrying on in the ordinary course the company's business or business of the kind carried on by the company binds the company, unless the member had no authority to act for the company in the particular matter and the person with whom the member was dealing knew or had notice that the member lacked authority; and

(3) an act of a member which is not apparently for carrying on in the ordinary course the company's business or business of the kind carried on by the company binds the company only if the act was authorized by the other members.

(b) Subject to subsection (c), in a manager-managed limited liability company:

(1) a member is not an agent of the company for the purpose of its business solely by reason of being a member;

(2) each manager is an agent of the company for the purpose of its business;

(3) an act of a manager, including the signing of an instrument in the company name, for apparently carrying on in the ordinary course the company's business or business of the kind carried on by the company binds the company, unless the manager had no authority to act for the company in the particular matter and the person with whom the manager was dealing knew or had notice that the manager lacked authority; and

(4) an act of a manager which is not apparently for carrying on in the ordinary course the company's business or business of the kind carried on by the company binds the company only if the act was authorized under Section 404(b)(2).

(c) Unless the articles of organization limit their authority, any member of a member-managed limited liability company, or any manager of a manager-managed company, may sign and deliver any instrument transferring or affecting the company's interest in real property. The instrument is conclusive in favor of a person who gives value without knowledge of the lack of authority of the person signing and delivering the instrument.

SECTION 302. LIMITED LIABILITY COMPANY LIABLE FOR MEMBER'S OR MANAGER'S ACTIONABLE CONDUCT. A limited liability company is liable for loss or injury caused to a person, or for a penalty incurred, as a result of a wrongful act or omission, or other actionable conduct, of a member or manager acting in the ordinary course of business of the company or with authority of the company.

SECTION 303. LIABILITY OF MEMBERS AND MANAGERS.

(a) Except as otherwise provided in subsection (c), the debts, obligations, and liabilities of a limited liability company, whether arising in contract, tort, or otherwise, are solely the debts, obligations, and liabilities of the company. A member or manager is not personally liable for debt, obligation, or liability of the company solely by reason of being or acting as a member or manager.

(b) The failure of a limited liability company to observe the usual company formalities or requirements relating to the exercise of its company powers or management of its business is not a ground for imposing personal liability on the members or managers for liabilities of the company.

(c) All specified members of a limited liability company are liable in their capacity as members for all or specified debts, obligations, or liabilities of the company if:

(1) a provision to that effect is contained in the articles of organization; and

(2) a member so liable has consented in writing to the adoption of the provision or to be bound by the provision.

[ARTICLE] 4
RELATIONS OF MEMBERS TO EACH OTHER AND TO
LIMITED LIABILITY COMPANY

Section 401.	Form of Contribution.
Section 402.	Member's Liability for Contributions.
Section 403.	Member's and Manager's Rights to Payments and Reimbursement.
Section 404.	Management of Limited Liability Company.
Section 405.	Sharing of and Right to Distributions.
Section 406.	Limitations on Distributions.
Section 407.	Liability for Unlawful Distributions.
Section 408.	Member's Right to Information.
Section 409.	General Standards of Member's and Manager's Conduct.
Section 410.	Actions by Members.
Section 411.	Continuation of Limited Liability Company After Expiration of Specified Term.

SECTION 401. FORM OF CONTRIBUTION. A contribution of a member of a limited liability company may consist of tangible or intangible property or other benefit to the company, including money, promissory notes, services performed, or other obligations to contribute cash or property, or contracts for services to be performed.

SECTION 402. MEMBER'S LIABILITY FOR CONTRIBUTION.

(a) A member's obligation to contribute money, property, or other benefit to, or to perform services for, a limited liability company is not excused by the member's death, disability, or other inability to perform personally. If a member does not make the required contribution of property or services, the member is obligated at the option of the company to contribute money equal to that portion of the value of the stated contribution which has not been made.

(b) A creditor of a limited liability company who extends credit or otherwise acts in reliance on an obligation described in subsection (a), and without notice of any compromise under Section 404(c)(5), may enforce the original obligation.

SECTION 403. MEMBER'S AND MANAGER'S RIGHTS TO PAYMENTS AND REIMBURSEMENT.

(a) A limited liability company shall reimburse a member or manager for payments made and indemnify a member or manager for liabilities incurred by the member or manager in the ordinary course of the business of the company or for the preservation of its business or property.

(b) A limited liability company shall reimburse a member for an advance to the company beyond the amount of contribution the member agreed to make.

(c) A payment or advance made by a member which gives rise to an obligation of a limited liability company under subsection (a) or (b) constitutes a loan to the company upon which interest accrues from the date of the payment or advance.

(d) A member is not entitled to remuneration for services performed for a limited liability company, except for reasonable compensation for services rendered in winding up the business of the company.

SECTION 404. MANAGEMENT OF LIMITED LIABILITY COMPANY.

(a) In a member-managed limited liability company:

(1) each member has equal rights in the management and conduct of the company's business; and

(2) except as otherwise provided in subsection (c) or in Section 801(3)(i), any matter relating to the business of the company may be decided by a majority of the members.

(b) In a manager-managed company:

(1) the managers have the exclusive authority to manage and conduct the company's business;

(2) except as specified in subsection (c) or in Section 801(3)(i), any matter relating to the business of the company may be exclusively decided by the manager or, if there is more than one manager, by a majority of the managers; and

(3) a manager:

(i) must be designated, appointed, elected, removed, or replaced by a vote, approval, or consent of a majority of the members; and

(ii) holds office until a successor has been elected and qualified, unless sooner resigns or is removed.

(c) The only matters of a limited liability company's business requiring the consent of all of the members are:

(1) the amendment of the operating agreement under Section 103.

(2) the authorization or ratification of acts or transactions under Section 103(b)(2)(ii) which would otherwise violate the duty of loyalty;

(3) an amendment to the articles of organization under Section 204;

(4) the compromise of an obligation to make a contribution under Section 402(b);

(5) the compromise, as among members, of an obligation of a member to make a contribution or return money or property paid or distributed in violation of this [Act];

(6) the making of interim distributions under Section 405(a);

(7) the admission of a new member;

(8) the use of the company's property to redeem an interest subject to a charging order;

(9) the consent to dissolve the company under Section 801(2);

(10) a waiver of the right to have the company's business wound up and the company terminated under Section 802(b);

(11) the consent of members to merge with another entity under Section 904(c)(1); and

(12) the sale, lease, exchange, or other disposal of all, or substantially all, of the company's property with or without goodwill.

(d) Action requiring the consent of members or managers under this [Act] may be taken with or without meeting. In the event a meeting is otherwise required and a written action in lieu thereof is not prohibited, the written action must be evidenced by one or more consents reflected in a record describing the action taken and signed by all of the members or managers entitled to vote on the action.

(e) A member or manager may appoint a proxy to vote or otherwise act for the member or manager by signing an appointment instrument, either personally or by the member's or manager's attorney-in-fact. An appointment of a proxy is valid for 11 months unless a different time is specified in the appointment instrument. An appointment is revocable by the member or manager unless the appointment form conspicuously states that it is irrevocable and the appointment is coupled with an interest, in which case the appointment is revoked when the interest is extinguished.

SECTION 405. SHARING OF AND RIGHT TO DISTRIBUTIONS.

(a) Any distributions made by a limited liability company before its dissolution and winding up must be in equal shares.

(b) A member has no right to receive, and may not be required to accept, a distribution in kind.

(c) If a member becomes entitled to receive a distribution, the member has the status of, and is entitled to all remedies available to, a creditor of the limited liability company with respect to distribution.

SECTION 406. LIMITATIONS ON DISTRIBUTIONS.

(a) A distribution may not be made if:

(1) the limited liability company would not be able to pay its debts as they become due in the ordinary course of business; or

(2) the company's total assets would be less than the sum of its total liabilities plus the amount that would be needed, if the company were to be dissolved, wound up, and terminated at the time of the distribution, to satisfy the preferential rights upon dissolution, winding up, and termination of members whose preferential rights are superior to those receiving the distribution.

(b) A limited liability company may base a determination that a distribution is not prohibited under subsection (a) on financial statements prepared on the basis of accounting practices and principles that are reasonable in the circumstances or on a fair valuation or other method that is reasonable in the circumstances.

(c) Except as otherwise provided in subsection (e), the effect of a distribution under subsection (a) is measured:

(1) in the case of distribution by purchase, redemption, or other acquisition of a distributional interest in a limited liability company, as of the date money or other property is transferred or debt incurred by the company; and

(2) in all other cases, as of the date the:

(i) distribution is authorized if the payment occurs within 120 days after the date of authorization; or

(ii) payment is made if it occurs more than 120 days after the date of authorization.

(d) A limited liability company's indebtedness to a member incurred by reason of a distribution made in accordance with this section is at parity with the company's indebtedness to its general, unsecured creditors.

(e) Indebtedness of a limited liability company, including indebtedness issued in connection with or as part of a distribution, is not considered a liability for purposes of determination under subsection (a) if its terms provide that payment of principal and interest are made only if and to the extent that payment of a distribution to members could then be made under this section. If the indebtedness is issued as a distribution, each payment of principal or interest on the indebtedness is treated as a distribution, the effect of which is measured on the date the payment is made.

SECTION 407. LIABILITY FOR UNLAWFUL DISTRIBUTIONS.

(a) A member of a member-managed limited liability company or a member or manager of a manager-managed company who votes for or assents to a distribution made in violation of Section 406, the articles of organization, a written operating agreement, or a signed record is personally liable to the company for the amount of the distribution which exceeds the amount that could have been distributed without violating Section 406, the articles of organization, a written operating agreement, or a signed record if it is established that the member or manager did not perform the member's or manager's duties in compliance with Section 409.

(b) A member of a manager-managed limited liability company who knew a distribution was made in violation of Section 406 is personally liable to the limited liability company, but only to the extent that the distribution received by the member exceeded the amount that could properly have been paid under Section 406.

(c) A member or manager against whom an action is brought under this section may implead in the action all:

(1) other members or managers who voted for or assented to the distribution in violation of subsection (a) and may compel contribution from them; and

(2) members who received a distribution in violation of subsection (b) and may compel contributions from the member in the amount received in violation of subsection (b)

(d) A proceeding under this section is barred unless it is commenced within two years after the distribution.

SECTION 408. MEMBER'S RIGHT TO INFORMATION.

(a) A limited liability company shall provide members and their agents and attorneys access to any of its records at reasonable locations specified in the operating agreement. The company shall provide former members and their agents and attorneys access for proper purposes to records pertaining to the period during which they were members. The right of access provides the opportunity to inspect and copy records during ordinary business hours. The company may impose a reasonable charge, limited to the costs of labor and material, for copies of records furnished.

(b) A limited liability company shall furnish to a member, and to the legal representative of a deceased member or member under legal disability:

(1) without demand, information concerning the company's business or affairs reasonably required for the proper exercise of the member's right and performance of the member's duties under the operating agreement or this [Act]; and

(2) on demand, other information concerning the company's business or affairs, except to the extent the demand or the information demanded is unreasonable or otherwise improper under the circumstances.

(c) A member has the right upon a signed record given to the limited liability company to obtain at the company's expense a copy of any operating agreement in record form.

SECTION 409. GENERAL STANDARDS OF MEMBER'S AND MANAGER'S CONDUCT.

(a) The only fiduciary duties a member owes to a member-managed limited liability company and its other members are the duty of loyalty and the duty of care imposed by subsections (b) and (c).

(b) A member's duty of loyalty to a member-managed limited liability company and its other members is limited to the following:

(1) to account to the company and to hold as trustee for it any property, profit, or benefit derived by the member in the conduct or winding up of the company's business or derived from a

use by the member of the company's property, including the appropriation of a company's opportunity;

(2) to refrain from dealing with the company in the conduct or winding up of the company's business as or on behalf of a party having an interest adverse to the company; and

(3) to refrain from competing with the company in the conduct of the company's business before the dissolution of the company.

(c) A member's duty of care to a member-managed limited liability company and its other members in the conduct of and winding up of the company's business is limited to refraining from engaging in grossly negligent or reckless conduct, intentional misconduct, or a knowing violation of law.

(d) A member shall discharge the duties to a member-managed limited liability company and its other members under this [Act] or under the operating agreement and exercise any rights consistently with the obligation of good faith and fair dealing.

(e) A member of a member-managed limited liability company does not violate a duty or obligation under this [Act] or under the operating agreement merely because the member's conduct furthers the member's own interest.

(f) A member of a member-managed limited liability company may lend money to and transact other business with the company. As to each loan or transaction, the rights and obligations of the members are the same as those of a person who is not a member, subject to other applicable law.

(g) This section applies to a person winding up the limited liability company's business as the personal or legal representative of the last surviving member as if the person were a member.

(h) In a manager-managed limited liability company:

(1) a member who is not also a manager owes no duties to the company or to the other members solely by reason of being a member;

(2) a manager is held to the same standards of conduct prescribed for members in subsections (b) through (f);

(3) a member who pursuant to the operating agreement exercises some or all of the rights of a manager in the management and conduct of the company's business is held to the standards of conduct in subsections (b) through (f) to the extent that the member exercises the managerial authority vested in a manager by this [Act]; and

(4) a manager is relieved of liability imposed by law for violations of the standards prescribed by subsections (b) through (f) to the extent of the managerial authority delegated to the members by the operating agreement.

SECTION 410. ACTIONS BY MEMBERS.

(a) A member may maintain an action against a limited liability company or another member for legal or equitable relief, with or without an accounting as to the company's business, to enforce:

(1) the member's rights under the operating agreement;

(2) the member's rights under this [Act]; and

(3) the rights and otherwise protect the interests of the member, including rights and interests arising independently of the member's relationship to the company.

(b) The accrual, and any time limited for the assertion, of a right of action for a remedy under this section is governed by other law. A right to an accounting upon a dissolution and winding up does not revive a claim barred by law.

SECTION 411. CONTINUATION OF LIMITED LIABILITY COMPANY AFTER EXPIRATION OF SPECIFIED TERM.

(a) If a limited liability company having a specified term is continued after the expiration of the term, the rights and duties of the members and managers remain the same as they were at the expiration of the term except to the extent inconsistent with rights and duties of members and managers of an at-will company.

(b) If the members in a member-managed limited liability company or the managers in a manager-managed company continue the business without any winding up of the business of the company, it continues as an at-will company.

[ARTICLE] 5
TRANSFEREES AND CREDITORS OF MEMBER

Section 501. Member's Distributional Interest.
Section 502. Transfer of Distributional Interest.
Section 503. Rights of Transferee.
Section 504. Rights of Creditor.

SECTION 501. MEMBER'S DISTRIBUTIONAL INTEREST.

(a) A member is not a co-owner of, and has no transferable interest in, property of a limited liability company.

(b) A distributional interest in a limited liability company is personal property and, subject to Sections 502 and 503, may be transferred in whole or in part.

(c) An operating agreement may provide that a distributional interest may be evidenced by a certificate of the interest issued by the limited liability company and, subject to Section 503, may also provide for the transfer of any interest represented by the certificate.

SECTION 502. TRANSFER OF DISTRIBUTIONAL INTEREST. A transfer of a distributional interest does not entitle the transferee to become or to exercise any rights of a member. A transfer entitles the transferee to receive, to the extent transferred, only the distributions to which the transferor would be entitled. A member ceases to be a member upon transfer of all of the member's distributional interest, other than a transfer for security purposes, or a court order charging the member's distributional interest, which has not been foreclosed.

SECTION 503. RIGHTS OF TRANSFEREE.

(a) A transferee of a distributional interest may become a member of a limited liability company if and to the extent that the transferor give the transferee the right in accordance with authority described in the operating agreement or all other members consent.

(b) A transferee who has become a member, to the extent transferred, has the rights and powers, and is subject to the restrictions and liabilities, of a member under the operating agreement of a limited liability company and this [Act]. A transferee who becomes a member also is liable for the transferor member's obligations to make contributions under Section 402 and for obligations under Section 407 to return unlawful distributions, but the transferee is not obligated for the transferor member's liabilities unknown to the transferee at the time the transferee becomes a member and is not personally liable for any obligation of the company incurred before the transferee's admission as a member.

(c) Whether or not a transferee of a distributional interest becomes a member under subsection (a), the transferor is not released from liability to the limited liability company under the operating agreement or this [Act].

(d) A transferee who does not become a member is not entitled to participate in the management or conduct of the limited liability company's business, require access to information concerning the company's transactions, or inspect or copy any of the company's records.

(e) A transferee who does not become a member is entitled to:

(1) receive, in accordance with the transfer, distributions to which the transferor would otherwise be entitled;

(2) receive, upon dissolution and winding up of the limited liability company's business:

(i) in accordance with the transfer, the net amount otherwise distributable to the transferor;

(ii) a statement of account only from the date of the latest statement of account agreed to by all the members;

(3) seek under Section 801(6) a judicial determination that it is equitable to dissolve and wind up the company's business.

(f) A limited liability company need not give effect to a transfer until it has notice of the transfer.

SECTION 504. RIGHTS OF CREDITOR.

(a) On application by a judgment creditor of a member of a limited liability company or of a member's transferee, a court having jurisdiction may charge the distributional interest of the judgment debtor to satisfy the judgment. The court may appoint a receiver of the share of the distributions due or to become due to the judgment debtor and make all other orders, directions, accounts, and inquiries the judgment debtor might have made or which the circumstances may require to give effect to the charging order.

(b) A charging order constitutes a lien on the judgment debtor's distributional interest. The court may order a foreclosure of a lien on a distributional interest subject to the charging order at any time. A purchaser at the foreclosure sale has the rights of a transferee.

(c) At any time before foreclosure, a distributional interest in a limited liability company which is charged may be redeemed:

(1) by the judgment debtor;

(2) with property other than the company's property, by one or more of the other members; or

(3) with the company's property, but only if permitted by the operating agreement.

(d) This [Act] does not affect a members' right under exemption laws with respect to the member's distributional interest in a limited liability company.

(e) This section provides the exclusive remedy by which a judgment creditor of a member or a transferee may satisfy a judgment out of the judgment debtor's distributional interest in a limited liability company.

[ARTICLE] 6
MEMBER'S DISSOCIATION

Section 601. Events Causing Member's Dissociation.
Section 602. Member's Power to Dissociate; Wrongful Dissociation.
Section 603. Effect of Member's Dissociation.

SECTION 601. EVENTS CAUSING MEMBER'S DISSOCIATION. A member is dissociated from a limited liability company upon the occurrence of any of the following events:

(1) the company's having notice of the member's express will to withdraw upon the date of notice or on a later date specified by the member;

(2) an event agreed to in the operating agreement as causing the member's dissociation;

(3) the member's expulsion pursuant to the operating agreement;

(4) the member's expulsion by unanimous vote of the other members if:

(i) it is unlawful to carry on the company's business with the member;

(ii) there has been a transfer of substantially all of the member's distributional interest, other than a transfer for security purposes, or a court order charging the member's distributional interest, which has not been foreclosed.

(iii) within 90 days after the company notifies a corporate member that it will be expelled because it has filed a certificate of dissolution or the equivalent, its charter has been revoked, or its right to conduct business has been suspended by the jurisdiction of its incorporation, the member fails to obtain a revocation of the certificate of dissolution or a reinstatement of its charter or its right to conduct business; or

(iv) a partnership or a limited liability company that is a member has been dissolved and its business is being wound up;

(5) on application by the company or another member, the member's expulsion by judicial determination because the member:

(i) engaged in wrongful conduct that adversely and materially affected the company's business;

(ii) willfully or persistently committed a material breach of the operating agreement or of a duty owed to the company or the other members under Section 409; or

(iii) engaged in conduct relating to the company's business which makes it not reasonably practicable to carry on the business with the member;

(6) the member's:

(i) becoming a debtor in bankruptcy;

(ii) executing an assignment for the benefit of creditors;

(iii) seeking, consenting to, or acquiescing in the appointment of a trustee, receiver, or liquidator of the member or of all or substantially all of the member's property; or

(iv) failing, within 90 days after the appointment, to have vacated or stayed the appointment of a trustee, receiver, or liquidator of the member or of all or substantially all of the member's property obtained without the member's consent or acquiescence, or failing within 90 days after the expiration of a stay to have the appointment vacated;

(7) in the case of a member who is an individual:

(i) the member's death;

(ii) the appointment of a guardian or general conservator for the member; or

(iii) a judicial determination that the member has otherwise become incapable of performing the member's duties under the operating agreement;

(8) in the case of a member that is a trust or is acting as a member by virtue of being a trustee of a trust, distribution of the trust's entire rights to receive distributions from the company, but not merely by reason of the substitution of a successor trustee;

(9) in the case of a member that is an estate or is acting as a member by virtue of being a personal representative of an estate, distribution of the estate's entire rights to receive distributions from the company, but not merely the substitution of a successor personal representative;

(10) termination of the existence of a member if the member is not an individual, estate, or trust other than a business trust; or

(11) a termination of a member's continued membership in a limited liability company for any other reason.

SECTION 602. MEMBER'S POWER TO DISSOCIATE; WRONGFUL DISSOCIATION.

(a) A member has the power to dissociate from a limited liability company at any time, rightfully or wrongfully, by express will pursuant to Section 601(1).

(b) A member's dissociation from a limited liability company is wrongful only if:

(1) it is in breach of an express provision of the operating agreement; or

(2) before the expiration of the term of a company having a specified term:

(i) the member withdraws by express will;

(ii) the member is expelled by judicial determination under Section 601(5);

(iii) the member is dissociated by becoming a debtor in bankruptcy; or

(iv) in the case of a member who is not an individual, trust other than a business trust, or estate, the member is expelled or otherwise dissociated because it willfully dissolved or terminated its existence.

(c) A member who wrongfully dissociates from a limited liability company is liable to the company and to the other members for damages caused by the dissociation. The liability is in addition to any other obligation of the member to the company or to the other members.

(d) If a limited liability company does not dissolve and wind up its business as a result of a member's wrongful dissociation under subsection (b), damages sustained by the company for the wrongful dissociation must be offset against distributions otherwise due the member after the dissociation.

SECTION 603. EFFECT OF MEMBER'S DISSOCIATION.

(a) If under Section 801 a member's dissociation from a limited liability company results in a dissolution and winding up of the company's business, [Article] 8 applies. If a member's dissociation from the company does not result in a dissolution and winding up of the company's business under Section 801:

(1) in an at-will company, the company must cause the dissociated member's distributional interest to be purchased under [Article] 7; and

(2) in a company having a specified term:

(i) if the company dissolves and winds up its business on or before the expiration of its specified term, [Article] 8 applies to determine the dissociated member's rights to distributions; and

(ii) if the company does not dissolve and wind up its business on or before the expiration of its specified term, the company must cause the dissociated member's distributional interest to be purchased under [Article] 7 on the date of the expiration of the term specified at the time of the member's dissociation.

(b) Upon a member's dissociation from a limited liability company:

(1) the member's right to participate in the management and conduct of the company's business terminates, except as otherwise provided in Section 803, and the member ceases to be a member and is treated the same as a transferee of a member;

(2) the member's duty of loyalty under Section 409(b)(3) terminates; and

(3) the member's duty of loyalty under Section 409(b)(1) and (2) and duty of care under Section 409(c) continue only with regard to matters arising and events occurring before the member's dissociation, unless the member participates in winding up the company's business pursuant to Section 803.

[ARTICLE] 7
MEMBER'S DISSOCIATION WHEN BUSINESS NOT WOUND UP

Section 701. Company Purchase of Distributional Interest.
Section 702. Court Action to Determine Fair Value of Distributional Interest.
Section 703. Dissociated Member's Power to Bind Limited Liability Company.
Section 704. Statement of Dissociation.

SECTION 701. COMPANY PURCHASE OF DISTRIBUTIONAL INTEREST.

(a) A limited liability company shall purchase a distributional interest of a:

(1) member of an at-will limited liability company for its fair value determined as of the date of the member's dissociation if the member's dissociation does not result in a dissolution and winding up of the company's business under Section 801; or

(2) member of a company having a specified term for its fair value determined as of the date of the expiration of the specified term that existed on the member's dissociation if the expiration of the specified term does not result in a dissolution and winding up of the company's business under Section 801.

(b) A limited liability company must deliver a purchase offer to the dissociated member whose distributional interest is entitled to be purchased not later than 30 days after the date determined under subsection (a). The purchase offer must be accompanied by:

(1) a statement of the company's assets and liabilities as of the date determined under subsection (a);

(2) the latest available balance sheet and income statement, if any; and

(3) an explanation of how the estimated amount of the payment was calculated.

(c) If the price and other terms of a purchase of a distributional interest are fixed or are to be determined by the operating agreement, the price and terms so fixed or determined govern the purchase unless the purchaser defaults. In that case the dissociated member is entitled to commence a proceeding to have the company dissolved under Section 801(5)(iv).

(d) If an agreement to purchase the distributional interest in not made within 120 days after the date determined under subsection (a), the dissociated member, within another 120 days, may commence a proceeding against the limited liability company to enforce the purchase. The company at its expense shall notify in writing all of the remaining members, and any other person the court directs, of the commencement of the proceeding. The jurisdiction of the court in which the proceeding is commenced under this subsection is plenary and exclusive.

(e) The court shall determine the fair value of the distributional interest in accordance with the standards set forth in Section 702 together with the terms for the purchase. Upon making these determinations, the court shall order the limited liability company to purchase or cause the purchase of the interest.

(f) Damages for wrongful dissociation under Section 602(b), and all other amounts owing, whether or not currently due, from the dissociated member to a limited liability company, must be offset against the purchase price.

SECTION 702. COURT ACTION TO DETERMINE FAIR VALUE OF DISTRIBUTIONAL INTEREST.

(a) In an action brought to determine the fair value of a distributional interest in a limited liability company, the court shall:

(1) determine the fair value of the interest, considering among other relevant evidence the going concern value of the company, and agreement among some or all of its members fixing the price or specifying a formula for determining value of distributional interests for any purpose, the recommendations of any appraiser appointed by the court, and any legal constraints on the company's ability to purchase the interest;

(2) specify the terms of the purchase, including, if appropriate, terms for installment payments, subordination of the purchase obligation to the rights of the company's other creditors, security for a deferred purchase price, and a covenant not to compete or other restriction on a dissociated member; and

(3) require the dissociated member to deliver an assignment of the interest to the purchaser upon receipt of the purchase price or the first installment of the purchase price.

(b) After an order to purchase is entered, a party may petition the court to modify the terms of the purchase and the court may do so if it finds that changes in the financial or legal ability of the limited liability company or other purchaser to complete the purchase justify a modification.

(c) After the dissociated member delivers the assignment, the dissociated member has no further claim against the company, its members, officers, or managers, if any, other than a claim to any unpaid balance of the purchase price and a claim under any agreement with the company or remaining members that is not terminated by the court.

(d) If the purchase is not completed in accordance with the specified terms, the company is to be dissolved upon application under Section 801(5)(iv). If a limited liability company is so dissolved, the dissociated member has the same rights and priorities in the company's assets as if the sale had not been ordered.

(e) If the court finds that a party to the proceedings acted arbitrarily, vexatiously, or not in good faith, it may award one or more other parties their reasonable expenses, including attorney's fees and the expenses of appraisers or other experts, incurred in the proceeding. The finding may be based on the company's failure to make an offer to pay or to comply with Section 701(b).

(f) Interest must be paid on the amount awarded from the determined under Section 701(a) to the date of payment.

SECTION 703. DISSOCIATED MEMBER'S POWER TO BIND LIMITED LIABILITY COMPANY.

For two years after a member dissociates without the dissociation resulting in a dissolution and winding up of a limited liability company's business, the company, including a surviving company under [Article] 9, is bound by an act of the dissociated member which would have bound the company under Section 301 before dissociation only if at the time of entering into the transaction the other party:

(1) reasonably believed that the dissociated member was then a member;

(2) did not have notice of the member's dissociation; and

(3) is not deemed to have had notice under Section 704.

SECTION 704. STATEMENT OF DISSOCIATION.

(a) A dissociated member or a limited liability company may file in the office of the [Secretary of State] a statement of dissociation stating the name of the company and that the member is dissociated from the company.

(b) For the purposes of Sections 301 and 703, a person not a member is deemed to have notice of the dissociation 90 days after the statement of dissociation is filed.

[ARTICLE 8]
WINDING UP COMPANY'S BUSINESS

Section 801. Events Causing Dissolution and Winding Up of Company's Business.
Section 802. Limited Liability Company Continues After Dissolution.
Section 803. Right to Wind Up Limited Liability Company's Business.
Section 804. Member's or Manager's Power and Liability as Agent After Dissolution.
Section 805. Articles of Termination.
Section 806. Distribution of Assets in Winding Up Limited Liability Company's Business.
Section 807. Known Claims Against Dissolved Limited Liability Company.
Section 808. Other Claims Against Dissolved Limited Liability Company.
Section 809. Grounds for Administrative Dissolution.
Section 810. Procedure for and Effect of Administrative Dissolution.
Section 811. Restatement Following Administrative Dissolution.
Section 812. Appeal from Denial of Reinstatement.

SECTION 801. EVENTS CAUSING DISSOLUTION AND WINDING UP OF COMPANY'S BUSINESS.

A limited liability company is dissolved, and its business must be wound up, upon the occurrence of any of the following events:

(1) an event specified in the operating agreement;

(2) consent of the number or percentage of members specified in the operating agreement;

(3) dissociation of a member-manager or, if none, a member of an at-will company, and dissociation of a member-manager or, if none, a member of a company having a specified term but only if the dissociation was for a reason provided in Section 601(6) through (10) and occurred before the expiration of the specified term, but the company is not dissolved and required to be wound up by reason of the dissociation:

(i) if, within 90 days after the dissociation, a majority in interest of the remaining members agree to continue the business of the company; or

(ii) the business of the company is continued under a right to continue stated in the operating agreement;

(4) an event that makes it unlawful for all or substantially all of the business of the company to be continued, but any cure of illegality within 90 days after notice to the company of the event is effective retroactively to the date of the event for purposes of this section;

(5) an application by a member or a dissociated member, upon entry of a judicial decree that:

(i) the economic purpose of the company is likely to be unreasonably frustrated;

(ii) another member has engaged in conduct relating to the company's business that makes it not reasonably practicable to carry on the company's business with that member;

(iii) it is not otherwise reasonably practicable to carry on the company's business in conformity with the articles of organization and the operating agreement;

(iv) the company failed to purchase the petitioner's distributional interest as required by Section 701; or

(v) the managers or members in control of the company have acted, are acting, or will act in a manner that is illegal, oppressive, fraudulent, or unfairly prejudicial to the petitioner;

(6) on application by a transferee of a member's interest, a judicial determination that it is equitable to wind up the company's business:

(i) after the expiration of the specified term, if the company was for a specified term at the time the applicant became a transferee by member dissociation, transfer, or entry of a charging order that gave rise to the transfer; or

(ii) at any time, if the company was at will at the time the applicant became a transferee by member dissociation, transfer, or entry of a charging order that gave rise to the transfer; or

(7) the expiration of a specified term.

SECTION 802. LIMITED LIABILITY COMPANY CONTINUES AFTER DISSOLUTION.

(a) Subject to subsection (b), a limited liability company continues after dissolution only for the purpose of winding up its business.

(b) At any time after the dissolution of a limited liability company and before the winding up of its business is completed, the members, including a dissociated member whose dissociation caused the dissolution, may unanimously waive the right to have the company's business wound up and the company terminated. In that case:

(1) the limited liability company resumes carrying on its business as if dissolution had never occurred and any liability incurred by the company or a member after the dissolution and before the waiver is determined as if the dissolution had never occurred; and

(2) the rights of a third party accruing under Section 804(a) or arising out of conduct in reliance on the dissolution before the third party knew or received a notification of the waiver are not adversely affected.

SECTION 803. RIGHT TO WIND UP LIMITED LIABILITY COMPANY'S BUSINESS.

(a) After dissolution, a member who has not wrongfully dissociated may participate in winding up a limited liability company's business, but on application of any member, member's legal representative, or transferee, the [designate the appropriate court], for good cause shown, may order judicial supervision of the winding up.

(b) A legal representative of the last surviving member may wind up a limited liability company's business.

(c) A person winding up a limited liability company's business may preserve the company's business or property as a going concern for a reasonable time, prosecute and defend actions and proceedings, whether civil, criminal, or administrative, settle and close the company's business, dispose of and transfer the company's property, discharge the company's liabilities, distribute the assets of the company pursuant to Section 806, settle disputes by mediation or arbitration, and perform other necessary acts.

SECTION 804. MEMBER'S OR MANAGER'S POWER AND LIABILITY AS AGENT AFTER DISSOLUTION.

(a) A limited liability company is bound by a member's or manager's act after dissolution that:

(1) is appropriate for winding up the company's business; or

(2) would have bound the company under Section 301 before dissolution, if the other party to the transaction did not have notice of the dissolution.

(b) A member or manager who, with knowledge of the dissolution, subjects a limited liability company to liability by an act that is not appropriate for winding up the company's business is liable to the company for any damage caused to the company arising from the liability.

SECTION 805. ARTICLES OF TERMINATION.

(a) At any time after dissolution and winding up, a limited liability company may terminate its existence by filing with the [Secretary of State] articles of termination stating:

(1) the name of the company;

(2) the date of the dissolution; and

(3) that the company's business has been wound up and the legal existence of the company has been terminated.

(b) The existence of a limited liability company is terminated upon the filing of the articles of termination, or upon a later effective date, if specified in the articles of termination.

SECTION 806. DISTRIBUTION OF ASSETS IN WINDING UP LIMITED LIABILITY COMPANY'S BUSINESS.

(a) In winding up a limited liability company's business, the assets of the company must be applied to discharge its obligations to creditors, including members who are creditors. Any surplus must be applied to pay in money the net amount distributable to members in accordance with their right to distributions under section (b).

(b) Each member is entitled to a distribution upon the winding up of the limited liability company's business consisting of a return of all contributions which have not previously been returned and a distribution of any remainder in equal shares.

SECTION 807. KNOWN CLAIMS AGAINST DISSOLVED LIMITED LIABILITY COMPANY.

(a) A dissolved limited liability company may dispose of the known claims against it by following the procedure described in this section.

(b) A dissolved limited liability company shall notify its known claimants in writing of the dissolution. The notice must:

(1) specify the information required to be included in a claim;

(2) provide a mailing address where the claim is to be sent;

(3) state the deadline for receipt of the claim, which may not be less than 120 days after the date the written notice is received by the claimant; and

(4) state that the claim will be barred if not received by the deadline.

(c) A claim against a dissolved limited liability company is barred if the requirements of subsection (b) are met, and;

(1) the claim is not received by the specified deadline; or

(2) in the case of a claim that is timely received but rejected by the dissolved company, the claimant does not commence a proceeding to enforce the claim within 90 days after the receipt of the notice of the rejection.

(d) For purposes of this section, "claim" does not include a contingent liability or a claim based on an event occurring after the effective date of dissolution.

SECTION 808. OTHER CLAIMS AGAINST DISSOLVED LIMITED LIABILITY COMPANY.

(a) A dissolved limited liability company may publish notice of its dissolution and request persons having claims against the company to present them in accordance with the notice.

(b) The notice must:

(1) be published at least once in a newspaper of general circulation in the [county] in which the dissolved limited liability company's principal office is located or, if none in this State, in which its designated office is or was last located;

(2) describe the information required to be contained in a claim and provide a mailing address where the claim is to be sent; and

(3) state that a claim against the limited liability company is barred unless a proceeding to enforce the claim is commenced within five years after publication of the notice.

(c) If a dissolved limited liability company publishes a notice in accordance with subsection (b), the claim of each of the following claimants is barred unless the claimant commences a proceeding to enforce the claim against the dissolved company within five years after the publication date of the notice:

(1) a claimant who did not receive written notice under Section 807;

(2) a claimant whose claim was timely sent to the dissolved company but not acted on; and

(3) a claimant whose claim is contingent or based on an event occurring after the effective date of dissolution.

(d) A claim not barred under this section may be enforced:

(1) against the dissolved limited liability company, to the extent of its undistributed assets; or

(2) if the assets have been distributed in liquidation, against a member of the dissolved company to the extent of the member's proportionate share of the claim or the company's assets distributed to the member in liquidation, whichever is less, but a member's total liability for all claims under this section may not exceed the total amount of assets distributed to the member.

SECTION 809. GROUNDS FOR ADMINISTRATIVE DISSOLUTION. The [Secretary of State] may commence a proceeding to dissolve a limited liability company administratively if the company does not:

(1) pay any franchise taxes or penalties imposed by this [Act] or other law within 60 days after they are due;

(2) deliver its annual report to the [Secretary of State] within 60 days after it is due, or

(3) file articles of termination under Section 805 following the expiration of the specified term designated in its articles of organization.

SECTION 810. PROCEDURE FOR AND EFFECT OF ADMINISTRATIVE DISSOLUTION.

(a) If the [Secretary of State] determines that a ground exists for administratively dissolving a limited liability company, the [Secretary of State] shall enter a record of the determination and serve the company with a copy of the record.

(b) If the company does not correct each ground for dissolution or demonstrate to the reasonable satisfaction of the [Secretary of State] that each ground determined by the [Secretary of State] does not exist within 60 days after service of the notice, the [Secretary of State] shall administratively dissolve the company by signing a certification of the dissolution that recites the ground for dissolution and its effective date. The [Secretary of State] shall file the original of the certificate and serve the company with a copy of the certificate.

(c) A company administratively dissolved continues its existence but may carry on only business necessary to wind up and liquidate its business and affairs under Section 802 and to notify claimants under Sections 807 and 808.

(d) The administrative dissolution of a company does not terminate the authority of its agent for service of process.

SECTION 811. REINSTATEMENT FOLLOWING ADMINISTRATIVE DISSOLUTION.

(a) A limited liability company administratively dissolved may apply to the [Secretary of State] for reinstatement within two years after the effective date of dissolution. The application must:

(1) recite the name of the company and the effective date of its administrative dissolution;

(2) state that the ground for dissolution either did not exist or have been eliminated;

(3) state that the company's name satisfies the requirements of Section 105; and

(4) contain a certificate from the [taxing authority] reciting that all taxes owed by the company have been paid.

(b) If the [Secretary of State] determines that the application contains the information required by subsection (a) and that the information is correct, the [Secretary of State] shall cancel the certificate of dissolution and prepare a certificate of reinstatement that recites this determination and the effective date of reinstatement, file the original of the certificate, and serve the company with a copy of the certificate.

(c) When reinstatement is effective, it relates back to and takes effect as of the effective date of the administrative dissolution and the company may resume its business as if the administrative dissolution had never occurred.

SECTION 812. APPEAL FROM DENIAL OF REINSTATEMENT.

(a) If the [Secretary of State] denies a limited liability company's application for reinstatement following administrative dissolution, the [Secretary of State] shall serve the company with a record that explains the reason or reasons for denial.

(b) The company may appeal the denial of reinstatement to the [name appropriate] court within 30 days after service of the notice of denial is perfected. The company appeals by petitioning the court to set aside the dissolution and attaching to the petition copies of the [Secretary of State's] certificate of dissolution, the company's application for reinstatement, and the [Secretary of State's] notice of denial.

(c) The court may summarily order the [Secretary of State] to reinstate the dissolved company or may take other action the court considers appropriate.

(d) The court's final decision may be appealed as in other civil proceedings.

[ARTICLE] 9
CONVERSIONS AND MERGERS

Section 901.	Definitions.
Section 902.	Conversion of Partnership or Limited Partnership To Limited Liability Company.
Section 903.	Effect of Conversion; Entity Unchanged.
Section 904.	Merger of Entities.
Section 905.	Articles of Merger.
Section 906.	Effect of Merger.
Section 907.	[Article] Not Exclusive.

SECTION 901. DEFINITIONS. In this [article]:

(1) "Corporation" means a corporation under [the State Corporation Act], a predecessor law, or comparable law of another jurisdiction.

(2) "General partner" means a partner in a partnership and a general partner in a limited partnership.

(3) "Limited partner" means a limited partner in a limited partnership.

(4) "Limited partnership" means a limited partnership created under [the State Limited Partnership Act], a predecessor law, or comparable law of another jurisdiction.

(5) "Partner" includes a general partner and a limited partner.

(6) "Partnership" means a general partnership under [the State Partnership Act], a predecessor law, or comparable law of another jurisdiction.

(7) "Partnership agreement" means an agreement among the partners concerning the partnership or limited partnership.

(8) "Shareholder" means a shareholder in a corporation.

SECTION 902. CONVERSION OF PARTNERSHIP OR LIMITED PARTNERSHIP TO LIMITED LIABILITY COMPANY.

(a) A partnership or limited partnership may be converted to a limited liability company pursuant to this section.

(b) The terms and conditions of a conversion of a partnership or limited partnership to a limited liability company must be approved by all of the partners or by a number or percentage of the partners required for conversion in the partnership agreement.

(c) An agreement of conversion must set forth the terms and conditions of the conversion of the interests of partners of a partnership or of a limited partnership, as the case may be, into interests in the converted limited liability company or the cash or other consideration to be paid or delivered as a result of the conversion of the interests of the partners, or a combination thereof.

(d) After a conversion is approved under subsection (b), the partnership or limited partnership shall file articles of organization in the office of the [Secretary of State] which satisfy the requirements of Section 203 and contain:

(1) a statement that the partnership or limited partnership was converted to a limited liability company from a partnership or limited partnership, as the case may be;

(2) its former name;

(3) a statement of the number of votes cast by the partners entitled to vote for and against the conversion and, if the vote is less than unanimous, the number or percentage required to approve the conversion under subsection (b); and

(4) in the case of a limited partnership, a statement that the certificate of limited partnership is to be canceled as of the date the conversion took effect.

(e) In the case of a limited partnership, the filing of articles of organization under subsection (d) cancels its certificate of limited partnership as of the date the conversion took effect.

(f) A conversion takes effect when the articles of organization are filed in the office of the [Secretary of State] or at any later date specified in the articles of organization.

(g) A general partner who becomes a member of a limited liability company as a result of a conversion remains liable as a partner for an obligation incurred by the partnership or limited partnership before the conversion takes effect.

(h) A general partner's liability for all obligations of the limited liability company incurred after the conversion takes effect is that of a member of the company. A limited partner who becomes a member as a result of a conversion remains liable only to the extent the limited partner was liable for an obligation incurred by the limited partnership before the conversion takes effect.

SECTION 903. EFFECT OF CONVERSION; ENTITY UNCHANGED.

(a) A partnership or limited partnership that has been converted pursuant to this [article] is for all purposes the same entity that existed before the conversion.

(b) When a conversion takes effect:

(1) all property owned by the converting partnership or limited partnership is vested in the limited liability company;

(2) all debts, liabilities, and other obligations of the converting partnership or limited partnership continue as obligations of the limited liability company;

(3) an action of proceeding pending by or against the converting partnership or limited partnership may be continued as if the conversion has not occurred;

(4) except as prohibited by other law, all of the rights, privileges, immunities, powers, and purposes of the converting partnership or limited partnership are vested in the limited liability company; and

(5) except as otherwise provided in the agreement of conversion under Section 902(c), all of the partners of the converting partnership continue as members of the limited liability company.

SECTION 904. MERGER OF ENTITIES.

(a) Pursuant to a plan of merger approved under subsection (c), a limited liability company may be merged with or into one or more limited liability companies, foreign limited liability companies, corporations, foreign corporations, partnerships, foreign partnerships, limited partnerships, foreign limited partnerships, or other domestic or foreign entities.

(b) A plan of merger must set forth:

(1) the name of each entity that is a party to the merger;

(2) the name of the surviving entity into which the other entities will merge;

(3) the type of organization of the surviving entity;

(4) the terms and conditions of the merger;

(5) the manner and basis for converting the interests of each party to the merger into interests or obligations of the surviving entity, or into money or other property in whole or in part; and

(6) the street address of the surviving entity's principal place of business.

(c) A plan of merger must be approved:

(1) in the case of a limited liability company that is a party to the merger, by the members representing the percentage of ownership specified in the operating agreement, but not fewer than the members holding a majority of the ownership or, if provision is not made in the operating agreement, by all the members;

(2) in the case of a foreign limited liability company that is a party to the merger, by the vote required for approval of a merger by the law of the State or foreign jurisdiction in which the foreign limited liability company is organized;

(3) in the case of a partnership or domestic limited partnership that is a party to the merger, by the vote required for approval of a conversion under Section 902(b); and

(4) in the case of any other entities that are parties to the merger, but the vote required for approval of a merger by the law of this State or of the State or foreign jurisdiction in which the entity is organized and, in the absence of such a requirement, by all the owners of interests in the entity.

(d) After a plan of merger is approved and before the merger takes effect, the plan may be amended or abandoned as provided in the plan.

(e) The merger is effective upon the filing of the articles of merger with the [Secretary of State], or at such later date as the articles may provide.

SECTION 905. ARTICLES OF MERGER.

(a) After approval of the plan of merger under Section 904(c), unless the merger is abandoned under Section 904(d), articles of merger must be signed on behalf of each limited liability company and other entity that is a party to the merger and delivered to the [Secretary of State] for filing. The articles must set forth:

(1) the name and jurisdiction of formation or organization of each of the limited liability companies and other entities that are parties to the merger;

(2) for each limited liability company that is to merge, the date its articles of organization were filed with the [Secretary of State];

(3) that a plan of merger has been approved and signed by each limited liability company and other entity that is to merge;

(4) the name and address of the surviving limited liability company or other surviving entity;

(5) the effective date of the merger;

(6) if a limited liability company is the surviving entity, such changes in its articles of organization as are necessary by reason of the merger;

(7) if a party to a merger is a foreign limited liability company, the jurisdiction and date of filing of its initial articles of organization and the date when its application for authority was filed by the [Secretary of State] or, if an application has not been filed, a statement to that effect; and

(8) if the surviving entity is not a limited liability company, an agreement that the surviving entity may be served with process in this State in any action or proceeding for the enforcement of any liability or obligation of any limited liability company previously subject to suit in this State which is to merge, and for the enforcement, as provided in this [Act], of the right of members of any limited liability company to receive payment for their interest against the surviving entity.

(b) If a foreign limited liability company is the surviving entity of a merger, it may not do business in this State until an application for that authority is filed with the [Secretary of State].

(c) The surviving limited liability company or other entity shall furnish a copy of the plan of merger, on request and without cost, to any member of any limited liability company or any person holding an interest in any other entity that is to merge.

(d) Articles of merger operate as an amendment to the limited liability company's articles of organization.

SECTION 906. EFFECT OF MERGER.

(a) When a merger takes effect:

(1) the separate existence of each limited liability company and other entity that is a party to the merger, other than the surviving entity, terminates;

(2) all property owned by each of the limited liability companies and other entities that are party to the merger vests in the surviving entity;

(3) all debts, liabilities, and other obligations of each limited liability company and other entity that is party to the merger become the obligations of the surviving entity;

(4) an action or proceeding pending by or against a limited liability company or other party to a merger may be continued as if the merger had not occurred or the surviving entity may be substituted as a party to the action or proceeding; and

(5) except as prohibited by other law, all the rights, privileges, immunities, powers, and purposes of every limited liability company and other entity that is a party to a merger become vested in the surviving entity.

(b) The [Secretary of State] is an agent for service of process in an action or proceeding against the surviving foreign entity to enforce an obligation of any party to a merger if the surviving foreign entity fails to appoint or maintain an agent designated for service of process in this State or the agent for service of process cannot with reasonable diligence be found at the designated office. Upon receipt of process, the [Secretary of State] shall send a copy of the process by registered or certified mail, return receipt requested, to the surviving entity at the address set forth in the articles of merger. Service is effected under this subsection at the earliest of:

(1) the date the company receives the process, notice, or demand;

(2) the date shown on the return receipt, if signed on behalf of the company; or

(3) five days after its deposit in the mail, if mailed postpaid and correctly addressed.

(c) A member of the surviving limited liability company is liable for all obligations of a party to the merger for which the member was personally liable before the merger.

(d) Unless otherwise agreed, a merger of a limited liability company that is not the surviving entity in the merger does not require the limited liability company to wind up its business under this [Act] or pay its liabilities and distribute its assets pursuant to this [Act].

(e) Articles of merger serve as articles of dissolution for a limited liability company that is not the surviving entity in the merger.

SECTION 907. [ARTICLE] NOT EXCLUSIVE. This [article] does not preclude an entity from being converted or merged under another law.

[ARTICLE] 10
FOREIGN LIMITED LIABILITY COMPANIES

Section 1001.	Law Governing Foreign Limited Liability Companies.
Section 1002.	Application for Certificate of Authority.
Section 1003.	Activities Not Constituting Transacting Business.
Section 1004.	Issuance of Certificate of Authority.
Section 1005.	Name of Foreign Limited Liability Company.
Section 1006.	Revocation of Certificate of Authority.
Section 1007.	Cancellation of Authority.
Section 1008.	Effect of Failure to Obtain Certificate of Authority.
Section 1009.	Action by [Attorney General]

SECTION 1001. LAW GOVERNING FOREIGN LIMITED LIABILITY COMPANIES.

(a) The laws of the State or other jurisdiction under which a foreign limited liability company is organized govern its organization and internal affairs and the liability of its managers, members and their transferees.

(b) A foreign limited liability company may not be denied a certificate of authority by reason of any difference between the laws of another jurisdiction under which the foreign company is organized and the laws of this State.

(c) A certificate of authority does not authorize a foreign limited liability company to engage in any business or exercise any power that a limited liability company may not engage in or exercise in this State.

SECTION 1002. APPLICATION FOR CERTIFICATE OF AUTHORITY.

(a) A foreign limited liability company may apply for a certificate of authority to transact business in this State by delivering an application to the [Secretary of State] for filing. The application must set forth:

(1) the name of the foreign company or, if its name is unavailable for use in this State, a name that satisfies the requirements of Section 1005;

(2) the name of the State or country under whose law it is organized;

(3) the street address of its principal office;

(4) the address of its initial designated office in this State;

(5) the name and street address of its initial agent for service of process in this State;

(6) whether the duration of the company is for a specified term and, if so, the period specified;

(7) whether the company is manager-managed, and, if so, the name and address of each initial manager; and

(8) whether the members of the company are to be liable for its debts and obligations under a provision similar to Section 303(c).

(b) A foreign limited liability company shall deliver with the completed application a certificate of existence or a record of similar import authenticated by the secretary of state or other official having custody of company records in the State or country under whose law it is organized.

SECTION 1003. ACTIVITIES NOT CONSTITUTING TRANSACTING BUSINESS.

(a) Activities of a foreign limited liability company that do not constitute transacting business within the meaning of this [article] include:

(1) maintaining, defending, or settling an action or proceeding;

(2) holding meetings of its members or managers or carrying on any other activity concerning its internal affairs;

(3) maintaining bank accounts;

(4) maintaining offices or agencies for the transfer, exchange, and registration of the foreign company's own securities or maintaining trustees or depositories with respect to those securities;

(5) selling through independent contractors;

(6) soliciting or obtaining orders, whether by mail or through employees or agents or otherwise, if the orders require acceptance outside this State before they become contracts;

(7) creating or acquiring indebtedness, mortgages, or security interests in real or personal property;

(8) securing or collecting debts or enforcing mortgages or other security interests in property securing the debts, and holding, protecting, and maintaining property so acquired;

(9) conducting an isolated transaction that is completed within 30 days and is not one in the course of similar transactions of a like manner; and

(10) transacting business in interstate commerce.

(b) For purposes of this [article] the ownership in this State of income-producing real property or tangible personal property, other than property excluded under subsection (a), constitutes transacting business in this State.

(c) This section does not apply in determining the contacts or activities that may subject a foreign limited liability company to service of process, taxation, or regulation under any other law of this State.

SECTION 1004. ISSUANCE OF CERTIFICATE OF AUTHORITY. Unless the [Secretary of State] determines that an application for a certificate of authority fails to comply as to form with the filing requirements of this [Act], the [Secretary of State], upon payment of all filing fees, shall file the application and send a receipt for it and the fees to the limited liability company or its representative.

SECTION 1005. NAME OF FOREIGN LIMITED LIABILITY COMPANY.

(a) If the name of a foreign limited liability company does not satisfy the requirements of Section 105, the company, to obtain or maintain a certificate of authority to transact business in this State, must use a fictitious name to transact business in this State if its real name is unavailable and it delivers to the [Secretary of State] for filing a copy of the resolution of its managers, in the case of a manager-managed company, or of its members, in the case of a member-managed company, adopting the fictitious name.

(b) Except as authorized by subsections (c) and (d), the name, including a fictitious name, or a foreign limited liability company must be distinguishable upon the records of the [Secretary of State] from:

(1) the name of any corporation, limited partnership, or company incorporated, organized, or authorized to transact business in this State;

(2) a company name reserved or registered under Section 106 or 107;

(3) the fictitious name of another foreign limited liability company authorized to transact business in this State.

(c) A foreign limited liability company may apply to the [Secretary of State] for authority to use in this State a name that is not distinguishable upon the records of the [Secretary of State] from a name described in subsection (b). The [Secretary of State] shall authorize use of the name applied for if:

(1) the present user, registrant, or owner of a reserved name consents to the use in a record and submits an undertaking in form satisfactory to the [Secretary of State] to change its name to a name that is distinguishable upon the records of the [Secretary of State] from the name of the foreign applying limited liability company; or

(2) the applicant delivers to the [Secretary of State] a certified copy of a final judgment of a court establishing the applicant's right to use the name applied for in this State.

(d) A foreign limited liability company may use in this State the name, including the fictitious name, of another domestic or foreign entity that is used in this State if the other entity is incorporated, organized, or authorized to transact business in this State and the foreign limited liability company:

(1) has merged with the other entity;

(2) has been formed by reorganization of the other entity; or

(3) has acquired all or substantially all of the assets, including the name, of the other entity.

(e) If a foreign limited liability company authorized to transact business in this State changes its name to one that does not satisfy the requirements of Section 105, it may not transact business in this State under the name as changed until it adopts a name satisfying the requirements of Section 105 and obtains an amended certificate of authority.

SECTION 1006. REVOCATION OF CERTIFICATE OF AUTHORITY.

(a) A certificate of authority of a foreign limited liability company to transact business in this State may be revoked by the [Secretary of State] in the manner provided in subsection (b) if:

(1) the company fails to:

(i) pay any fees prescribed by law;

(ii) appoint and maintain an agent for service of process as required by this [article]; or

(iii) file a statement of a change in the name or business address of the agent as required by this [article]; or

(2) a misrepresentation has been made of any material matter in any application, report, affidavit, or other record submitted by the company pursuant to this [article].

(b) The [Secretary of State] may not revoke a certificate of authority of a foreign limited liability company unless the [Secretary of State] sends the company notice of revocation, at least 60 days before its effective date, by a record addressed to its agent for service of process in this State, or if the company fails to appoint and maintain a proper agent in this State, addressed to the office required to be maintained by Section 108. The notice must identify the cause for the revocation of the certificate of authority. The authority of the company to transact business in this State ceases on the effective date of the revocation unless the foreign limited liability company cures the failure before that date.

SECTION 1007. CANCELLATION OF AUTHORITY. A foreign limited liability company may cancel its authority to transact business in this State by filing in the office of the [Secretary of State] a certificate of cancellation. Cancellation does not terminate the authority of the [Secretary of State] to accept service of process on the company for [claims for relief] arising out of the transactions of business in this State.

SECTION 1008. EFFECT OF FAILURE TO OBTAIN CERTIFICATE OF AUTHORITY.

(a) A foreign limited liability company transacting business in this State may not maintain an action or proceeding in this State unless it has a certificate of authority to transact business in this State.

(b) The failure of a foreign limited liability company to have a certificate of authority to transact business in this State does not impair the validity of a contract or act of the company or prevent the foreign limited liability company from defending an action or proceeding in this State.

(c) Limitations on personal liability of managers, members, and their transferrees are not waived solely by transacting business in this State without a certificate of authority.

(d) If a foreign limited liability company transacts business in this State without a certificate of authority, it appoints the [Secretary of State] as its agent for service of process for [claims for relief] arising out of the transaction of business in this State.

SECTION 1009. ACTION BY [ATTORNEY GENERAL]. The [Attorney General] may maintain an action to restrain a foreign limited liability company from transacting business in this State in violation of this [article].

[ARTICLE] 11
DERIVATIVE ACTIONS

Section 1101.   Right of Action.
Section 1102.   Proper Plaintiff.
Section 1103.   Pleading.
Section 1104.   Expenses.

SECTION 1101. RIGHT OF ACTION. A member of a limited liability company may maintain an action in the right of the company if the members or managers having authority to do so have refused to commence the action or an effort to cause those members to commence the action is not likely to succeed.

SECTION 1102. PROPER PLAINTIFF. In a derivative action for a limited liability company, the plaintiff must be a member of the company when the action is commenced; and:

(1) must have been a member at the time of the transaction of which the plaintiff complains; or

(2) the plaintiff's status as a member must have devolved upon the plaintiff by operation of law or pursuant to the terms of the operating agreement from a person who was a member at the time of the transaction.

SECTION 1103. PLEADING. In a derivative action for a limited liability company, the complaint must set forth with particularity the effort of the plaintiff to secure initiation of the action by a member or manager or the reasons for not making the effort.

SECTION 1104. EXPENSES. If a derivative action for a limited liability company is successful, in whole or in part, or if anything is received by the plaintiff as a result of a judgment, compromise, or settlement of an action or claim, the court may award the plaintiff reasonable expenses, including reasonable attorney's fees, and shall direct the plaintiff to remit to the limited liability company the remainder of the proceeds received.

[ARTICLE] 12
MISCELLANEOUS PROVISIONS

Section 1201. Uniformity of Application and Construction.
Section 1202. Short Title.
Section 1203. Severability Clause.
Section 1204. Effective Date.
Section 1205. Transitional Provisions.
Section 1206. Savings Clause.

SECTION 1201. UNIFORMITY OF APPLICATION AND CONSTRUCTION. This [Act] shall be applied and construed to effectuate its general purpose to make uniform the law with respect to the subject of this [Act] among States enacting it.

SECTION 1202. SHORT TITLE. This [Act] may be cited as the Uniform Limited Liability Company Act.

SECTION 1203. SEVERABILITY CLAUSE. If any provision of this [Act] or its application to any person or circumstance is held invalid, the invalidity does not affect other provisions or applications of this [Act] which can be given effect without the invalid provision or application, and to this end the provisions of this [Act] are severable.

SECTION 1204. EFFECTIVE DATE. This [Act] takes effect [_____].

SECTION 1205. TRANSITIONAL PROVISIONS.

(a) Before January 1, 199__, this [Act] governs only a limited liability company organized:

(1) after the effective date of this [Act], unless the company is continuing the business of a dissolved limited liability company under [Section of the existing Limited Liability Company Act]; and

(2) before the effective date of this [Act], which elects, as provided by subsection (c), to be governed by this [Act].

(b) On and after January 1, 199__, this [Act] governs all limited liability companies.

(c) Before January 1, 199__, a limited liability company voluntarily may elect, in the manner provided in its operating agreement or by law for amending the operating agreement, to be governed by this [Act].

SECTION 1206. SAVINGS CLAUSE. This [Act] does not affect an action or proceeding commenced or right accrued before the effective date of this [Act].

APPENDIX 2
STATE-BY-STATE DIRECTORY OF INFORMATION

Filing fees: These filing fees are in effect as of May 1, 1997.

Forms: The forms following the state listings are included solely for informational purposes and as guides when drafting an LLC's Articles of Organization. Contact the appropriate secretary of state for official forms, instructions, and guidance on other necessary forms to be filed and fees to be paid.

Professional assistance: Forming and operating an LLC can be very complex. You may need the assistance of professionals such as LLC lawyers and tax advisers. Those who have little or no experience with LLCs may be unaware of important tax and legal implications. Anyone who forms and operates an LLC without professional assistance does so at his or her own risk.

ALABAMA

Secretary of State
Business Division
P.O. Box 5616
Montgomery, AL 36103
(205) 242-5324

Filing fee: $75 ($35 to probate judge and $40 to secretary of state)

Number of members required: at least two

Statutory citation: Alabama Statute § 10-12-1

State-specific considerations: Articles of Organization must be executed by all members forming the company. Original and two copies of the Articles of Organization must be submitted to the probate judge in the county where the initial registered office is located. Organizers must also file a Report of Domestic Limited Liability Company with the secretary of state along with a $5 filing fee within 30 days of filing the Articles of Organization.

Individuals who render professional services may do business as LLCs. Contributions may take the form of an obligation to contribute cash, property, or service. Alabama law allows the registration of foreign LLCs.

ALASKA

The State of Alaska
Division of Banking, Securities,
and Corporations
P.O. Box 110808
Juneau, AK 99811-0808
(907) 465-2530

Filing fee: $250

Number of members required: one

Statutory citation: Alaska Statute § 10.50.075

State-specific considerations: An original and copy of the Articles of Organization must be filed with the secretary of state. Organizers must use 8 ½" X 11" paper for the Articles of Organization and include a statement that the documents are being filed under the Alaska Limited Liability Act. The Articles of Organization must list the Standard Industrial Classification (SIC) codes that best describe the LLC's activities. The Articles of Organization must be signed either by the manager set out in the Articles or by the members set out in the Articles.

The LLC name may not contain the words "city" or "borough" or otherwise imply that the LLC is a municipality. The name must also be distinct from trade names on record with the Division of Banking, Securities, and Corporations.

Alaska requires payment of a biennial license fee of $100. Alaska allows registration of foreign LLCs. The filing fee for foreign LLC registration is $350. Foreign LLCs must pay a biennial license fee of $200.

ARIZONA

Arizona Corporation Commission
Division: Corporation Filing Section
1300 W. Washington Street
Phoenix, AZ 85007-2929
(602) 542-3135

Filing fee: $50

Number of members required: two or more

Statutory citation: Arizona Statute § 29-6-1

State-specific considerations: Notice of the filing of the Articles of Organization must be published within 60 days after the filing in a newspaper of general circulation in the county of the known place of business of the LLC in Arizona. Proof of publication by affidavit must be filed.

A name may be reserved for 120 days for a $10 fee. The statutory agent must have a street address and must have been an Arizona resident for at least three years. The Arizona LLC law sets forth a list of records required to be kept. Foreign LLCs may register in Arizona. The foreign LLC filing fee is $150.

ARKANSAS

Secretary of State
State Capitol
Little Rock, AR 72201-1094,
(501) 682-1010

Filing fee: $50

Number of members required: One is required to form an LLC, and there is no separate statutory provision regarding the required number of members.

Statutory citation: Arkansas Statute § 4-32-1301

State-specific considerations: The registered agent must sign Articles of Organization acknowledging acceptance of appointment. If forming a manager-managed LLC, the Articles of Organization must also contain a statement to that effect.

Professionals are allowed to form LLCs. Arkansas LLCs must pay an annual franchise tax. In order to receive the annual franchise tax reporting form, the LLC must complete and file a franchise tax form at the time the Articles of Organization are filed.

Foreign LLCs may obtain authority to do business in Alabama. The filing fee for foreign LLCs is $300.

CALIFORNIA

Secretary of State
Limited Liability Company Unit
1500 - 11th Street
P.O. Box 944228
Sacramento, CA 94244-2280
(916) 653-3795

Filing fee: $70

Number of members required: two or more

Statutory citation: California Corporations Code §17050

State-specific considerations: The Articles of Organization need not be executed by members but they must state whether the LLC is manager managed. The members must enter into an Operating Agreement. A Statement of Information form must be filed within 90 days after the filing of the Articles of Organization. The Statement of Information must also be filed annually.

The LLC name may not contain the words "bank," "insurance," "trust," "trustee," "incorporated," "inc.," "corporation," or "corp." Names may be reserved for 60 days for a fee of $10.

Professional LLCs are prohibited from forming and registering in California. The applicant must determine whether it may form as an LLC. Foreign LLCs must register in California before conducting business there. Unregistered foreign LLCs conducting business in California are subject to penalties.

LLCs must pay an $800 annual fee (franchise tax), and this fee is increased on a tiered basis if the LLC's total income is $250,000 or more.

COLORADO

Secretary of State
Corporations Section
1560 Broadway, Suite 200
Denver, CO 80202
(303) 894-2251
(303) 894-2242 fax

Filing fee: $50

Number of members required: two or more

Statutory citation: Colorado Statute § 29-80-101

State-specific considerations: Two copies of the Articles of Organization must be submitted. Articles of Organization must state whether the LLC will be member managed or manager managed. The Colorado secretary of state will provide a computer disk containing the Colorado Business Corporation Act and 36 forms, including LLC forms.

The Colorado LLC Act sets forth a list of records that are required to be kept.

CONNECTICUT

Secretary of State
30 Trinity Street
P.O. Box 150470
Hartford, CT 06115-0470

Filing fee: $60, $30 name

Number of members required: two or more

Statutory citation: P.A. #93-363, P.A. #93-267

State-specific considerations: The person forming a Connecticut LLC must have capacity to act as an organizer under Connecticut law. The statutory agent must sign the Articles of Organization acknowledging acceptance of appointment. The Operating Agreement need not be in writing.

Members have the power to vote on the election or removal of managers. Foreign LLCs must register in Connecticut. The Connecticut LLC Act lists records required to be kept.

DELAWARE

Department of State
Division of Corporations
P.O. Box 898
Dover, DE 19903
(302) 739-3073

Filing fee: $70, $100 annual

Number of members required: two or more

Statutory citation: Delaware Statute § 18-101

State-specific considerations: Strict guidelines should be followed in document preparation because the Delaware secretary of state uses computer imaging equipment to process documents. LLC need not state a specific date of dissolution in the Certificate of Formation. The Operating Agreement must be in writing.

LLC continuation requires unanimous consent within 90 days after a member dissociates. LLC mergers are allowed with all types of business entities. Members have the right to access to records on demand for a proper purpose. Members have the power to vote on the election or removal of managers.

Foreign LLCs must register in Delaware. Domestic and foreign corporations, and the LLC itself, may act as a registered agent. The Delaware LLC Act lists certain types of businesses that may not operate as LLCs. Delaware LLC Act contains a list of records required to be kept.

FLORIDA

Division of Corporations
Florida Department of State
P.O. Box 6327
Tallahassee, FL 32314
(904) 487-6052

Filing fee: $250, $35 designation of agent

Number of members required: two or more

Statutory citation: Florida Statute § 608.401

State-specific considerations: The Articles of Organization must be executed by at least one member. A separate Certificate of Designation of the LLC's initial registered office must accompany the Articles of Organization. The registered office must have a Florida street address. The LLC organizer must file an affidavit declaring that the LLC has at least two members, the amount of cash contributed at formation, the agreed value of contributed property, and the total amount of cash and property anticipated to be contributed. The registered agent must sign a statement acknowledging acceptance of appointment.

Foreign LLCs must register. The Florida LLC Act contains a list of records required to be kept.

GEORGIA

Secretary of State
Business Services and Regulation
#2 Martin Luther King, Jr. Drive, S.E.
Suite 306, West Tower
Atlanta, GA 30334
(404) 656-2817

Filing fee: $75

Number of members required: No separate provision regarding the number of required owners. Two or more organizers required.

Statutory citation: Georgia Statute § 14-11-1

State-specific considerations: The original Articles of Organization must be signed by at least one organizer of the LLC. A copy of the Articles of Organization must be filed with the original. A name may be reserved by use of a BSR Form 231 transmittal form and a later filing of a name reservation certificate. The name cannot exceed 80 characters. A transmittal form must also be filed to accompany the Articles of Organization.

Georgia LLCs may not merge with corporations. Provisions are made for conversion from corporation or limited partnership to an LLC. The Georgia LLC Act addresses member derivative suits in detail. Members have the right to remove assignors.

Foreign LLCs must register. Records must be kept from which voting rights may be determined.

HAWAII

Department of Commerce and Consumer Affairs
Business Registration Division
1010 Richards Street
P.O. Box 40
Honolulu, HI 96810
(808) 586-2727

Filing fee: $100 (expedited for additional $80)

Number of members required: two or more

Statutory citation: Hawaii Revised Statutes § 428-201 et seq.

State-specific considerations: Name must include the term "Limited Liability Company" or the abbreviation "L.L.C." or "LLC." Foreign LLCs must register and pay a $100 fee. An annual report must be filed together with a $25 filing fee. Record keeping requirements include keeping a list of the names and addresses of all past and present members and managers and the date on which each became a member.

The Operating Agreement and all amendments to it also must be kept along with a copy of the Articles of Organization and all amendments. Period of duration of the LLC may be "at will" or a specified duration. All organizers must sign the Articles of Organization in black ink and the articles must be prepared in black ink.

IDAHO

Secretary of State
Statehouse, Room 203
P.O. Box 83720
Boise, ID 83720-0080
(208) 334-2301

Filing fee: $100 typed with no attachments, $120 not typed with attachments

Number of members required: one or more persons required to form an LLC, but no provision as to required number of owners.

Statutory citation: Idaho Statute § 53-601

State-specific considerations: The name and address of at least one manager in a manager-managed LLC must be listed in the Articles of Organization, and at least one manager so listed must sign the articles. The same is true of at least one member in a member-managed LLC. The registered agent must sign the Articles of Organization.

Professionals may conduct business as Idaho LLCs. The Idaho LLC statute lists those professions authorized to practice as LLCs.

Foreign LLCs must register in Idaho if doing business there. Both foreign and domestic LLCs must file annual reports. The Idaho LLC Act contains a list of the records LLCs are required to keep.

ILLINOIS

Secretary of State
Department of Business Services
Limited Liability Company Division
Howlett Building, Room 359
Springfield, IL 62756
(217) 782-7880

Filing fee: $500 initial, $300 annual, $300 name registration

Number of members required: two or more

Statutory citation: Illinois Statute ch. 805 § 180/1-10

State-specific considerations: The Articles of Organization must state whether the LLC will be transacting business under an assumed name, and contain the LLCs SIC code.

Illinois LLCs may not carry on the business of banking or insurance. LLCs also may not carry on the practice of dentistry unless all the members are licensed Illinois dentists.

Managers need not be members of the LLC. A promise by a member to contribute to an LLC is enforceable only if it is in writing and signed by the member. Members may bring derivative actions against the LLC.

Foreign LLCs must register before transacting business in Illinois. LLCs must file annual reports. The Illinois LLC Act contains a listing of the records the LLC is required to keep.

INDIANA

Secretary of State
302 West Washington Street, Room E018
Indianapolis, IN 46204
(317) 232-6576

Filing fee: $90

Number of members required: one person required for formation and no statutory provision regarding required number of members.

Statutory citation: Indiana Statute § 23-16-10.1-1

State-specific considerations: The Operating Agreement need not be in writing.

The Indiana LLC Act lists things that may be done during winding up. Notice of dissolution limits a member's authority to bind the LLC. LLCs may merge with other LLCs. Derivative actions by members are authorized. Members have the right to remove an assignor. The LLC may be served with process if it does not have a registered agent or the registered agent cannot be found.

A foreign LLC authorized to do business in Indiana under the Indiana Revised Uniform Limited Partnership Act is subject to the Indiana LLC Act, but it is not required to register to do business in Indiana. A foreign LLC may not conduct the business of the type prohibited by a domestic LLC.

The LLC Act lists records that are required to be kept.

IOWA

Secretary of State
Business Services Division
Hoover Building
Des Moines, IA 50319
(515) 281-5204
(515) 242-5953 fax

Filing fee: $50

Number of members required: two or more

Statutory citation: Iowa Statute § 490A.100

State-specific considerations: Organizer must file an application for Certificate of Registration. The application must be signed by a manager or the person forming the LLC. The Articles of Organization must be attached to the application. Applications may be delivered by fax. The Operating Agreement must be in writing unless otherwise provided in the Articles of Organization.

Members may agree that a member may not resign prior to dissolution. Members cannot agree to vary the statutory right to continue the LLC. LLCs may merge with limited partnerships and corporations. Professionals may form LLCs in Iowa. Foreign LLCs must register in Iowa before conducting business there.

KANSAS

Secretary of State
State Capitol, 2nd Floor
300 S.W. 10th Avenue
Topeka, KS 66612-1594
(913) 296-4564

Filing fee: $150

Number of members required: two or more

Statutory citation: Kansas Statute § 17-7601

State-specific considerations: An LLC may not transact business until the Articles of Organization are filed. The address of the registered agent and the registered office must be identical. The Articles of Organization must state whether the members have the right to admit additional members and the terms and conditions of that right. The articles must also address continuation rights and whether the LLC is member managed or manager managed. The names and addresses of managers in a manager-managed LLC or the members in a member-managed LLC must be included in the articles. The articles must be signed by the person forming the LLC or by any member or manager. The original and a copy of the articles must be submitted. The Operating Agreement need not be in writing.

Kansas LLCs must file an annual report and pay an annual franchise tax. Financial information on the annual reports may be kept confidential upon application. A Kansas LLC dissolves when a member unsuccessfully demands the return of his or her contribution. The Kansas LLC Act provides for liability for omission of required words in an LLC name. Foreign LLCs must register in Kansas.

KENTUCKY

Secretary of State
P.O. Box 718
Frankfort, KY 40602-0718
(502) 564-3490

Filing fee: $40

Number of members required: One person may form an LLC and two or more members are required

Statutory citation: § 275.001

State-specific considerations: Professionals may form an LLC in Kentucky. The permissible professional services which may be provided through an LLC are defined by the LLC statute. An LLC membership interest may be obtained in exchange for a promise to render services. The LLC statutes explicitly governs conversions from partnership to LLC status.

Foreign LLCs must register to do business in Kentucky. LLCs must file an annual report and pay an annual fee of $15. The LLC statute sets forth the records the LLC must keep at its principal office.

LOUISIANA

Secretary of State
P.O. Box 94125
Baton Rouge, LA 70804-9125
(504) 925-4704

Filing fee: $20

Number of members required: no separate provision in LLC law regarding number of members required, but two persons are required for formation.

Statutory citation: Louisiana Statute § 1301

State-specific considerations: LLC organizers must file an LLC Initial Report along with the Articles of Organization. The Initial Report must be signed by each person who signs the Articles of Organization. If no managers or members have been selected at the time the Initial Report and Articles of Organization are filed, the LLC must later file a Supplemental Report setting forth their names and addresses. The Operating Agreement need not be in writing.

The registered agent must acknowledge appointment before a notary public. LLCs may merge with domestic LLCs, partnerships, or corporations. The Operating Agreement may restrict or enlarge the management rights of members. LLC membership interest is defined as an *incorporeal movable*. The LLC's name may not indicate that the LLC is formed for an unlawful purpose or falsely suggest a charitable or nonprofit nature. Foreign LLCs must register in order to do business in Louisiana. Certain businesses may not be operated as Louisiana LLCs. LLC statute provides a list of records required to be kept.

MAINE

Secretary of State
Bureau of Corporations, Elections,
and Commissions
Statehouse, Station 101
Augusta, ME 04333-0101
(207) 287-4195

Filing fee: $250

Number of members required: one or more persons

Statutory citation: Public Law Chapter 718

State-specific considerations: All organizers must sign the Articles of Organization. The registered agent must accept appointment by signature in the Articles of Organization. The Articles of Organization, once filed, are considered notice of the facts contained therein.

The LLC may purchase insurance for a member, manager, agent, or employee. Members have the right to bring a derivative action against the LLC. LLCs may merge with other LLCs.

Maine allows professionals to form LLCs. Foreign LLCs must register to do business in Maine. Domestic and foreign LLCs are required to file annual reports. The Maine LLC Act sets forth the records required to be kept.

MARYLAND

State of Maryland
Department of Assessments and Taxation
Business Services and Finance Division
301 W. Preston Street, Room 809
Baltimore, MD 21201
(410) 767-1350
1-800-735-2258

Filing fee: $50

Number of members required: two or more

Statutory citation: Maryland Statute § 4A-101

State-specific considerations: The Articles of Organization may be signed by any adult individual authorized by the persons forming the LLC. The Articles of Organization must be filed with the Maryland Department of Assessments and Taxation, Business Services and Finance Division. There are no fill-in-the-blanks forms available from this department. The Operating Agreement must be in writing unless otherwise provided in the Articles of Organization.

Members may agree that a member may not resign prior to dissolution. Nonmembers may be granted agency power through the Articles of Organization. Member contributions must be set forth in the Operating Agreement or Articles of Organization. Members have the right to inspect certain records, but there is no statutory record keeping requirement. Foreign LLCs must register to do business in Maryland.

MASSACHUSETTS

Corporations Division
Secretary of State
One Ashburton Place
Boston, MA 02108
(617) 727-2850

Filing fee: $500

Number of members required: one

Statutory citation: 950 CMR 112.0 et seq.

State-specific considerations: Name must include the terms "Limited Liability Company," "Limited Company," or the abbreviations "LC," "L.C.," "L.L.C.," or "LLC." Must provide an address of an office in Massachusetts while filing. There must be a specific dissolution date stated in the Articles of Organization. The name and address of each manager, if any, and the purpose of the LLC must be stated in the Articles of Organization. Foreign LLCs must register within 10 days of doing business in Massachusetts and must appoint a resident agent.

MICHIGAN

State of Michigan
Department of Commerce
Corporation & Securities Bureau
P.O. Box 30054
Lansing, MI 48909
(517) 334-6302

Filing fee: $50

Number of members required: two or more

Statutory citation: Michigan Statute § 450.4101

State-specific considerations: A form must be filed with the Articles of Organization stating the name, address, and business telephone number of the person forming the LLC. A post office box may not be listed as the address for the registered office. Form 701 is to be used if the LLC will be providing a service for which a license or legal authorization is required. The Articles of Organization must be signed by two or more members. The Operating Agreement must be in writing.

A member who wrongfully withdraws from the LLC is not entitled to the fair value of his or her membership interest. Members may bring a derivative action against the LLC if the LLC is manager managed and the Operating Agreement does not grant members the right to bring suit. Foreign LLCs must register to do business in Michigan.

MINNESOTA

Secretary of State
100 Constitution Avenue
State Office Building, Suite 180
Saint Paul, MN 55155-1299
(612) 297-1455

Filing fee: $135

Number of members required: two or more

Statutory citation: Minnesota Statute § 322B.01

State-specific considerations: The LLC name may not include the words "incorporated" or "corporation" or abbreviations of these words. The registered office must be a Minnesota address and cannot be a post office box. The duration of the LLC must be stated in years and cannot exceed 30 years from the date of filing. The Articles of Organization must include the SIC code which best matches the nature of the LLC's business. The articles must also address dissolution rights upon member withdrawal or expiration of a business continuation agreement. The LLC must meet the requirement of Minnesota Statutes section 500.24 in order to own agricultural land. The organizers must sign the Articles of Organization.

There is no requirement that the LLC have a registered agent. Members are entitled to receive annual financial statements on written request. Member control agreements must be in writing. The LLC Act lists the record keeping requirements. A foreign LLC must register to do business in Minnesota.

MISSISSIPPI

Secretary of State
P.O. Box 136
Jackson, MS 39205-0136
(601) 359-1333

Filing fee: $50

Number of members required: no requirement stated

Statutory citation: § 79-29-101

State-specific considerations: Special forms are required to allow the filing agency's computers to scan the formation documents. A Federal Tax ID number must be listed on the Certificate of Formation. An evidenced copy of the filed Certificate of Formation is provided if a stamped, self-addressed envelope is provided to the filing agency at the time of filing.

Professionals may do business as LLCs. The permissible professional services are defined. The professional service must be of the type licensed by the state, and excludes clerks, bookkeepers, secretaries, and technicians.

Certain words, such as "bank," "banker," "trust," and "incorporated" may not be used.

Mississippi has a statute authorizing the registration of foreign registered limited liability partnerships. The LLC statute sets forth the records that must be kept at the principal place of business.

MISSOURI

Secretary of State
P.O. Box 778
Jefferson City, MO 65102
(314) 751-1310

Filing fee: $105

Number of members required: No separate provision addresses the required number of members. One person may form a Missouri LLC.

Statutory citation: Missouri Statute § 347.010

State-specific considerations: The Articles of Organization must state the rights, if any, of remaining members to continue the LLC after a member withdraws. The names and addresses of each organizer must be listed in the Articles of Organization. The Articles of Organization must state whether the LLC is to be considered a corporation for tax purposes. The Articles of Organization must be amended if there is a change in the LLC name, form of management, or time of dissolution. The Operating Agreement need not be in writing.

Upon dissolution, distributions are based on the agreement made regarding interim distributions. An assignor may be released from liability with the written consent of all members. Service of process may be made on the organizer if the registered agent cannot be found. Foreign LLCs must register to do business in Missouri.

MONTANA

Secretary of State
P.O. Box 202801
Helena, MT 59620-2801
(406) 444-3665

Filing fee: $70

Flexible or bulletproof: flexible

Number of members required: One person may form an LLC. There is no separate statutory provision regarding the required number of members.

Statutory citation: Montana Statute § 35-8-101

State-specific considerations: An LLC may be formed as a professional LLC by so designating in the Articles of Organization. If the LLC will be a professional LLC, the Articles of Organization must contain a statement of the services to be provided. The Articles of Organization must be signed by the organizer. The Articles of Organization need not state the business purpose of the LLC. The Operating Agreement need not be in writing.

Montana LLCs must file an annual report. Members of professional LLCs remain personally liable for their negligent or wrongful acts, and their relationship with their clients is the same as if they performed their services as a sole proprietor. Foreign LLCs must obtain a Certificate of Authority to transact business in Montana.

NEBRASKA

Nebraska Department of State
Secretary of State
1301 State Capitol
Lincoln, NE 68509-4608
(402) 471-4079

Filing fee: $100

Flexible or bulletproof: bulletproof

Number of members required: two or more

Statutory citation: Neb. Rev. Stat. § 21-2601 et seq.

State-specific considerations: The Articles of Organization must state the total amount of cash contributed to stated capital and a description of the agreed value of property other than cash contributed. In addition, the Articles of Organization must state the total additional contributions agreed to be made by all members and the times at which or event upon the happening of which the contributions will be made. The Articles of Organization must also set forth the right, if any, of the members to admit additional members and the terms and conditions of the admission. The Operating Agreement need not be in writing.

Certain businesses may not be operated as LLCs in Nebraska. Foreign LLCs must register to do business in Nebraska.

NEVADA

Secretary of State
State Capitol
Carson City, NV 89710
(702) 687-5203

Filing fee: $125

Number of members required: Two people are required to form an LLC, but there is no separate statutory provision regarding the required number of members.

Statutory citation: Nevada Statute § 86.011

State-specific considerations: Execution of Articles of Organization must be verified. The Operating Agreement must be in writing. The LLC records must disclose the arrangements made for the return of contributions.

An LLC may be identified by "Co." or "Ltd." Certain businesses may not do business as LLCs. Foreign LLCs may register by complying with the procedures for foreign limited partnerships.

NEW HAMPSHIRE

Department of State
107 N. Main Street
Statehouse, Room 204
Concord, NH 03301-4989
(603) 271-3244

Filing fee: $85

Number of members required: two or more

Statutory citation: New Hampshire Statute § 304-C:1

State-specific considerations: The Certificate of Formation must state whether the membership interests will be sold within the meaning of the New Hampshire Securities Act. The Certificate of Formation must be accompanied by a form LLC 1A containing sworn statements about the application of the New Hampshire Securities Act. The person executing the Certificate of Formation must sign and state the capacity in which he or she signs. The Operating Agreement must be in writing, and it is enforceable against a member who does not sign if the agreement so provides.

The LLC name may contain the name of a member or manager. New Hampshire LLCs may not be formed for the purpose of carrying on banking, construction, and maintenance of railroads, the business of making contracts for the payment of money at a fixed date or upon the happening of some contingency, or the business of a trust, surety, indemnity, or safe deposit company. Professional LLCs may be formed in New Hampshire.

NEW JERSEY

Department of State
Division of Commercial Recording
CN 308
Trenton, NJ 08625
(609) 984-1900

Filing fee: $100

Number of members required: two or more

Statutory citation: New Jersey Statute NJSA 42

State-specific considerations: The Articles of Organization must contain a signed representation that the filing complies with the applicable statute and that the LLC has two or more members. The Operating Agreement must be in writing, and members are bound by the Operating Agreement even if they do not sign it.

Members may agree that a member may not resign prior to dissolution. Contributions to the LLC may take any form. Foreign LLCs must register to do business in New Jersey. Members are permitted to inspect records, but there is no duty to keep records.

NEW MEXICO

State Corporation Commission
P.O. Drawer 1269
Santa Fe, NM 87504-1269
(505) 827-4511

Filing fee: $50

Number of members required: One person may form an LLC, and the New Mexico LLC Statute contains no provision regarding the required number of members.

Statutory citation: New Mexico Statute § 53-19-1

State-specific considerations: The person forming the LLC need not be a member. The initial registered agent must submit an affidavit of acceptance of appointment. The Operating Agreement must be in writing.

Consent to transfer management rights must be in writing unless the Operating Agreement provides otherwise. Promissory notes and promises to provide services in the future may not be contributed unless the Operating Agreement so provides. An LLC may be dissolved by a majority vote.

Foreign LLCs must register in New Mexico before doing business there.

NEW YORK

Department of State
Division of Corporations
41 State Street
Albany, NY 12231
(518) 473-2492

Filing fee: $200

Number of members required: one

Statutory citation: Chapter 34 of the Consolidated Laws of New York

State-specific considerations: The Articles of Organization should be submitted with a backer or cover sheet with the title of the certificate and the name of the filer typed thereon. The Articles of Organization must state the members who will be liable for specified LLC debts and obligations.

The New York LLC law contains a long list of names that may not be included in an LLC name. Professionals may form LLCs in New York. Foreign professional LLCs must register before doing business in New York.

NORTH CAROLINA

Corporations Division
Secretary of State
300 N. Salisbury Street
Raleigh, NC 27603-5909
(919) 733-4201

Filing fee: $100

Number of members required: Two are required to form an LLC, but there is no separate statutory provision regarding the required number of members.

Statutory citation: North Carolina Statute § 57C-1-01

State-specific considerations: The Operating Agreement need not be in writing unless the Articles of Organization so provides. Consent to transfer management rights must be in writing unless otherwise provided in the Operating Agreement.

The members may agree that a member may not resign prior to dissolution. All members are managers unless otherwise provided.

LLCs formed in order to render professional services must contact the appropriate North Carolina licensing board to determine whether additional licensing requirements are mandated by law. Foreign LLCs must register in order to do business in North Carolina and must submit a Certificate of Existence certified by the property state or county official.

NORTH DAKOTA

Secretary of State
600 E. Boulevard Avenue
Bismarck, ND 58505-0500
(701) 328-4284

Filing fee: $125

Number of members required: One or more may organize, but the LLC must have two or more members at the time of formation.

Statutory citation: North Dakota Statute § 10-32-01

State-specific considerations: The Articles of Organization must be dated and signed by all organizers named in the articles. The Operating Agreement need not be in writing.

The Federal ID number or Social Security number of registered agents must be provided. The registered agent must sign a *consent to serve* form.

The LLC name may not include the words "bank," "banker," or "banking," or any other words of like import. An LLC may be used as an insurance agency engaged in the sale of insurance products, but not as an insurance company backing the claims. LLCs engaged in farming or ranching must be organized according to North Dakota Century Code Chapter 10-06.1. Professionals may do business as an LLC as long as they comply with North Dakota Century Code Chapter 10-31.1.

Foreign LLCs must register to do business in North Dakota.

OHIO

Secretary of State
30 E. Broad Street, 14th Floor
Columbus, OH 43266-0418
(614) 466-3251

Filing fee: $85

Number of members required: two or more

Statutory citation: Ohio Statute § 1705.01

State-specific considerations: The Articles of Organization must list the address to which interested persons may direct requests for copies of any operating agreement or bylaws of the LLC. All organizers must sign the Articles of Organization. The registered agent must sign an Acceptance of Appointment and it must be filed with the Articles of Organization. The Operating Agreement must be in writing.

A promise to perform services may be exchanged for an LLC membership interest. Foreign LLCs must register in order to do business in Ohio. The LLC statute lists the records that must be kept at the principal office.

OKLAHOMA

Secretary of State
101 State Capitol
Oklahoma City, OK 73105-4897
(405) 521-3911

Filing fee: $100

Number of members required: Two are required to form an LLC, but there is no separate statutory provision regarding the required number of members.

Statutory citation: Oklahoma Statute § 2000

State-specific considerations: At least one person, who need not be a member of the LLC, must sign the Articles of Organization. The names of the organizers, managers, and members need not be disclosed in the Articles of Organization. The Operating Agreement need not be in writing.

Records must be kept from which members' voting rights may be determined. Certain businesses may not operate as Oklahoma LLCs. Foreign LLCs must register in order to do business in Oklahoma.

OREGON

Secretary of State
Corporation Division
Public Service Building
255 Capitol Street N.E., Suite 151
Salem, OR 97310-1327
(503) 986-2200
(503) 378-4381 fax

Filing fee: $40

Number of members required: two or more

Statutory citation: Oregon Rev. Stat. § 63.001

State-specific considerations: Articles of Organization must include SIC Code. Filing fees may be paid with Visa or MasterCard, and documents may be filed by fax. The Operating Agreement need not be in writing.

Minutes of meetings and consents to action must be kept as LLC records. All members are managers unless otherwise provided.

Foreign LLCs must register in order to do business in Oregon, and no foreign LLC may transact business in Oregon if it has only one member.

PENNSYLVANIA

Secretary of the Commonwealth
Department of State
P.O. Box 8722
Harrisburg, PA 17105-8722
(717) 787-1057

Filing fee: $100

Number of members required: One or more persons may organize a Pennsylvania LLC.

Statutory citation: Senate Bill No. 1059

State-specific considerations: Filings must be accompanied by Docketing Statement DSCB 15-134-A. Pennsylvania also has a limited liability partnership law.

An LLC may be divided into two or more LLCs. Professional associations may elect LLC status. Certain professions may fall within the category of a restricted professional company and thereby be subject to additional statutory provisions. LLCs may not be used for banking or insurance purposes. Foreign LLCs and LLPs must register to do business in Pennsylvania. Much of the Pennsylvania LLC law is patterned after the prototype LLC law.

RHODE ISLAND

Secretary of State
Corporations Division
100 N. Main Street
Providence, RI 02903-1335
(401) 277-3040

Filing fee: $150, $50 name, $50 annual report fee

Number of members required: Two are required to form an LLC, and there is no separate statutory provision regarding the required number of members.

Statutory citation: Rhode Island Statute § 7-16-1

State-specific considerations: The Articles of Organization must state whether the LLC is intended to be treated as a corporation or a partnership for federal tax purposes. The Articles of Organization must be amended if the LLC name or duration changes. The Operating Agreement need not be in writing.

The LLC name may be reserved by calling the secretary of state. Professionals may not form a Rhode Island LLC. Foreign LLCs must register to do business in Rhode Island. An annual report must be filed every year along with a $50 filing fee.

SOUTH CAROLINA

Jim Miles
Secretary of State
P.O. Box 11350
Columbia, SC 29211
(803) 734-2155

Filing fee: $110

Number of members required: two or more

Statutory citation: South Carolina Statute § 33-43-103

State-specific considerations: The Articles of Organization must designate whether the LLC is managed by a manager or managers. All initial members must sign the Articles of Organization.

SOUTH DAKOTA

Secretary of State
State Capitol, Suite 204
500 E. Capitol Street
Pierre, SD 57501-5070
(605) 773-4845

Filing fee: $50-sliding scale, $50 annual

Number of members required: two or more

Statutory citation: South Dakota Statute § 47-34-1

State-specific considerations: The Articles of Organization must state the total amount of cash contributed and provide a description and agreed value of property or services contributed or to be contributed. The Articles of Organization must also state the total additional contributions, if any, agreed to be made by all members and when they shall be made. The terms related to the right to admit additional members and to continue the LLC must also be included in the Articles of Organization. The Articles of Organization must be signed by two or more members in the presence of a notary public. The Operating Agreement must be in writing. An annual tax of $50 must be paid.

TENNESSEE

Secretary of State
Corporations Section
James K. Polk Building, 18th Floor
Nashville, TN 37243-0306
(615) 741-0537

Filing fee: $10 name, $50 per member for articles (min. $300, max. $3,000)

Number of members required: two or more

Statutory citation: Tennessee Statute § 48A-5-101

State-specific considerations: The Articles of Organization must state whether the LLC will be board managed or member managed, the number of members at the date of filing, whether the LLC has the power to expel a member, and whether the members have preemptive rights.

Tennessee has a professional LLC law. Board-managed LLCs must have meetings at least annually. An annual report must be filed, with a fee based on a sliding scale ($50 per member, minimum $300, but not to exceed $3,000). A list of records required to be kept is set forth in the LLC statute.

TEXAS

Secretary of State
Statutory Filings Division
Corporations Section
P.O. Box 13697
Austin, TX 78711-3697
1-800-735-2989
(512) 463-5709 fax

Filing fee: $200

Number of members required: One person may form a Texas LLC, and there is no separate statutory provision regarding the required number of members.

Statutory citation: Texas Statute § Article 1528n

State-specific considerations: The Articles of Organization must state whether the LLC is member managed or manager managed, and they must also include the name and address of each organizer. The State of Texas does not provide a sample for Articles of Organization; the filer must create the form. The organizer must sign the Articles of Organization. The Operating Agreement need not be in writing.

Preliminary name availability may be checked by telephone. Members may agree that a member may not resign prior to dissolution. LLCs are subject to state franchise taxes. LLC statute sets forth the records that must be kept.

UTAH

Department of Commerce
Division of Corporations and Commercial Code
Heber M. Wells Building
160 East 300 South
P.O. Box 146705
Salt Lake City, UT 84114-6705
(801) 530-4849

Filing fee: $50

Number of members required: Two are required to form, and there is no separate statutory provision regarding the required number of members.

Statutory citation: Utah Statute § 48-2b-102

State-specific considerations: The state filing agency does not provide forms. Managers must be identified in the Articles of Organization. At least two members must sign the Articles of Organization, and the registered agent must sign an acknowledgment of acceptance of appointment. The Operating Agreement need not be in writing. The Operating Agreement may provide for termination of a member's interest.

Members have the authority to bind the LLC unless the Articles of Organization state otherwise. Distributions may be made in cash or other assets. An LLC may be involuntarily dissolved if it fails to maintain a registered agent.

LLC name may not include the terms "association," "corporation," "incorporated," "limited partnership," "limited," or abbreviations of these terms.

An annual report is required with a $15 fee. Records must be kept of any right to a return of contributions.

VERMONT

Secretary of State
109 State Street
Montpelier, VT 05609-1104
(802) 828-2366

Filing fee: $75

Number of members required: one

Statutory citation: 11 V.S.A. § 3001 et seq.

State-specific considerations: An LLC may be formed for any purpose except to transact business as a bank, savings and loan association, credit union, insurance company, or railroad company. Professionals may do business as LLCs, but are also governed by the licensing laws of their professions and the Vermont Professional Corporation Act. Every LLC must have an Operating Agreement, but it is not to be filed with the secretary of state. Operating Agreements may not vary the power of members to withdraw, the right of members to expel another member, or the requirement to wind up business if the articles specify such an event or in case of certain judicially recognized events listed in the LLC law. The words "limited liability company," "limited company," "LLC," "L.L.C.," LC," or "L.C.," must be used in the LLC name. "Company" or "Limited" may be abbreviated as "Co." or "Ltd." LLC names may be reserved for 120 days.

Foreign LLCs may obtain a certificate of authority from the Vermont Secretary of State by filing a form and paying a fee of $100. Every member has a right to access to information and documents relating to the company. The company may impose a reasonable charge for providing this information. All LLCs must — both foreign and domestic — file an annual report with the secretary of state within two-and-a-half months of the end of the company's fiscal years. There is a $15 fee for the annual report of domestic LLCs and a $100 fee for foreign LLCs.

VIRGINIA

State Corporation Commission
P.O. Box 1197
Richmond, VA 23209-1197
(804) 371-9733

Filing fee: $100

Number of members required: two or more

Statutory citation: Virginia Statute § 13.1-1000

State-specific considerations: The Operating Agreement need not be in writing unless so provided in the Operating Agreement or Articles of Organization.

Members have no right to vary the continuation terms set forth in the LLC statute. The liability of members and managers for breach of their duty of care is limited to the greater of $100,000 or last year's compensation. The registered agent must be a member, manager, member of the bar, professional corporation, or professional LLC.

WASHINGTON

Secretary of State
Corporations Division
505 E. Union Avenue
Republic Building, 2nd Floor
P.O. Box 40234
Olympia, WA 98504-0234
(306) 753-7115

Filing fee: $175 Articles of Organization

Number of members required: One person may form an LLC, and there is no separate statutory provision regarding the required number of members.

Statutory citation: Washington Statute § 25.15

State-specific considerations: The registered agent must be a resident of the State of Washington or an active corporation, limited partnership, or limited liability company registered in Washington. The registered agent must sign a consent to appointment. The registered office address must have a Washington street address identical to the business address of the registered agent. The LLC's principal place of business must be stated.

Professionals may do business as LLCs. An annual report must be filed. Certain types of terms, such as "bank," "banking," "trust," and "incorporated" may not be used in the LLC name.

Foreign LLCs must register to do business in Washington by submitting a Certificate of Existence from the state or country of formation. An annual report must be filed.

WEST VIRGINIA

Secretary of State
State Capitol
1900 Kanawha Boulevard E.
Charleston, WV 25305-0770
(304) 342-8000

Filing fee: $10 duplicate originals must be filed. In other words, two forms need to be filled out, signed, and submitted. You cannot fill out just one form and make a copy of it.

Number of members required: Two members are required to form an LLC, but there is no separate statutory provision regarding the required number of owners.

Statutory citation: West Virginia Stat., Chapter 31, Article 1A

State-specific considerations: The name and address of the person preparing Articles of Organization must be stated in the articles. The Operating Agreement need not be in writing.

Members may agree that a member may not resign prior to dissolution. Mergers with other LLCs are allowed. No statutory provision regarding records are required to be kept.

WISCONSIN

Secretary of State
Corporations Division
P.O. Box 7846
Madison, WI 53707-7846
(608) 266-3590

Filing fee: $130

Number of members required: two or more

Statutory citation: Wisconsin Statutes, Chapter 183

State-specific considerations: Articles of Organization must state whether they were drafted in Wisconsin and the name of the drafter. The Operating Agreement must be in writing.

LLC dissolves when it has only one member, but does not dissolve upon the expiration of its agreed duration.

WYOMING

Secretary of State
Corporation Division
State Capitol
Cheyenne, WY 82002-0020
(307) 777-7311

Filing fee: sliding scale

Number of members required: two or more

Statutory citations: Wyoming Statute § 17-15-101

State-specific considerations: The Articles of Organization must list the total amount of cash contributed, and a description and agreed value of property other than cash contributed. The Articles of Organization must also address when additional contributions will be made, the right to admit additional members, and the continuation rights of members upon a dissolution event. The registered agent must sign a consent to appointment. The Operating Agreement need not be in writing.

A foreign LLC may do business in Wyoming by complying with the limited partnership act, as long as doing so is consistent with the LLC act. Last words of the LLC name must be "Limited Liability Company."

ALABAMA

STATE OF ALABAMA
DOMESTIC LIMITED LIABILITY COMPANY
ARTICLES OF ORGANIZATION

INSTRUCTIONS:
STEP 1: A LIMITED LIABILITY COMPANY MUST BE FORMED AND EXECUTED BY TWO OR MORE PERSONS AS MEMBERS; THE "ARTICLES" MUST ALSO SET FORTH THE RIGHT, TERMS AND CONDITIONS, IF GIVEN, TO ADMIT ADDITONAL MEMBERS; THE RIGHT, IF GIVEN, BY REMAINING MEMBERS TO CONTINUE BUSINESS AFTER DISSOCIATION; AND ANY OTHER PROVISIONS NOT INCONSISTENT WITH THE LAW.
STEP 2: THE NAME OF THE LIMITED LIABILITY COMPANY MUST CONTAIN THE WORDS LIMITED LIABILITY COMPANY OR **L.L.C.**
STEP 3: FILE THE ORIGINAL AND TWO COPIES OF THE ARTICLES OF ORGANIZATION IN THE COUNTY WHERE THE **LLC'S** REGISTERED OFFICE IS LOCATED. THE JUDGE OF PROBATE'S FILING FEE IS **$35** AND THE SECRETARY OF STATE'S FILING FEE IS **$40**.
STEP 4: FILE A COMPLETED REPORT OF DOMESTIC LIMITED LIABILITY COMPANY WITH THE SECRETARY OF STATE WITHIN 30 DAYS OF FILING THE ARTICLES OF ORGANIZATION WITH THE JUDGE OF PROBATE. THE FILING FEE IS **$5**.

PURSUANT TO THE PROVISIONS OF THE ALABAMA LIMITED LIABILITY COMPANY ACT, THE UNDERSIGNED HEREBY ADOPTS THE FOLLOWING ARTICLES OF ORGANIZATION.

Article I The name of the Limited Liability Company.
Damman Legal Research, L.L.C.

Article II The duration of the Limited Liability Company is perpetual.

Article III The Limited Liability Company has been organized for the following purpose(s):
any lawful business

Article IV The street address (NO PO BOX) of registered office 117 N. 6th st. and the name of registered agent at that office Gregory C. Damman.

Article V The names and addresses of the initial Members. (Attach additional sheets if necessary.)
Gregory C. Damman, 1688 Karol Kay Blvd., Seward, AL 68434

Susan C. Damman, 1688 Karol Kay Blvd., Seward, AL 68434

Article VI If the Limited Liability Company is to be managed by one or more managers, list the names and addresses of the managers who are to serve until the first annual meeting of members or until their successors are elected and qualify.
n/a

Any provision, not inconsistent with the law, for the regulation of the internal affairs of the Limited Liability Company are permitted to be set out in the operating agreement of the LLC.

IN WITNESS THEREOF, the undersigned members executed these Articles of Organization on this, the _____ day of _____, 19_____.

THIS DOCUMENT PREPARED BY:

Signature of Member

Signature of Member

ALASKA

Please do not write in this space (FOR DEPARTMENT USE ONLY)

ARTICLES OF ORGANIZATION
(Domestic Limited Liability Company)

The undersigned persons acting as organizers of a limited liability company under the Alaska Limited Liability Act (AS 10.50) hereby adopt the following Articles of Organization:

ARTICLE I

The name of the Limited Liability Company (LLC) is:

Damman Legal Research, L.L.C.

ARTICLE II

The purpose for which the LLC is organized:

Any lawful business

S.I.C. Codes: Primary _____   Secondary _____   Other _____

ARTICLE III

1. The name of the LLC's registered agent:

   Gregory C. Damman

2. The mailing address of the LLC's registered agent (if the mailing address is a P.O. Box, include a physical address):

   117 N. 6th St., Seward, AK   68434

ARTICLE IV

If applicable, the latest date or event which will cause the LLC to cease to exist:

n/a

ALASKA

ARTICLE V

1. The affairs of the LLC will be: (check one box)

   ☒ Managed by the members   ☐ Managed by a manager

2. If applicable, the name and address of the LLC's manager (optional):

   n/a

3. If member managed, the names and addresses of the LLC's members (optional):

   Gregory C. Damman, 1688 Karol Kay Blvd., Seward, AK 68434

   Susan C. Damman, 1688 Karol Kay Blvd., Seward, NE 68434

Attach list of additional names if necessary.

ARTICLE VI

If applicable, the terms and conditions restricting a member's ability to assign their interest in the LLC:

n/a

Attach additional pages if necessary.

Attach additional pages for including any other optional articles governing the regulation of the internal affairs of the LLC, consistent with this Act and the laws of this state.

Signed this _____ day of _____, _____.

Name   Address

ARIZONA

STATE OF ARIZONA

OFFICE OF THE

CORPORATION COMMISSION

The following is a list of the mandatory information required in the Articles of Organization of an Arizona Limited Liability Company. (This is not intended for use as a blank form, but as a guideline only.) You may include any other provision in your Articles that is consistent with the Arizona Limited Liability Company Act (A.R.S. §29-601 et seq.)

ARTICLES OF ORGANIZATION

Pursuant to A.R.S. §29-632 the undersigned states as follows:

1. The name of the limited liability company is

    Damman Legal Research, L.L.C.

2. The address of the registered office in Arizona is

    605 South 14th St., Ste 412, Lincoln, AZ 68508

    located in the County of Lancaster

3. The name and address of the statutory agent is: (This may be either an individual (past three year) resident of this State, a domestic corporation, a limited liability company or a foreign corporation or limited liability company authorized to transact business in this state) Gregory C. Damman

    605 South 14th St., Ste. 412, Lincoln, AZ 68508

4. There are or will be two or more members at the time the limited liability company is formed (A.R.S. §29-632.A.3.)

5. The latest date on which the limited liability company is to dissolve is July 9, 2025

6. A. (Check appropriate Box.)

    [ ] Management of the limited liability company is vested in a manager or managers. The names and addresses of each person who is a manager AND each member who owns a twenty percent or greater interest in the capital or profits of the limited liability company are:

ARIZONA

[x] Management of the limited liability company is reserved to the members. The names and addresses of each person who is a member are:

Gregory C. Damman   [x] member [ ] manager

605 South 14th St., Ste. 412   [ ] member [ ] manager

Lincoln, AZ 68508   [ ] member [ ] manager

Susan C. Damman   [x] member [ ] manager
(same address as above)

Signed: _____   Date _____

Signed: _____   Date _____

The person(s) executing this document need not be member(s) of the limited liability company at the time of formation or after formation has occurred.

I, _____, having been designated to act as Statutory Agent, hereby consent to act in that capacity until removed or resignation is submitted in accordance with the Arizona Revised Statutes.

_____
(Signature of Statutory Agent)

Filing Fee: $50.00 (U.S.)
(Please make check payable to the Arizona Corporation Commission)

ARKANSAS

Instructions: File in <u>**DUPLICATE**</u> with the Secretary of State, State Capitol, Little Rock, Arkansas 72201-1094. A copy will be returned after filing has been completed.
PLEASE TYPE OR CLEARLY PRINT IN INK

State of Arkansas - Office of Secretary of State
ARTICLES OF ORGANIZATION

The undersigned authorized manager or member or person forming this Limited Liability Company under the Small Business Entity Tax Pass Through Act, Act 1003 of 1993, adopt the following Articles of Organization of such Limited Liability Company:

First: The Name of the Limited Liability Company is:

Damman Legal Research, L.L.C.

Must contain the words "Limited Liability Company," "Limited Company," or the abbreviation "L.L.C.," "L.C.," "LLC," or "LC." The word "Limited" may be abbreviated as "Ltd.", and the word "Company" may be abbreviated as "Co." Companies which perform **PROFESSIONAL SERVICE MUST** additionally contain the words "Professional Limited Liability Company," "Professional Limited Company," or the abbreviations "P.L.L.C.," "P.L.C.," "PLLC," or "PLC." The word "Limited" may be abbreviated as "Ltd." and the word "Company" may be abbreviated as "Co."

Second: Address of registered office of the Limited Liability Company which may be, but need not be, the place of business shall be:

605 South 14th St., Ste. 412

Lincoln, Arkansas 68508

Third: The name of the registered agent and the business residence or mailing address of said agent shall be:

Gregory C. Damman

605 South 14th St. Ste. 412

Lincoln, Arkansas 68508

(a) Acknowledgment and acceptance of appointment **MUST** be signed. I hereby acknowledge and accept the appointment of registered agent for and on behalf of the above named Limited Liability Company.

Please sign here

Fourth: The latest date (month, day, year) upon which this Limited Liability Company is to dissolve:

July 9, 2025

Fifth: IF THE MANAGEMENT OF THIS COMPANY IS VESTED IN A MANAGER OR MANAGERS, A STATEMENT TO THAT EFFECT MUST BE INCLUDED IN THE SPACE PROVIDED OR BY ATTACHMENT:

PLEASE TYPE OR PRINT CLEARLY IN INK THE NAME OF THE PERSON (S) AUTHORIZED TO EXECUTE THIS DOCUMENT.

Gregory C. Damman

Signature of authorized manager, member, or person forming this Company: _____
Filing Fee $50.00

LL-01

CALIFORNIA

BILL JONES
SECRETARY OF STATE

LLC-1

LIMITED LIABILITY COMPANY
ARTICLES OF ORGANIZATION

IMPORTANT - Read the instructions before completing the form.
This document is presented for filing pursuant to Section 17050 of the California Corporations Code.

1. Limited liability company name: Damman Legal Research, L.L.C.
   (End the name with "LLC" or "Limited Liability Company". No periods between the letters in "LLC". "Limited" and "Company" may be abbreviated to "Ltd." and "Co.")

2. Latest date (month/day/year) on which the limited liability company is to dissolve: 8/4/2025

3. The purpose of the limited liability company is to engage in any lawful act or activity for which a limited liability company may be organized under the Beverly-Killea Limited Liability Company Act.

4. Enter the name of initial agent for service of process and check the appropriate provision below:

   Gregory C. Damman _____, which is

   [X] an individual residing in California. Proceed to Item 5.

   [ ] a corporation which has filed a certificate pursuant to Section 1505 of the California Corporations Code. Skip Item 5 and proceed to Item 6.

5. If the initial agent for service of process is an individual, enter a business or residential street address in California:
   Street address: 3794 H St.
   City: Lincoln   State: CALIFORNIA   Zip Code: 68510

6. The limited liability company will be managed by : (check one)

   [ ] one manager   [ ] more than one manager   [X] limited liability company members

7. If other matters are to be included in the Articles of Organization attach one or more separate pages.
   Number of pages attached, if any: none

8. It is hereby declared that I am the person who executed this instrument, which execution is my act and deed.

   _____
   Signature of organizer

   Gregory C. Damman
   Type or print name of organizer

   Date: _____, 19 ___

   For Secretary of State Use

LLC-1
Filing Fee $80

Approved by the Secretary of State
1/95

CALIFORNIA

INSTRUCTIONS FOR COMPLETING THE ARTICLES OF ORGANIZATION (LLC-1)

All references are to the California Corporations Code unless otherwise indicated.
Type or legibly print in black ink.

DO NOT ALTER THE FORM

Item 1. Enter the name of the limited liability company which must end with the words "LLC" or "Limited Liability Company". Do not enter periods between the letters in "LLC". The words "Limited" and "Company" may be abbreviated to "Ltd." and "Co." Section 17051(a)(1). The name of the limited liability company may not contain the words "bank", "insurance", "trust", "trustee", "incorporated", "inc.", "corporation", or "corp." Section 17052(d).

Professional limited liability companies are prohibited from forming or registering in California.

Item 2. Enter the latest date (month/day/year) on which the limited liability company is to dissolve. Section 17051(a)(2).

Item 3 The articles of organization must contain the following statement of purpose which is preprinted on the form and may not be altered: "The purpose of the limited liability company is to engage in any lawful act or activity for which a limited liability company may be organized under the Beverly-Killea Limited Liability Company Act". Section 17051(a)(3). If provisions limiting or restricting the business of the limited liability company are desired refer to Item 7 for instructions on attaching additional pages.

Item 4. Enter the name of the initial agent for service of process. Check the appropriate provision indicating whether the initial agent is an individual residing in California or a corporation which has filed a certificate pursuant to Section 1505. If an individual is designated proceed to Item 5. If a corporation is named skip Item 5 and proceed to Item 6. Section 17051(a)(5).

Item 5. If an individual is designated as the initial agent for service of process, enter a business or residential street address in California. Box numbers and "in care of" (c/o) are not acceptable. Do not enter an address if a corporation is designated as the initial agent for service of process. Section 17051(a)(5).

Item 6. Check the appropriate provision indicating whether the limited liability company is to be managed by one manager, more than one manager, or the limited liability company members. Section 17051(a)(6).

Item 7. The articles of organization may contain additional provisions including, but not limited to, provisions limiting or restricting the business in which the limited liability company may engage, powers that the limited liability company may exercise, admission of members, events that will cause a dissolution, or limitations on the authority of managers or members to bind the limited liability company. Such matters must be submitted on single-sided, standard white paper. Number and identify each page as an attachment to the articles of organization. Enter the number of pages attached to the form, if any, in Item 7. Section 17051(c).

Item 8. The articles of organization must be executed with an original signature. Facsimiles and photocopies of the articles of organization are not acceptable for the purpose of filing with the Secretary of State. The person executing the articles of organization need not be a member or manager of the limited liability company. Section 17051(a).

- The fee for filing the articles of organization with the Secretary of State is eighty dollars ($80). Section 17701(b).

- Return the acknowledgment of filing to:

  Name: _____
  Firm/Company: _____
  Address: _____
  City: _____
  State: _____ Zip Code: _____

- Send the executed document and filing fee to:

  Office of the Secretary of State
  Limited Liability Company Unit
  P.O. Box 944228
  Sacramento, California 94244-2280

1/95

COLORADO

Mail to: Secretary of State
Corporations Section
1560 Broadway, Suite 200
Denver, CO 80202
(303) 894-2251
Fax (303) 894-2242

For office use only

MUST BE TYPED
FILING FEE: $50.00
MUST SUBMIT TWO COPIES

Please include a typed
self-addressed envelope

ARTICLES OF ORGANIZATION

I/We the undersigned natural person(s) of the age of eighteen years or more, acting as organizer(s) of a limited liability company under the Colorado Limited Liability Company Act, adopt the following Articles of Organization for such limited liability company:

FIRST: The name of the limited liability company is: Damman Legal Research, L.L.C.

SECOND: Principal place of business (if known): 605 South 14th St., Ste. 412
Lincoln, CO 68508

THIRD: The street address of the initial registered office of the limited liability company is:
605 South 14th St., Ste. 412, Lincoln, CO 68508

The mailing address (if different from above) of the initial registered office of the limited liability company is:
same as above

The name of its proposed registered agent in Colorado at that address is:
Gregory C. Damman

FOURTH: The management is vested in managers/members (circle one)

FIFTH: The names and business addresses of the initial manager or managers or if the management is vested in the members, rather than managers, the names and addresses of the member or members are:

NAME	ADDRESS (include zip codes)
Gregory C. Damman	3794 H Street
	Lincoln, CO 68510

SIXTH: The name and address of each organizer is:

NAME	ADDRESS (include zip code)
Gregory C. Damman	3794 H St., Lincoln CO 68508
Susan C. Damman	3794 H St., Lincoln, CO 68508

Signed_____
Organizer

Signed_____
Organizer

CONNECTICUT

Secretary of the State
30 Trinity Street
Hartford, CT 06106

NOTE: This form constitutes only the minimum statutory requirements for filing with the Office of the Secretary of the State. Should you wish to include additional information, you may attach a plain sheet of 8½x11 paper to the document.

1. The name of the limited liability company:

    Damman Legal Research, L.L.C.

2. The nature of business to be transacted or the purpose to be promoted or carried out by the limited liability company is as follows:

    Any lawfull business

3. Principal office address: (P.O. Box is **not** acceptable) _____

    605 South 14th St., Ste. 412, Lincoln, CT 68508

4. Statutory agent for service of process, P.A. 93-267 §5:
    Name: Gregory C. Damman   Business Address: 605 S. 14th St., Ste. 412
                                                  Lincoln, CT 68508
                               Residence Address: 3794 H St.
                                                  Lincoln, CT 68510

5. The latest date upon which the limited liability company will dissolve:
    July 9, 2025

EXECUTION

6. Dated this _____ day of _____, 19____

7. Gregory C. Damman   8. _____
   Name of Organizer (print or type)   Signature

9. Acceptance of appointed statutory agent.

    Gregory C. Damman   10. _____
    Name (print or type)   Signature

For Official Use Only | Rec; CC:
                         |_____
                         |_____
                         |_____
                         |_____
                         |_____
                         |_____
                         Please provide filer's name and
                         complete address for mailing receipt

DELAWARE

STATE *of* DELAWARE
CERTIFICATE *of* FORMATION *of*

▶ FIRST: The name of the limited liability company is <u>Damman Legal Research, L.L.C.</u>

▶ SECOND: The address of its registered office in the State of Delaware is <u>605 S. 14th St.,</u> <u>Ste. 412</u> in the City of <u>Lincoln</u>, County of <u>Lancaster</u>. The name of its Registered Agent at such address is <u>Gregory C. Damman</u>

▶ THIRD: (Use this paragraph only if the company is to have a specific date of dissolution: "The latest date on which the limited liability company is to dissolve is <u>none</u>.")

▶ FOURTH: (Insert any other matters the members determine to include herein.)
<u>none</u>

▶ IN WITNESS WHEREOF, the undersigned have executed this Certificate of Formation of _____ this day of _____ , 19 _____ .

Authorized Person(s)
Gregory C. Damman
<u>3794 H St., Lincoln, CT 68508</u>

FLORIDA

ARTICLES OF ORGANIZATION FOR FLORIDA LIMITED LIABILITY COMPANY

ARTICLE I - Name:
The name of the Limited Liability Company is:

Damman Legal Research, L.L.C.

ARTICLE II - Address:
The mailing address and street address of the principal office of the Limited Liability Company is:

Damman Legal Research, L.L.C.
605 S. 14th St., Ste. 412
Lincoln, FL 68508

ARTICLE III - Duration:
The period of duration for the Limited Liability Company shall be:

30 years

ARTICLE IV - Management:
(check and complete the appropriate statement)

☐ The Limited Liability Company is to be managed by a manager or managers and the name(s) and address(es) of such manager(s) who is/are to serve as manager(s) is/are:

☒ The Limited Liability Company is to be managed by the members and the name(s) and address(es) of the managing member(s) is/ are:

Gregory C. Damman
3794 H St.
Lincoln, FL 68508

FLORIDA

ARTICLE V - Admission of Additional Members:
The right, if given, of the remaining members to admit additional members and the terms and conditions of the admissions shall be:

The remaining members may admit additional members upon the majority vote of the remaining members consenting to the admission of the additional member.

ARTICLE VI - Members Rights to Continue Business:
The right, if given, of the remaining members of the limited liability company to continue the business on the death, retirement, resignation, expulsion, bankruptcy, or dissolution of a member or the occurrence of any other event which terminates the continued membership of a member in the limited liability company shall be:

The remaining members have the right to continue the business on the death, retirement, resignation, expulsion, bankruptcy, or dissolution of a member or the occurrence of any other event which terminates the continued membership of a member in the limited liability company upon the majority vote of the remaining members.

FLORIDA

AFFIDAVIT OF MEMBERSHIP AND CONTRIBUTIONS

The undersigned member or authorized representative of a member of _____

_____ deposes and says:

1) the above named limited liability company has at least two members

2) the total amount of cash contributed by the member(s) is $ _____ .

3) if any, the agreed value of property other than cash contributed by member(s) is
   $ _____ . A description of the property is attached and made a part hereto.

4) the total amount of cash or property anticipated to be contributed by member(s) is
   $ _____ . This total includes amounts from 2 and 3 above.

_____
Signature of a member or authorized representative of a member.
(In accordance with section 608.408(3), Florida Statutes, the execution of this affidavit constitutes an affirmation under the penalties of perjury that the facts stated herein are true.)

FILING FEE: $ 250 for Articles of Organization and Affidavit

GEORGIA

MAX CLELAND
Secretary of State
State of Georgia

BUSINESS SERVICES AND REGULATION
Suite 315, West Tower
2 Martin Luther King Jr., Drive
Atlanta, Georgia 30334-1530
(404) 656-2817

J. F. GULLION
Director

TRANSMITTAL INFORMATION FOR GEORGIA LIMITED LIABILITY COMPANIES

DO NOT WRITE IN SHADED AREA - SOS USE ONLY

DOCKET # _____ PENDING CONTROL # _____ CONTROL # _____

Docket Code _____ LLC Type _____

Date Filed _____ Amount Received $ _____ Check/Receipt # _____

Jurisdiction (County) Code _____

Examiner _____ Date Completed _____

NOTICE TO APPLICANT: PRINT PLAINLY OR TYPE REMAINDER OF THIS FORM.
INSTRUCTIONS ARE ON THE BACK OF THIS FORM.

1. editor's note: obtain the number from the Secretary of State.
   LLC Name Reservation Number
   Damman Legal Research, L.L.C.
   LLC Name (exactly as appears on name reservation)

2. Gregory C. Damman   (402) 476-8330
   Applicant/Attorney   Telephone Number
   3794 H Street, Lincoln, GA 68508
   Address   City   State   Zip Code

3. Name and Address of each organizer (attach additional sheets if necessary)
   Gregory C. Damman   3794 H Street, Lincoln, GA 68508
   Organizer   Address   City   State   Zip Code
   Susan C. Damman   3794 H Street, Lincoln, GA 68508
   Organizer   Address   City   State   Zip Code

4. Gregory C. Damman
   Name of Registered Agent in Georgia
   Gregory C. Damman 3794 H Street, Lincoln, GA 68508
   Registered Office Street Address in Georgia
                                              GA
   City   County   State   Zip Code

5. 605 South 14th St., Ste. 412, Lincoln, GA 68508
   Principal Place of Business Mailing Address   City   State   Zip Code

6. NOTICE: This form does not replace the articles of organization. Mail or deliver to the Secretary of State at the above address the following: (1) an original and one copy of this form; (2) an original and one copy of the articles of organization; and (3) a filing fee of $75.00 (make check payable to "Secretary of State").

_____   _____
Authorized Signature   Date
(Member, Manager, or Organizer)

BR231 (03-94)

IDAHO

ARTICLES OF ORGANIZATION
LIMITED LIABILITY COMPANY

(Instructions on back of application)

1. The name of the limited liability company is: <u>Damman Legal Research L.L.C.</u>

2. The address of the initial registered office is: <u>117 N. 6th St., Seward, ID 68434</u>
   (not a PO Box)

   ———————————————————————— and the name of the initial registered agent at that address is: <u>Gregory C. Damman</u>

   Signature of registered agent : _____

3. Is management of the limited liability company vested in a manager or managers?
   ☐ Yes   ☒ No   (check appropriate box)

4. If management is vested in one or more manager(s), list the name(s) and address(es) of at least one initial manager. If management is vested in the members, list the name(s) and address(es) of at least one initial member.

Name:	Address:
Gregory C. Damman	1688 Karol Kay Blvd., Seward ID 68434

5. Signature of at least one person listed in #4 above:

   _____

Secretary of State use only

Revised 6/97

ILLINOIS

Form **LLC-5.5**
January 1995

George H. Ryan
Secretary of State
Department of Business Services
Limited Liability Company Division
Room 359, Howlett Building
Springfield, IL 62756
http://www.sos.state.il.us

Payment must be made by certified check, cashier's check, Illinois attorney's check, Illinois C.P.A.'s check or money order, payable to "Secretary of State."

Illinois Limited Liability Company Act
Articles of Organization

Filing Fee $500.
SUBMIT IN DUPLICATE
Must be typewritten

This space for use by Secretary of State

Date
Assigned File #
Filing Fee $500.00
Approved:

This space for use by Secretary of State

1. Limited Liability Company Name: __Damman Legal Research, L.L.C.__

   (The LLC name must contain the words limited liability company or L.L.C. and cannot contain the terms corporation, corp., incorporated, inc., ltd., co., limited partnership, or L.P.)

2. Transacting business under an assumed name: ☐ Yes   ☒ No.
   (If YES, a Form LLC-1.20 is required to be completed and attached to these Articles.)

3. The address, including county, of its principal place of business: (Post office box alone and c/o are unacceptable.) __117 N. 6th St., Seward, IL 68434__

4. Federal Employer Identification Number (F.E.I.N.): __57-0098765__

5. The Articles of Organization are effective on: (Check one)

   a) __x__ the filing date, or b) _____ another date later than but not more than 60 days subsequent to the filing date: _____
   (month, day, year)

6. The registered agent's name and registered office address is:

   Registered agent: __Gregory__   __C.__   __Damman__
                       First Name   Middle Initial   Last Name

   Registered Office: __117 N. 6th St.__
   (P.O. Box alone and   Number   Street   Suite #
   c/o are unacceptable) __Seward, IL 68545__   __Seward__
                          City   Zip Code   County

7. Purpose or purposes for which the LLC is organized: Include the business code # (from IRS Form 1065)
   (If not sufficient space to cover this point, add one or more sheets of this size.)

   Any lawful business

8. The latest date the company is to dissolve __perpetual__.
   (month, day, year)

   And other events of dissolution enumerated on an attachment. (Optional)

   n/a

ILLINOIS

LLC-5.5

9. Other provisions for the regulation of the internal affairs of the LLC per Section 5-5 (a) (8) included as attachment:

    ☐ Yes ☒ No

    If yes, state the provisions(s) and the statutory cite(s) from the ILLCA.

10. a) Management is vested, in whole or in part, in managers: ☐ Yes ☒ No
    If yes, list their names and business addresses.

    b) Management is retained, in whole or in part, by the members: ☒ Yes ☐ No
    If yes, list their names and addresses.
    If no, the company has 2 or more members pursuant to S. 5-1 of the ILLCA.

    ```
    Gregory C. Damman              Susan C. Damman
    1688 Karol Kay Blvd.           1688 Karol Kay Blvd.
    Seward, IL  68434              Seward, IL  68434
    ```

11. The undersigned affirms, under penalties of perjury, having authority to sign hereto, that these articles of organization are to the best of my knowledge and belief, true, correct and complete.

    Dated _____ 19____

Signature(s) and Name(s) of Organizer(s)

1. _____
   Signature
   _____
   (Type or print name and title)
   _____
   (Name if a corporation or other entity)

2. _____
   Signature
   _____
   (Type or print name and title)
   _____
   (Name if a corporation or other entity)

3. _____
   Signature
   _____
   (Type or print name and title)
   _____
   (Name if a corporation or other entity)

Business Address(es)

1. _____
   Number   Street
   _____
   City/Town
   _____
   State   Zip Code

2. _____
   Number   Street
   _____
   City/Town
   _____
   State   Zip Code

3. _____
   Number   Street
   _____
   City/Town
   _____
   State   Zip Code

(Signatures must be in ink on an original document. Carbon copy, photocopy or rubber stamp signatures may only be used on conformed copies.)
LLC-4.2

INDIANA

ARTICLES OF ORGANIZATION
OF
Damman Legal Research, L.L.C.
An Indiana Limited Liability Company

I

The name of the limited liability company is:_____
Damman Legal Research, L.L.C._____.

II

The latest date on which the limited liability company is to dissolve is: July 25, 2025_____.

(Author's note: If the limited liability company is to have a perpetual existence, the above provision must be replaced by the following: The duration of the limited liability company is perpetual until dissolution in accordance with the Indiana Business Flexibility Act.)

III

The street address of the limited liability company's registered office in Indiana and the name of the registered agent at that office is: Gregory C. Damman, 605 S. 14th St., Ste. 412, Lincoln, IN 68508_____.

IV

These Articles of Organization do ( ) do not (x) provide for a manager or managers of the limited liability company.

V

Other provisions, not inconsistent with law, which the members agree to set out in these Articles of Organization, including any matters that are required to be or may be included in an operating agreement under Indiana Business Flexibility Act:_____
_____none_____
_____.

Executed this ____ day of _____, 19____.

Organizer's name and address: Gregory C. Damman_____
(type or print)   3794 H St._____
                               Lincoln, IN 68508_____

                               _____
                               Organizer's signature

(Note: The author created this form. The state filing agency may require the use of official forms.)

IOWA

ARTICLES OF ORGANIZATION
OF
Damman Legal Research, L.L.C.
An Iowa Limited Liability Company

I

The name of the limited liability company is:_____
Damman Legal Research, L.L.C._____.

II

The latest date on which the limited liability company is to dissolve, or its period of duration, is: July 25, 2025____.
(Author's note: The duration may not be perpetual.)

III

The address of the limited liability company's initial registered office is: 605 S. 14th St., Ste. 412, Lincoln, IA 68508
_____.

IV

The name and address of the limited liability company's initial resident agent at the above office is: Gregory C. Damman
605 S. 14th St., Ste. 412, Lincoln, IA 68508_____.

V

The street address of the principal office of the limited liability company is:_____
_____same as registered office_____.
(Author's note: This office may be the same as the registered office and need not be within the State of Iowa.)

XI

Any other provisions, not inconsistent with law, including, but not limited to, a statement of whether there are limitations on the authority of members to bind the limited liability company:___
_____none_____
_____.

Executed this ____ day of _____, 19____.

Organizer's name and address: Gregory C. Damman
(type or print)   3794 H St.
                               Lincoln, IA 68508

                               _____
                               Organizer's signature

(Note: The author created this form. The state filing agency may require the use of official forms.)

KANSAS

ARTICLES OF ORGANIZATION
OF
Damman Legal Research, L.L.C.
A Kansas Limited Liability Company

I

The name of the limited liability company is: __Damman Legal Research, L.L.C.__ .

II

The latest date on which the limited liability company is to dissolve, or its period of duration, is: __July 25, 2025__ .

III

The purpose for which the limited liability company is formed is: __any lawful purpose__ .

IV

The address of the limited liability company's registered office in this State is: __605 S. 14th St., Ste. 412, Lincoln, KS 68508__ .

V

The name and address of the limited liability company's initial resident agent in this State is: __Gregory C. Damman, 605 S. 14th St., Ste. 412, Lincoln, KS 68508__ .

VI

The right, if given, of the members to admit additional members and the terms and conditions of the admissions: __additional members may be admitted upon the majority vote of the members__ .

VII

The right, if given, of the remaining members of the limited liability company to continue the business on the death, retirement, resignation, expulsion, bankruptcy, or dissolution of a member or the occurrence of any other event which terminates the continued membership of a member in the limited liability company: __the company may continue business upon the majority vote of the remaining members__ .

KANSAS

VIII

The limited liability company is ( ) is not (x) to be managed by a manager or managers.

IX

If the limited liability company is to be managed by a manager or managers, the names and addresses of such managers who are to serve until their successors are elected and qualified are as follows:

n/a

X

If the limited liability company is to be managed by its members, the names and addresses of its members are:

Gregory C. Damman
3794 H St.
Lincoln, KS 68508

Susan C. Damman
3794 H St.
Lincoln, KS 68508

XI

Any other provisions, not inconsistent with law, which the members elect to set out in these Articles of Organization for the regulation of the internal affairs of the limited liability company, including any provisions which under the Kansas limited liability company act are required or permitted to be set out in the operating agreement of the limited liability company: none

Executed this ____ day of _____, 19____.

Organizer's name and address: Gregory C. Damman
(type or print)   3794 H St.
                               Lincoln, KS 68508

Organizer's signature

(Note: The author created this form. The state filing agency may require the use of official forms.)

KENTUCKY

ARTICLES OF ORGANIZATION
OF
Damman Legal Research, L.L.C.
A Kentucky Limited Liability Company

I

The name of the limited liability company is:
Damman Legal Research, L.L.C.

II

The latest date on which the limited liability company is to dissolve is: July 25, 2025.

III

The street address of the limited liability company's initial registered office and the name of its registered agent at that office is: Gregory C. Damman, 605 S. 14th St., Ste. 412, Lincoln, KY 68508.

IV

The mailing address of the initial principal office of the limited liability company is: 605 S. 14th St., Ste. 412, Lincoln, KY 68508.

V

The limited liability company has at least two (2) or more members.

VI

The limited liability is to be managed by (check one):

( ) A manager or managers

(x) Its members

VII

The professional services to be practiced through the limited liability company are: none.

(note: Complete this section only if the company to be formed is a professional limited liability company.)

KENTUCKY

VIII

Other provisions permitted to be set forth in an operating agreement, not inconsistent with law, which the members elect to set out in these Articles of Organization:_____
_____none_____
_____.

Executed this ____ day of _____, 19____.

_____
Signature of manager, member, or organizer

___Gregory C. Damman, member_____
Type or print name of person signing
the articles of organization, and state
whether person is signing as member, manager,
or organizer.

Registered Agent's Consent To Appointment

The undersigned hereby consents to serve as the Registered Agent for <u>Damman Legal Research, L.L.C.</u>, a Kentucky limited liability company.

___Gregory C. Damman_____
Type or Print Name

Address: ___3794 H St._____
___Lincoln, KY 68508_____
_____

_____
Signature of Registered Agent

(Note: The author created this form. The state filing agency may require the use of official forms.)

LOUISIANA

**W. Fox McKeithen
Secretary of State**

LIMITED LIABILITY COMPANY INITIAL REPORT
(R.S. 12:1305 (E))

1. The name of this limited liability company is: Damman Legal Research, L.L.C.

2. The location and municipal address, not a post office box only, of this limited liability company's registered office:
   605 S. 14th St., Ste. 412, Lincoln, LA 68508

3. The full name and municipal address, not a post office box only, of each of this limited liability company's registered agent(s) is/are:

   Gregory C. Damman, 3794 H St., Lincoln, LA 68501

4. The names and municipal addresses, not a post office box only, of the first managers, or the members:
   Gregory C. Damman, 3794 H St., Lincoln, LA 68501
   Susan C. Damman, 3794 H St., Lincoln, LA 68501

To be signed by each person who signed the articles of organization:

_____

_____

_____

_____

AGENT'S AFFIDAVIT AND ACKNOWLEDGEMENT OF ACCEPTANCE

I hereby acknowledge and accept the appointment of registered agent for and on behalf of the above named limited liability company.

Registered agent(s) signature(s):

_____

_____

Sworn to and subscribed before me this _____ day of _____, 19_____.

_____
Notary

#973 2/91   (See instructions on back)

MAINE

DOMESTIC LIMITED LIABILITY COMPANY

STATE OF MAINE

ARTICLES OF ORGANIZATION OF LIMITED LIABILITY COMPANY

(Check box only if applicable)

☐ This is a professional limited liability company formed pursuant to 31 MRSA §611 and 13 MRSA Chapter 22.

Filing Fee $250.00

_____
Deputy Secretary of State

A True Copy When Attested By Signature

_____
Deputy Secretary of State

Pursuant to 31 MRSA §622, the undersigned adopt(s) the following articles of organization:

FIRST: The name of the limited liability company is

Damman Legal Research, L.L.C.
(The name must contain one of the following: "Limited Liability Company", "L.L.C." or "LLC"; §603.1.A.)

SECOND: The name of its Registered Agent, an individual Maine resident or a corporation, foreign or domestic, authorized to do business or carry on activities in Maine, and the address of the registered office shall be

Gregory C. Damman
(name)

117 N. 6th St., Seward, ME 68434
(physical location - street (not P.O. Box), city, state and zip code)

_____
(mailing address if different from above)

THIRD: ("X" one box only)

☒ A. The management of the company is vested in a member or members.

☐ B. 1. The management of the company is vested in a manager or managers. The minimum number shall be _____ managers and the maximum number shall be _____ managers.

2. If the initial managers have been selected, the name and business, residence or mailing address of each manager is:

NAME	ADDRESS
_____	_____
_____	_____
_____	_____

☐ Names and addresses of additional managers are attached hereto as Exhibit ____, and made a part hereof.

MAINE

FOURTH: ("X" one box only) These articles may be amended upon approval of the following: (§623.4.)

☒ A.   A majority of the members (if no box is checked, the statute requires that).

☐ B.   A majority in interest of the members.

☐ C.   Other.

FIFTH: Other provisions of these articles, if any, that the members determine to include are set forth in Exhibit ____ attached hereto and made a part hereof.

ORGANIZER(S)*   **DATED** _____

_____   <u>Gregory C. Damman</u>_____
              (signature)   (type or print name)

_____   Susan C. Damman_____
              (signature)   (type or print name)

_____   _____
              (signature)   (type or print name)

For Organizer(s) which are Entities

Name of Entity _____

By _____   _____
        (authorized signature)   (type or print name and capacity)

Name of Entity _____

By _____   _____
        (authorized signature)   (type or print name and capacity)

Name of Entity _____

By _____   _____
        (authorized signature)   (type or print name and capacity)

MAINE

THE FOLLOWING SHALL BE COMPLETED BY THE REGISTERED AGENT _UNLESS_ THIS DOCUMENT IS ACCOMPANIED BY FORM MLLC-18 (§607.2.).

The undersigned hereby accepts the appointment as registered agent for the above named limited liability company.

REGISTERED AGENT   **DATED** _____

_____   _____
(signature)   (type or print name)

For Registered Agent which is a Corporation

Name of Corporation _____

By _____   _____
(authorized signature)   (type or print name and capacity)

---

*Articles must be signed by all **organizers** (§627.1.A.). The execution of the articles constitutes an oath or affirmation, under the penalties of false swearing under Title 17-A, section 453, that, to the best of the signers' knowledge and belief, the facts stated in the articles are true (§627.3.).

SUBMIT COMPLETED FORMS TO: CORPORATE EXAMINING SECTION, SECRETARY OF STATE,
101 STATE HOUSE STATION, AUGUSTA, ME 04333-0101
FORM NO. MLLC-6   Rev. 7/23/96   TEL. (207) 287-4195

MARYLAND

ARTICLES OF ORGANIZATION
OF
Damman Legal Research, L.L.C.
A Maryland Limited Liability Company

I

The name of the limited liability company is:_____
Damman Legal Research, L.L.C._____.

II

The latest date on which the limited liability company is to dissolve is: July 25, 2025_____.

III

The purpose for which the limited liability company is formed is: any lawful purpose_____.

IV

The address of the limited liability company's principal office in this State is: 605 S. 14th St., Ste. 412, Lincoln, MD 68508
_____.

V

The name and address of the limited liability company's resident agent is: Gregory C. Damman, 3794 H St., Lincoln, MD 68508
_____.

VI

Other provisions, not inconsistent with law, which the members elect to set out in these Articles of Organization:_____
                  none
_____.

Executed this ____ day of _____, 19____.

Gregory C. Damman, member
Type or print name of person authorized
by the limited liability company to
execute the articles of organization

_____
Signature of authorized person listed above

(Note: The author created this form. The state filing agency may require the use of official forms.)

MASSACHUSETTS

CERTIFICATE OF ORGANIZATION
OF
Damman Legal Research, L.L.C.

To the Secretary of State of the Commonwealth of Massachusetts

It is hereby certified that:

1. The name of the limited liability company is Damman Legal Research, L.L.C.

2. The address of the office of the company in the Commonwealth of Massachusetts is:

   Damman Legal Research
   Gregory C. Damman
   117 N. 6th St.
   Seward, MA 68434

3. The name and address of the company registered agent within the Commonwealth of Massachusetts is:

   Gregory C. Damman
   117 N. 6th St.
   Seward, ME 68434

4. The company's specific dissolution date is: (author's note: may be perpetual)

5. The name and address of each manager of the company at the time of formation are:

   (Author's note: If no managers, simply type "none")

6. The general character of the company's business as follows:

   Any lawful business

7. The name of each person authorized to execute documents to be filed with the Secretary of State is:

8. The name of each person authorized to execute, acknowledge, deliver, and record any recordable instrument purporting to affect an interest in real property, whether to be recorded with a Registry of Deeds or with a District Office of Land Court is:

IN WITNESS WHEREOF and under penalties of perjury, the person whose signature appears below does hereby affirm and execute this certificate of organization as an authorized person this   day of   , 19   .

_____
Authorized Person

MICHIGAN

C&S 700 (Rev. 8/93)

MICHIGAN DEPARTMENT OF COMMERCE - CORPORATION AND SECURITIES BUREAU

Date Received

(FOR BUREAU USE ONLY)

Name: Gregory C. Damman
Address: 3794 H St., Lincoln, MI 68508
City / State / Zip Code

EFFECTIVE DATE:

Document will be returned to the name and address you enter above

ARTICLES OF ORGANIZATION
For use by Domestic Limited Liability Companies
(Please read information and instructions on last page)

L C — ___

Pursuant to the provisions of Act 23, Public Acts of 1993, the undersigned execute the following Articles:

ARTICLE I
The name of the limited liability company is:

Damman Legal Research, L.L.C.

ARTICLE II
The purpose or purposes for which the limited liability company is formed is to engage in any activity within the purposes for which a limited liability company may be formed under the Limited Liability Company Act of Michigan.

ARTICLE III
The duration of the limited liability company is: 30 years

ARTICLE IV
1. The address of the registered office is:

   605 S. 14th St., Ste. 412, Lincoln (City), Michigan 58408 (ZIP Code)

2. The mailing address of the registered office if different than above:

   Same as above (P.O. Box), (City), Michigan ___ (ZIP Code)

3. The name of the resident agent at the registered office is: Gregory C. Damman

Signed this _____ day of _____, 19_____

By _____   _____   _____
      (Signature)   (Signature)   (Signature)

Gregory C. Damman   Susan C. Damman   _____
   (Type or Print Name)   (Type or Print Name)   (Type or Print Name)

MICHIGAN

Name of Person or Organization
Remitting Fees:

Gregory C. Damman

Preparer's Name and Business
Telephone Number:

Gregory C. Damman

(402) 476-8330

INFORMATION AND INSTRUCTIONS

1. The articles of organization cannot be filed until this form, or a comparable document, is submitted.

2. Submit one original of this document. Upon filing, the document will be added to the records of the Corporation and Securities Bureau. The original will be returned to the address you enter in the box on the front as evidence of filing.

   Since this document will be maintained on optical disc media, it is important that the filing be legible. Documents with poor black and white contrast, or otherwise illegible, will be rejected.

3. This document is to be used pursuant to the provisions of Act 23, P.A. of 1993, by two or more persons for the purpose of forming a domestic limited liability company. **Use form 701 if the Limited Liability Company will be providing a personal service for which a license or legal authorization is required pursuant to Article 9 of the Act.**

4. Article I - The name of a domestic limited liability company is required to contain one of the following words or abbreviations: "Limited Liability Company", "L.L.C.", or "L.C."

5. Article II - Under section 203(b) of the Act, it is sufficient to state substantially, alone or with specifically enumerated purposes, that the limited liability company is formed to engage in any activity within the purposes for which a limited liability company may be formed under the Act.

6. Article III - The term of existence of the limited liability company must be stated.

7. Article IV - A post office box may not be designated as the address of the registered office.

8. This document is effective on the date endorsed "Filed" by the Bureau. A later effective date, no more than 90 days after the date of delivery, may be stated as an additional article.

9. The articles must be signed in ink by two or more of the persons who will be members. Names of person signing shall be stated beneath their signatures.

10. If more space is needed, attach additional pages. All pages should be numbered.

11. **FEES:** Make remittance payable to the State of Michigan. Include limited liability company name on check or money order. **Nonrefundable filing fee** $50.00

12. Mail form and fee to:

    Michigan Department of Commerce
    Corporation and Securities Bureau
    Corporation Division
    P.O. Box 30054
    Lansing, MI 48909-7554

    The office is located at:

    6546 Mercantile Way
    Lansing, MI 48910
    (517) 334-6302

MINNESOTA

STATE OF MINNESOTA
ARTICLES OF ORGANIZATION FOR
A LIMITED LIABILITY COMPANY
MINNESOTA STATUTES CHAPTER 322B

FOR OFFICE USE ONLY
Filing date: _____
Charter # _____ -LLC
Page # _____

PLEASE TYPE OR PRINT IN BLACK INK.

Before Completing this Form Please Read the Instructions on the Back.   FILING FEE $135.00

1. Name of Company: **Damman Legal Research, L.L.C.**

2. Registered Office Address:

   __117 N. 6th Street__   __Seward__   __MN__ __68434__
   Complete Street Address or Rural Route and Rural Route Box Number   City   State   ZIP Code
   (P.O. Box is Unacceptable)

3. Name of Registered Agent (optional): __Gregory C. Damman__

4. Business Mailing Address: (if different from registered office address)

   __same as above__
   Address   City   State   ZIP Code

5. Desired Duration of LLC: (in years) __perpetual__

6. List your SIC Code. __00__   Select one of the 2-digit SIC codes listed on the reverse side of this form that most accurately describes the nature of the business you are forming.

7. The members of this company **(check one)** do _x_ do not ____ have the power to avoid dissolution by giving dissolution avoidance consent in the case of occurrence of events listed in section 322B.80, subdivision 1, clause (5).

8. The members of this company **(check one)** do _x_ do not ____ have the power to enter into a business continuation agreement.

9. Does this LLC own, lease or have any interest in agricultural land or land capable of being farmed?
   (Check One)   Yes ____   No _x_

10. Name and Telephone Number of Contact Person for this LLC:

    Name __Gregory C. Damman__   Phone (402) __123-4567__

11. Name and Address of Organizer(s):

Name (print)	Complete Address	Original Signature (required)
Gregory C. Damman	1688 Karol Kay Blvd. Seward, MN 68434	
Susan C. Damman	1688 Karol Kay Blvd. Seward, MN 68434	

MISSISSIPPI

F0100 - Page 1 of 2

OFFICE OF THE MISSISSIPPI SECRETARY OF STATE
P.O. BOX 136, JACKSON, MS 39205-0136 (601) 359-1333
Certificate of Formation

The undersigned, pursuant to Senate Bill No. 2395, Chapter 402, Laws of 1994, hereby executes the following document and sets forth:

1. Name of the Limited Liability Company

⇨ Damman Legal Research, L.L.C.

2. The future effective date is (Complete if applicable)

3. Federal Tax ID

⇨ 57-0998763

4. Name and Street Address of the Registered Agent and Registered Office is

⇨ Name: Gregory C. Damman

⇨ Physical Address: 117 N. 6th St.

⇨ P.O. Box: P.O. Box 1041

⇨ City, State, ZIP5, ZIP4: Seward | MS | 68434 -

5. If the Limited Liability Company is to have a specific date of dissolution, the latest date upon which the Limited Liability Company is to dissolve

⇨ n/a

6. Is full or partial management of the Limited Liability Company vested in a manager or managers? (Mark appropriate box)

⇨ [ ] Yes [x] No

7. Other matters the managers or members elect to include

⇨ none

⇨

OFFICE OF THE MISSISSIPPI SECRETARY OF STATE
P.O. BOX 136, JACKSON, MS 39205-0136   (601) 359-1333
Certificate of Formation

By: Signature

Printed Name: Gregory C. Damman

Title: member

Street and Mailing Address

- Physical Address: 117 N. 6th St.
- P.O. Box: P.O. Box 1041
- City, State, ZIP5, ZIP4: Seward, MS 68434 -

By: Signature

Printed Name: Gregory C. Damman

Title:

Street and Mailing Address

- Physical Address: 117 N. 6th St.
- P.O. Box: P.O. Box 1041
- City, State, ZIP5, ZIP4: Seward, MS 68434 -

MISSOURI

State of Missouri

Judith K. Moriarty, Secretary of State
P.O. Box 778, Jefferson City, Mo. 65102

Corporation Division

Articles of Organization
(Submit in duplicate with filing fee of $105)

1. The name of the limited liability company is:
   Damman Legal Research, L.L.C.

2. The purpose(s) for which the limited liability company is organized: Any lawful business

3. The name and address of the limited liability company's registered agent in Missouri is:
   Gregory C. Damman, 605 S. 14th St., Ste. 412, Lincoln, MO 68508
   Name — Street address — City/State/Zip

4. The management of the limited liability company is vested in one or more managers. ☐ Yes ☒ No

5. The latest date on which the limited liability company is to dissolve is: July 10, 2025
   Month/Day/Year

6. Upon the withdrawal of any member, the remaining member(s) have the following right(s) (if any) to continue the business and affairs of the limited liability company:
   A majority vote of the remaining members

7. The name(s) and address(es) of each organizer:
   Gregory C. Damman, 3794 H St., Lincoln, MO 68510
   Susan C. Damman, 3794 H St., Lincoln, MO 68510

8. For tax purposes, is the limited liability company considered a corporation? ☐ Yes ☒ No

In affirmation thereof, the facts stated above are true:

_____ Organizer
_____ Organizer
_____ Organizer

MONTANA

STATE OF MONTANA

ARTICLES of ORGANIZATION for
DOMESTIC LIMITED LIABILITY COMPANY
(35-8-202, MCA)

Prepare, sign and **submit an ORIGINAL AND COPY** with fee.
This is the minimum information required.

(For use by the Secretary of State only)

MAIL TO: MIKE COONEY
Secretary of State
P.O. Box 202801
Helena, MT 59620-2801
☎(406)444-3665

Form: PLC-1
Filing Fee: $70.00

☐ Priority Filing (additional $20.00)

▶ *Executed by the undersigned for the purpose of forming a Montana Limited Liability Company.*

PLEASE CHECK ONE BOX:
☒ Limited Liability Company   ☐ Professional Limited Liability Company

▶ FIRST: The name of the limited liability company is (must contain "limited liability company", "limited company" or if Professional, "professional limited liability company", or an abbreviation)

Damman Legal Research, L.L.C.

▶ SECOND: The name and address of its registered office/agent in Montana:

Name Gregory C. Damman

Street Address 117 N. 6th St.

Mailing Address P.O. Box 1041

Seward, MONTANA Zip Code 68434

▶ THIRD: The address of its principal place of business in Montana:

Address 117 N. 6th St.

City Seward, MONTANA Zip Code 68434

▶ FOURTH: The latest date on which the LLC is to dissolve is perpetual.

▶ FIFTH: The LLC will be managed by a ☐ Manager or by its ☒ Members.

▶ SIXTH: The names of the Managers or Members and street addresses are:

Gregory C. Damman, 1688 Karol Kay Blvd., Seward, MT 68434

Susan C. Damman, 1688 Karol Kay Blvd., Seward, MT 68434

▶ SEVENTH: *If a Professional Limited Liability Company, the services to be provided*

n/a

Signature of Organizer   Date

Printed Name and Title

NEBRASKA

ARTICLES OF ORGANIZATION
LIMITED LIABILITY COMPANY
Submit in Duplicate

Scott Moore, Secretary of State
Room 1301 State Capitol, P.O. Box 94608
Lincoln, NE 68509
(402) 471-4079

Name of Limited Liability Company _Damman Legal Research, L.L.C._

Period of Duration _perpeutal_ (may be perpetual)

Purpose for which the limited liability company is organized

any lawful business

Principal place of business in Nebraska:

_117 N. 6th St._   _Seward_   NE _68434_
Street Address   City   Zip

Name and address of registered agent in Nebraska:

Registered Agent Name: _Gregory C. Damman_

Address: _117 N. 6th St., Seward_   NE _68434_
          Street Address   City   Zip

The total amount of cash contributed to stated capital of the LLC $ _1,000.00_

Description and agreed value of property other than cash contributed to stated capital:

Description of Property   Agreed Value

none

NEBRASKA

LLC ARTICLES OF ORGANIZATION (Continued)   Page 2

Total additional contributions agreed to be made by all members and the times at which, or events upon the happening of which such contributions shall be made:

___none___

Members __x__ shall or ____ shall not have the right to admit additional members (check)

If additional members are allowed the terms and conditions of admission:

___majority vote of members___

The company will be managed by ____ managers or __x__ members (check one). List the name and address of the managers or, if the management is reserved to the members, the name and address of the members:

Name	Address
Gregory C. Damman	117 N. 6th St., Seward, NE 68434
Susan C. Damman	117 N. 6th St., Seward, NE 68434

Attach additional pages if needed for additional managers or members. If the LLC has more than one class of membership please attach additional pages with the name or description of each class of membership and the names and addresses of the members in each class.

NEBRASKA

LLC ARTICLES OF ORGANIZATION (Continued)   Page 3

Any other provisions, not inconsistent with law, which the members elect to set out in the articles of organization for the limited liability company:

_____none_____
_____
_____
_____
_____
_____

Only one signature is required, additional members/managers may sign:

_____	Or	_____
Signature of Member		Signature of Manager
_____	Or	_____
Printed Name of Member		Printed Name of Manager
_____	Or	_____
Signature of Member		Signature of Manager
_____	Or	_____
Printed Name of Member		Printed Name of Manager
_____	Or	_____
Signature of Member		Signature of Manager
_____	Or	_____
Printed Name of Member		Printed Name of Manager
_____	Or	_____
Signature of Member		Signature of Manager
_____	Or	_____
Printed Name of Member		Printed Name of Manager
_____	Or	_____
Signature of Member		Signature of Manager
_____	Or	_____
Printed Name of Member		Printed Name of Manager

FILING FEE: $100.00 plus $5.00 per page and $10.00 for certificate of organization

NEVADA

Articles of Organization
Limited-Liability Company
(PURSUANT TO NRS 86)
STATE OF NEVADA
Secretary of State

Filing fee: $125

(For Office Use Only)

IMPORTANT: Read instructions on reverse side before completing this form.
TYPE OR PRINT (BLACK INK ONLY)

1. Name of Limited Liability Company: __Damman Legal Research, L.L.C.__
2. Dissolution Date (latest date upon which the company is to dissolve): __perpetual__
3. Resident Agent: (designated resident agent and the STREET ADDRESS in Nevada where process may be served)

   Name of Resident Agent: __Gregory C. Damman__

   Street Address: __117 N. 6th St., Seward, NV 68434__
               Street No.   Street Name   City   Zip

   Mailing Address (if different): __same as above__

4. Right of remaining members of the company to continue the business on the death, retirement, resignation, expulsion, bankruptcy, dissolution of a member or occurrence of any other event which terminates the continued membership of a member in the company:
   __X__ YES   ____ NO

5. Management: The company shall be managed by ____ manager(s) OR __X__ members
   Names and addresses of manager(s) or members: (attach additional pages if necessary)
   1. __Gregory C. Damman, 1688 Karol Kay Blvd., Seward, NV 68434__
   2. __Susan C. Damman, 1688 Karol Kay Blvd., Seward, NV 68434__
   If managed by members, members may contract debts on behalf of the company __X__ YES ____ NO

6. Other matters: This form includes the minimal statutory requirements to organize under NRS 86. Please attach any other information deemed appropriate. Number of pages attached _____.

7. Signature of organizer(s): The name(s) and address(es) of the organizer(s) executing the articles:
   (Signatures must be notarized) (Attach additional pages if there are more than two organizers.)

   __Gregory C. Damman__   __Susan C. Damman__
   Name (print)   Name (print)

   __1688 Karol Kay Blvd., Seward, NV 68434__   __same__
   Address   City/State/Zip   Address   City/State

   _____ Signature   Date   _____ Signature   Date

   This instrument was acknowledged before me on _____, 19__, by

   This instrument was acknowledged before me on _____, 19__

   _____ Name of Person _____   _____ Name of Person _____
   as organizer   as organizer
   of _____   of _____
   (name of party on behalf of whom instrument was executed)   (name of party on behalf of whom instrument was executed)

   _____ Notary Public Signature _____   _____ Notary Public Signature _____

   (affix notary stamp or seal)   (affix notary stamp or seal)

8. Certificate of acceptance of appointment of resident agent: I, _____
   hereby accept appointment as resident agent for the above named limited-liability company.

   _____ Signature of resident agent   _____ Date

NEW HAMPSHIRE

STATE OF NEW HAMPSHIRE

Fee for Form LLC 1A: $50.00
Filing fee: $35.00
Total fees $85.00
Use black print or type.
Leave 1" margins both sides.

Form No. LLC 1
RSA 304-C:12

CERTIFICATE OF FORMATION

THE UNDERSIGNED, UNDER THE NEW HAMPSHIRE LIMITED LIABILITY COMPANY LAWS SUBMITS THE FOLLOWING CERTIFICATE OF FORMATION:

FIRST: The name of the Limited Liability Company is _____ Damman Legal Research, L.L.C.

SECOND: The nature of the primary business or purposes are Any lawful business

THIRD: The name of the limited liability company's registered agent is Gregory C. Damman and the street address (including zip code and post office box, if any) of its registered office is (agent's business address) _____ 605 South 14th St., Ste. 412, Lincoln, NH 68508

FOURTH: The securities (generally, membership interests) will be sold or offered for sale within the meaning of RSA 421-B. (New Hampshire Securities Act).

FIFTH: The latest date on which the limited liability company is to dissolve is July 10, 2025.

SIXTH: The management of the limited liability company is not vested in a manager or managers.

Dated _____, 19___

Signature: _____
Print or Type Name: Gregory C. Damman
Title: _____

NEW JERSEY

**New Jersey Department of State
Division of Commercial Recording
Certificate of Formation, Limited Liability Company**

L-100 NJSA 42 (2/94)

This form may be used to record the formation of a Limited Liability Company under and by virtue of New Jersey State law. Applicants must insure strict compliance with NJSA 42, the New Jersey Limited Liability Company Act, and insure that all applicable filing requirements are met. Applicants are advised to seek out private legal assistance before submitting filings to the Secretary's office.

1. Name of Limited Liability Company: Damman Legal Research, L.L.C.

2. The purpose for which this Limited Liability Company is organized is: Any lawful purpose

3. Date of formation: July 10, 1995

4. Registered Agent Name & Address (must be in NJ): Gregory C. Damman
605 South 14th St., Ste. 412
Lincoln, NJ 68508

5. Dissolution date: July 10, 2025

6. Other provisions (list below or attach to certificate): none

The undersigned represent(s) that this Limited Liability Company has two or more members, and that this filing complies with requirements detailed in NJSA 42. The undersigned hereby attest(s) that they are authorized to sign this certificate on behalf of the Limited Liability Company.

Name	Date

NEW MEXICO

FEE: $50.00
Submit original and
one copy
Must be Typewritten

ARTICLES OF ORGANIZATION

OF

Damman Legal Research, L.L.C.
(NAME OF LIMITED LIABILITY COMPANY)

The undersigned, acting as organizer(s) of a limited liability company pursuant to the New Mexico Limited Liability Company Act, adopt the following Articles of Organization:

ARTICLE 1 NAME

The name of the limited liability company is _____

_Damman Legal Research, L.L.C._____.

ARTICLE 2 DURATION

The latest date upon which the Company is to dissolve is:_____

_July 10, 2025_____.

ARTICLE 3 AGENT AND ADDRESS

The street address and city of the Company's initial registered office and the name of its initial registered agent at that office is: _Gregory C. Damman, 605 South 14th St., Ste. 412,_

_Lincoln, NE 68508_____, and the street address and city of the Company's principal place of business, if different from its registered office, is _____

_same as above_____.

ARTICLE 4   MANAGEMENT

If management of the Company is vested to any extent in a manager then a statement to that effect and of the extent to which management is so vested is: (attach addendum, if needed)

n/a

ARTICLE 5   INTERNAL AFFAIRS

Any other provisions including provisions for the regulation of the internal affairs of the Company is: (attach addendum, if needed).

none

Dated:_____.

_____

_____

_____

Organizers' Signatures

NEW YORK

Basic Articles of Organization using an Affirmation Statement

SAMPLE

ARTICLES OF ORGANIZATION
OF
Under Section 203 of the Limited Liability Company Law

FIRST: The name of the limited liability company is: __Damman Legal Research, L.L.C._____.

SECOND: The county within this state in which the office of the limited liability company is to be located is: _Lancaster_____.

THIRD: (optional) The latest date on which the limited liability company is to dissolve is: * _July 10, 2025_____.

FOURTH: The secretary of state is designated as agent of the limited liability company upon whom process against it may be served. The post office address within or without this state to which the secretary of state shall mail a copy of any process against the limited liability company served upon him or her is: _605 South 14th St., Ste., 412, Lincoln, NY 68508_____.

FIFTH: (optional) The name and street address within this state of the registered agent of the limited liability company upon whom and at which process against the limited liability company can be served is: _Gregory C. Damman, 605 S. 14th St. Ste. 412, Lincoln, NY 68508_____.

SIXTH: The future effective date of the Articles of Organization, if not effective upon filing, is __effective on filing____.

SEVENTH: The limited liability company is to be managed by (check appropriate box):

☒ 1 or more members

☐ A class or classes of members

☐ 1 or more managers

☐ A class or classes of managers

EIGHTH: If all or specified members are to be liable in their capacity as members for all or specified debts, obligations or liabilities of the limited liability company as authorized pursuant to Section 609 of the Limited Liability Company Law, a statement that all or specified members are so liable.

IN WITNESS WHEREOF, this certificate has been subscribed this_____ day of _____ , 19 ___, by the undersigned who affirms that the statements made herein are true under the penalties of perjury.

_____   _____
(signature)   (name and capacity of signer)

*   If the limited liability company shall maintain more than one office in this state, set forth the county in which the principal office is to be located.

1)   The future effective date may not exceed 60 days from the date of filing and must be a date certain.

2)   The articles may include any other provisions not inconsistent with law.

Prepared by NYS Department of State 1994

NORTH CAROLINA

State of North Carolina
Department of the Secretary of State
LIMITED LIABILITY COMPANY
ARTICLES OF ORGANIZATION

Pursuant to §57C-2-20 of the General Statutes of North Carolina, the undersigned does hereby submit these Articles of Organization for the purpose of forming a limited liability company.

1. The name of the limited liability company is: __Damman Legal Research, L.L.C.__

2. The latest date on which the limited liability company is to dissolve is: __July 10, 2025__

3. The name and address of each organizer executing these articles of organization is as follows (at least two persons must execute this document; attach additional pages if necessary):

   Gregory C. Damman   Susan C. Damman
   3794 H Street   3794 H Street
   Lincoln, NC 68508   Lincoln, NC 68508

4. The street address and county of the initial registered office of the limited liability company is:

   Number and Street __605 South 14th St., Ste. 412__

   City, State, Zip Code __Lincoln, NC 68508__   County __Lancaster__

5. The mailing address **if different from the street address** of the initial registered office is: _____
   __Same as above__

6. The named of the initial registered agent is: __Gregory C. Damman__

7. Check one of the following:
   __x__ (i) Member-managed LLC: all of the members by virtue of their status as members shall be managers of this limited liability company.
   _____ (ii) Manager-managed LLC: except as provided by N.C.G.S. §57C-3-20(a), the members of this limited liability company shall not be managers by virtue of their status as members.

8. Any other provisions which the limited liability company elects to include are attached.

9. These articles will be effective upon filing, unless a date and/or time is specified: __none__

This the _____ day of _____ , 19_____

Signature	Signature
Gregory C. Damman	Susan C. Damman
Type or Print Name and Title	Type or Print Name and Title

NOTES:
1. Filing fee is $100. This document and one exact or conformed copy of these articles must be filed with the Secretary of State.
CORPORATIONS DIVISION   300 N. SALISBURY STREET   RALEIGH, NC 27603-5909

NORTH DAKOTA

**SAMPLE FORMAT
ARTICLES OF ORGANIZATION OF
LIMITED LIABILITY COMPANY**

(The **Bold** items are to be completed by the applicant)

I(We), the undersigned individual(s) of the age of eighteen years or more, acting as organizer(s) of a limited liability company organized under the North Dakota (**Limited Liability Company** or Limited Liability Company Farming) Act, adopt the following Articles of Organization for such limited liability company.

ARTICLE I: The name of the limited liability company is **NORTH DAKOTA ENTERPRISE LIMITED LIABILITY COMPANY.**

ARTICLE II: The address of the principal executive office is **8520 East Lansing, Bismarck, ND, 58501.** The telephone number at that address is **701-223-0000.**

ARTICLE III: The name of the registered agent is **John Doe** whose social security number is **501-77-3428.** The address of such agent is **2237 West Boulevard, Wilton, ND, 58579.** This address shall be the registered office in North Dakota.

ARTICLE IV: The names and addresses of the organizers are:

John Doe	**Jane Bishop**	**Mark Marzo**
2237 West Boulevard	**8518 N Crystal St**	**8520 E Lansing**
Wilton, ND, 58579	**Fargo, ND, 58102**	**Bismarck, ND, 58501**

ARTICLE V: The period of duration is **thirty years** from the date of filing of these Articles of Organization with the North Dakota Secretary of State, unless the limited liability company is sooner dissolved.

ARTICLE VI: The members **have (do not have)** the right to continue the limited liability company upon the occurrence of any event under N.D.C.C., subdivision e of Section 10-32-109 that terminates the continued membership of a member. The remaining members **will (will not)** have the power to avoid dissolution by giving dissolution avoidance consent.

ARTICLE VII: The members **have (do not have)** the power to enter into a business continuation agreement.

I(We), the above named organizer(s) have read the foregoing Articles of Organization, know the contents, and believe the statements made therein to be true.

Dated: *November 30*, 19*93*

John Doe   *Jane Bishop*   *Mark Marzo*

Prescribed by
Bob Taft, Secretary of State
30 East Broad Street, 14th Floor
Columbus, Ohio 43266-0418
Form LCA (July 1994)

OHIO
Approved _____
Date _____
Fee $85.00

ARTICLES OF ORGANIZATION

(Under Section 1705.04 of the Ohio Revised Code)
Limited Liability Company

The undersigned, desiring to form a limited liability company, under Chapter 1705 of the Ohio Revised Code, do hereby state the following:

FIRST: The name of said limited liability company shall be _____

__Damman Legal Research, L.L.C._____
(the name must include the words "limited liability company", "limited", "Ltd" or "Ltd.")

SECOND: This limited liability company shall exist for a period of __30 years__

THIRD: The address to which interested persons may direct requests for copies of any operating agreement and any bylaws of this limited liability company is:

__605 S. 14th St., Ste. 412_____
(street or post office box)

__Lincoln,   OH   68508_____
(city, village or township)   (state)   (zip code)

[ ]   Please check this box if additional provisions are attached hereto

Provisions attached hereto are incorporated herein and made a part of these articles of organization.

none

197

OHIO

FOURTH: Purpose (optional)

IN WITNESS WHEREOF, we have hereunto subscribed our names, this _____ day of _____, 19_____.

Signed:_____   Signed:_____

Signed:_____   Signed:_____

Signed:_____   Signed:_____

(If insufficient space for all signatures, please attach a separate sheet containing additional signatures)

INSTRUCTIONS

1. The fee for filing Articles of Organization for a limited liability company is $85.00.

2. Articles **will be returned unless** accompanied by a written appointment of agent signed by all or a majority of the members of the limited liability company which must include a written acceptance of the appointment by the named agent.

3. A limited liability company must be formed by a minimum of two persons.

4. Any other provisions that are from the operating agreement or that are not inconsistent with applicable Ohio law and that the members elect to set out in the articles for the regulation of the affairs of the limited liability company may be attached.

[Ohio Revised Code Section 1705.04]

OKLAHOMA

FEE: $100.00

ARTICLES OF ORGANIZATION

PLEASE PRINT CLEARLY

FOR OFFICE USE ONLY

FILE IN DUPLICATE

TO: **THE OKLAHOMA SECRETARY OF STATE**, 101 State Capitol, Oklahoma City, OK 73105

The undersigned, for the purpose of forming an Oklahoma limited liability company pursuant to the provisions of 18 O.S. 1993 Supp., Section 2004, does hereby execute the following articles:

1. The name of the limited liability company (**Note:** The name must contain either the words "limited liability company" or "limited company" or the abbreviations "L.L.C." or "L.C." The word "limited" may be abbreviated as "Ltd." and the word "Company" may be abbreviated as "Co."):

   Damman Legal Research, L.L.C.

2. The street address of its principal place of business in the state of Oklahoma:

   605 South 14th St., Ste. 412, Lincoln, OK 68508
   Street address   City   State   Zip Code

3. The name and address of the resident agent in the state of Oklahoma:

   Gregory C. Damman, 605 S. 14th St., Ste. 412, Lincoln, OK 68508
   Name   Street Address   City   State   Zip Code
   (P.O. Boxes are **not** acceptable.)

4. The latest date on which the limited liability company is to dissolve: July 10, 2025

Articles of organization must be signed by at least one person who need not be a member of the limited liability company.

Dated: _____

Signature: _____

Type or Print Name: Gregory C. Damman

Address: _____

(SOS FORM 0073-8/93)

OREGON

Articles of Organization—Limited Liability Company

Phone: (503) 986-2200
Fax: (503) 378-4381
Secretary of State
Corporation Division
255 Capitol St. NE, Suite 151
Salem, OR 97310-1327

For office use only

Registry Number: _____

Attach Additional Sheet if Necessary
Please Type or Print Legibly in **Black** Ink

1) NAME (Must contain the words "Limited Liability Company" or the abbreviations "LLC" or "L.L.C.")

Damman Legal Research, L.L.C.

2) DURATION (Please check one.)

☐ Latest date upon which the Limited Liability Company is to dissolve is _____

☒ Duration shall be perpetual.

3) NAME OF THE INITIAL REGISTERED AGENT

Gregory C. Damman

4) ADDRESS OF THE INITIAL REGISTERED AGENT (Must be an Oregon Street Address which is identical to the registered agent's business office.)

117 N. 6th St., Seward OR 68434

5) ADDRESS WHERE THE DIVISION MAY MAIL NOTICES

117 N. 6th St., Seward, OR 68434

6) NAME AND ADDRESS OF EACH ORGANIZER

Gregory C. Damman
117 N. 6th St.
Seward, OR 68434

7) CHECK THE FOLLOWING STATEMENT IF APPLICABLE.

☐ This limited liability company will be managed by a manager(s).

8) OPTIONAL PROVISIONS (Attach a separate sheet if necessary.)

9) EXECUTION (The title for each signer must be "Organizer.")

Printed Name: Gregory C. Damman

Signature:

Title:

10) CONTACT NAME

Gregory C. Damman

DAYTIME PHONE NUMBER

(402) 555-1234

FEES

Make check for $40 payable to "Corporation Division."

NOTE: Filing fees may be paid with VISA or MasterCard. The card number and expiration date should be submitted on a separate sheet for your protection.

PENNSYLVANIA

Microfilm Number _____

Entity Number _____

Filed with the Department of State on _____

_____
Secretary of the Commonwealth

CERTIFICATE OF ORGANIZATION-DOMESTIC LIMITED LIABILITY COMPANY
DSCB:15-8913 (Rev 95)

In compliance with the requirements of 15 Pa.C.S. § 8913 (relating to certificate of organization), the undersigned, desiring to organize a limited liability company, hereby state(s) that:

1. The **name** of the limited liability company is: Damman Legal Research, L.L.C.

2. The (a) **address** of this limited liability company's initial registered office in this Commonwealth or (b) **name** of its commercial registered office provider and the county of venue is:

    (a) 605 South 14th St., Ste. 412, Lincoln, PA 68508, Lancaster County
    Number and Street — City — State — Zip — County

    (b) c/o: n/a
    Name of Commercial Registered Office Provider — County

    For a limited liability company represented by a commercial registered office provider, the county in (b) shall be deemed the county in which the limited liability company is located for venue and official publication purposes.

3. The **name** and **address**, including street and number, if any, of each organizer are:

NAME	ADDRESS
Gregory C. Damman	3794 H St., Lincoln, PA 68508
Susan C. Damman	3794 H St., Lincoln, PA 68508

4. (Strike out if inapplicable): A member's interest in the company is to be evidenced by a certificate of membership interest.

5. (Strike out if inapplicable): Management of the company is vested in a manager or managers.

6. The **specified effective date**, if any is: none
    month — day — year — hour, if any

7. (Strike out if inapplicable): The company is a restricted professional company organized to render the following restricted professional service(s):

    n/a

8. For additional provisions of the certificate, if any, attach an 8 1/2 x 11 sheet.

    none

201

PENNSYLVANIA

DSCB:15-8913 (Rev 95)-2

   IN TESTIMONY WHEREOF, the organizer(s) has (have) signed this Certificate of Organization this _____ day of _____ , 19 ____ .

_____
(Signature)

_____
(Signature)

_____
(Signature)

RHODE ISLAND

Filing Fee $150.00   LLC I.D. #..............................

State of Rhode Island and Providence Plantations
OFFICE OF THE SECRETARY OF STATE

CORPORATIONS DIVISION
100 NORTH MAIN STREET
PROVIDENCE, RI 02903

LIMITED LIABILITY COMPANY

ARTICLES OF ORGANIZATION

Pursuant to the provisions of Chapter 7-16 of the General Laws, 1956, as amended, the following Articles of Organization are adopted for the limited liability company to be organized hereby:

FIRST. The name of the Limited Liability company is:
Damman Legal Research, L.L.C.

SECOND. There are at least two members who have agreed to form this limited liability company.

THIRD. The latest date on which the limited liability company is to dissolve is:
July 11, 2025

FOURTH. The name and address of the resident agent in the State of Rhode Island is:
Gregory C. Damman, 605 S. 14th St., Ste. 412, Lincoln, RI 68508

....
Signature of Resident Agent

FIFTH. Under the terms of these Articles of Organization and any written operating agreement made or intended to be made, the limited liability company is intended to be treated for purposes of federal income taxation as:

        ☒ a partnership;
or ☐ a corporation.

RHODE ISLAND

SIXTH. The address of the principal office of the limited liability company if it is determined: 605 S. 14th St., Ste. 412, Lincoln, RI 68508

SEVENTH. Additional provisions (if any) not inconsistent with law, which the members elect to have set forth in these Articles of Organization:

none

EIGHTH. Date these Articles of Organization are to become effective, if later than the date of filing, is: date of filing (not more than 30 days after the filing of these Articles of Organization)

Dated ...., 19..........

....
(Signature of Authorized Person)

SOUTH CAROLINA

STATE OF SOUTH CAROLINA
SECRETARY OF STATE
JIM MILES
ARTICLES OF ORGANIZATION
LIMITED LIABILITY COMPANY

The undersigned deliver the following articles of organization to form a South Carolina limited liability company pursuant to § 33-44-202 and § 33-44-203 of the 1976 South Carolina Code, as amended.

1. The name of the limited liability company which complies with § 33-44-105 of the South Carolina Code of 1976, as amended is _____
   Damman Legal Research, L.L.C.

2. The office of the initial designated office of the limited liability company in South Carolina is:
   Gregory C. Damman, 117 N. 6th St., Seward, SC 68434
   Street address
   Seward, SC 68434
   City   Zip Code

3. The initial agent for service of process of the limited liability company is
   Gregory C. Damman
   Name

   and the street address in South Carolina for this initial agent for service of process is:

   117 N. 6th St., Seward, SC 68434
   Street address
   Seward, SC 68434
   City   Zip Code

4. The name and address of each organizer is:

   (a) Gregory C. Damman
       Name
       117 N. 6th St.
       Street address
       Seward, SC 68434
       City   State   Zip Code

   (b) Susan C. Damman
       Name

205

SOUTH CAROLINA

      <u>117 N. 6th St.</u>
         Street address
      <u>Seward, SC 68434</u>
       City   State   Zip Code

(Add additional lines if necessary)

5.   [ ]   Check this box only if the company is to be term company. If so, provide the term specified:
_____
_____

6.   [ ]   Check this box only if management of the limited liability company is vested in a manager or managers. If this company is to be managed by managers, specify the name and address of each initial manager:

    (a)   _____
            Name
        _____
            Street address
        _____
            City   State   Zip Code

    (b)   _____
            Name
        _____
            Street address
        _____
            City   State   Zip Code

    (c)   _____
            Name
        _____
            Street address
        _____
            City   State   Zip Code

    (d)   _____
            Name
        _____
            Street address
        _____
            City   State   Zip Code

(Add additional lines if necessary)

SOUTH CAROLINA

7. [ ] Check this box only if one or more of the members of the company are to be liable for it debts and obligations under Section 33-44-303(c). If one or more members are so liable, specify which members, and for which debts, obligations or liabilities such members are liable in their capacity as members.

_____
_____
_____

8. Unless a delayed effective date is specified, these articles will be effective when endorsed for filing by the Secretary of State. Specify any delayed effective date and time:
_____

9. Set forth any other provisions not inconsistent with law which the organizers determine to include, including any provisions that are required or are permitted to be set forth in the limited liability company operating agreement.

10. Signature of each organizer:

_____
Signature of Organizer

_____
Signature of Organizer

Date:_____

FILING INSTRUCTIONS

1. File two copies of this form, the original and either a duplicate original or a conformed copy.

2. If space on this form is not sufficient, please attach additional sheets containing a reference to the appropriate paragraph in this form, or prepare this using a computer disk which will allow for expansion of the space on the form.

3. This form must be accompanied by the filing fee of $110.00 payable to the Secretary of State.

Form Approved by South Carolina
Secretary of State Jim Miles, June 1996

SOUTH DAKOTA

Secretary of State
State of South Dakota
500 E. Capitol
Pierre, SD 57501-5070
605-773-4845

ARTICLES OF ORGANIZATION
DOMESTIC LIMITED LIABILITY COMPANY

1. The name of the limited liability company is
   Damman Legal Research, L.L.C.

2. The period of duration is _perpetual_ years.

3. The purpose for which the limited liability company is organized:
   Any lawful business

4. The address of its principal place of business in South Dakota is
   117 N. 6th St., Seward, SD 68434

5. The name of the registered agent is Gregory C. Damman

   The address of the registered agent is 117 N. 6th St., Seward, SD 68434

6. The total amount of cash is $10,000.00, and a description and agreed value of property or services initially or to be initially contributed:
   n/a

7. The total additional contributions, if any, agreed to be made by all members and the times at which or events upon the happening of which they shall be made, including any consent or affirmative vote required for assessing the additional contributions:
   none

SOUTH DAKOTA

COMPLETE EITHER NUMBER EIGHT OR NINE

8. If the limited liability company is to be managed by a manager or managers, state the names and addresses of the manager or managers who are to serve as managers until the first annual meeting of members or until their successors are elected and qualify:

   n/a

9. If the management of a limited liability company is reserved to the members, the names and addresses of the members are:

   Gregory C. Damman, 117 N. 6th St., Seward, SD 68434
   Susan C. Damman, 117 N. 6th St., Seward, SD 68434

10. Any other provisions, not inconsistent with law, which the members elect to set out in the articles of organization for the regulation of the internal affairs of the limited liability company:

    none

Two or more members must sign in the presence of a notary public. Date _____

STATE OF _____
COUNTY OF _____   ss

I, _____, a notary public, do hereby certify that on this _____ day of _____ 19____, personally appeared before me _____ who, being by me first duly sworn, declared that he/she is the _____ of _____ that he/she signed the foregoing document as _____ of the limited liability company and the statements therein contained are true.

My Commission Expires _____   _____
                                          Notary Public

(Notarial Seal)

TENNESSEE

State of Tennessee
Department of State
Corporation Section
18th Floor, James K. Polk Building
Nashville, TN 37243-0306

TENNESSEE ARTICLES OF ORGANIZATION OF A LIMITED LIABILITY COMPANY

For Office Use Only

The undersigned acting as organizer(s) of a Limited Liability Company under the provisions of the Tennessee Limited Liability Company Act, § 48A-5-101, adopts the following Articles of Organization.

1. The name of the Limited Liability Company is:
   Damman Legal Research, L.L.C.
   (NOTE: Pursuant to the provisions of § 48A-7-101, each limited Liability Company name must contain the words "Limited Liability Company" or the abbreviation "LLC" or "L.L.C.")

2. The name and address of the Limited Liability Company's initial registered agent and office located in the state of Tennessee is:
   Gregory C. Damman
   (Name)
   117 N. 6th St., Seward, TN 68434
   (Street Address) (City) (State/Zip Code)
   Seward
   (County)

3. List the name and address of the members organizing and/or members in this Limited Liability Company.
   Greg Damman, 117 N. 6th St., Seward, TN 68434
   (Name) (Address: Include City, State and Zip Code)
   Susan Damman, 117 N. 6th St., Seward, TN 68434
   (Name) (Address: Include City, State and Zip Code)
   _____
   (Name) (Address: Include City, State and Zip Code)

4. At the date and time of formation there are two (2) or more members. Number of members .

5. The Limited Liability Company will be: *(NOTE: PLEASE MARK APPLICABLE BOX)*
   ☐ Board Managed   ☒ Member Managed

6. Number of members at the date of filing 2 .

7. If the document is not to be effective upon filing by the Secretary of State, the delayed effective date and time is:
   Date n/a , 19 , Time

8. The complete address of the Limited Liability Company's principal office is:
   117 N. 6th St., Seward, TN 68434
   (Street Address) (City) (State/Country/Zip Code)

9. Period of Duration: perpetual

10. Other Provisions:

11. Do the members, parties (other than the LLC) to a contribution agreement or a contribution allowance agreement, have preemptive rights? *(NOTE: PLEASE MARK THE APPLICABLE BOX)*
    ☐ Yes   ☒ No

_____
Signature Date

Signature *(manager or member authorized to sign by the Limited Liability Company)*

_____
Signer's Capacity

Name *(typed or printed)*

SS-4249 (Rev. 8/96)   RDA Pending

TEXAS

ARTICLES OF ORGANIZATION

OF

Damman Legal Research, L.L.C.
A Texas Limited Liability Company

I

The name of the limited liability company is:
Damman Legal Research, L.L.C.

II

The latest date on which the limited liability company is to dissolve is: perpetual duration.
(Author's note: Duration may be perpetual.)

III

The purpose for which the limited liability company is formed is: any lawful business.

IV

The street address of the limited liability company's initial registered office in this State, and the name of its initial registered agent at that address is: Gregory C. Damman 605 S. 14th St., Ste. 412, Lincoln, TX 65808.

V

The limited liability company is ( ) is not (X) to be managed by a manager or managers, and if the limited liability company is to be managed by a manager or managers, the names and addresses of the initial managers are as follows:

n/a

VI

The limited liability company will ( ) will not (X) be managed by managers, and the names and addresses of its initial members are:

Gregory C. Damman
3794 H St.
Lincoln, NE 68508

Susan C. Damman
3794 H St.
Lincoln, NE 68508

TEXAS

VII

The name and address of each organizer is as follows:

Gregory C. Damman
3794 H St.
Lincoln, NE 68508

VIII

Other provisions, not inconsistent with law, which the members elect to set out in these Articles of Organization: _____
none
_____
_____.

Executed this ____ day of _____, 19____.

Organizer's name and address: Gregory C. Damman
(type or print)   3794 H St.
                               Lincoln, TX 68508

                               _____
                               Organizer's signature

(Note: The author created this form. The state filing agency may require the use of official forms.)

UTAH

Articles of Organization
of
Ellipse Productions, L.C.

The undersigned natural persons of the age of eighteen years or more, acting as members of a limited liability company under the Utah Limited Liability Company Act, adopt the following Articles of Organization for such limited liability company:

1. **Name of the Limited Liability Company.** The name of the limited liability company is **Ellipse Productions, L.C.**

2. **Period of Duration of the Limited Liability Company.** The period of duration of the limited liability company shall be from the date these articles of organization are duly filed with the Division of Corporations and Commercial Code of the Utah Department of Commerce through and including December 31, 1999.

3. **Business Purposes For Which the Limited Liability Company Is Organized.** The purposes for which the limited liability company is organized are:

    (a) to engage in the business of the production and distribution of video products, and

    (b) to engage in any other lawful business activities for which limited liability companies may be organized pursuant to the Utah Limited Liability Company Act.

4. **Registered Office and Registered Agent.** The street address of the limited liability company's initial registered office is 265 East First South, Suite 300, Salt Lake City, Utah 84110-3358, and the name of its original registered agent at such street address is Krege B. Christensen.

5. **Appointment of the Director of the Division of Corporations and Commercial Code of the Utah Department of Commerce as Agent For Service of Process.** The Director of the Division of Corporations and Commercial Code of the Utah Department of Commerce is hereby appointed the agent of the limited liability company for service of process if the registered agent has resigned, the registered agent's authority has been revoked, or the registered agent cannot be found or served with the exercise of reasonable diligence.

6. **Principal Place of Business.** The principal place of business of the limited liability company shall be 1185 South 300 West, Salt Lake City, Utah 84101.

UTAH

7. **Management of the Limited Liability Company is Reserved to the Members; Names and Street Addresses of the Members.** The management of the limited liability company is reserved to the members. The name and street address of each of the members of the limited liability company are as follows:

Ron Hill	1185 South 300 West Salt Lake City, Utah 84101
Mark Nelson	435 South 300 East Salt Lake City, Utah 84111
Brian Twede	435 South 300 East Salt Lake City, Utah 84111

Under penalties of perjury, the undersigned members do hereby declare that these Articles of Organization have been examined by us and are, to the best of our knowledge and belief, true, correct, and complete on or as of July 1, 1991.

"Member"   _____
                    Ron Hill

"Member"   _____
                    Mark Nelson

"Member"   _____
                    Brian Twede

The undersigned hereby accepts appointment as registered agent for the above named limited liability company.

_____
Krege B. Christensen

KBC/hs

Articles of Organization   Ellipse Productions, L.C.

VERMONT

VERMONT SECRETARY OF STATE
Location: 81 River Street Mail: 109 State Street
Montpelier, VT 05609-1104 (802) 828-2386

LIMITED LIABILITY COMPANY ARTICLES OF ORGANIZATION

Name of LLC: Damman Legal Research, L.L.C.
(Name must contain the words Limited Liability Company, Limited Company, LLC, LC; limited may be abbrev as Ltd and Company as Co.)

Organized under the laws of the state (or country) of: Vermont

A *Foreign* LLC (non VT) must attach a *good standing certificate*, dated no earlier than 30 days prior to filing, from its state of origin.

Address of principal office: 117 N. 6th St.   *City* Seward   *State* VT   *Zip* 68434

Name of process agent: Gregory C. Damman

Agents address: 117 N. 6th St.   *City* Seward   VT   *Zip* 68434
An agent is the person or "corporation", residing IN Vt, who is authorized to receive service of process. An LLC cannot be an agent.

The fiscal year ends the month of 12. (DEC will be designated as the month your year ends unless you state differently.)

Is the company a TERM Limited Liability Company? no   *if YES, state the duration of its term:* _____
(An LLC is an *At-Will Company* unless it is designated in its articles of organization as a *Term Company*)

This is a MANAGER-MANAGED company.   [ ] YES   [X] NO

If the LLC is Manager-Managed list the name and address of each initial MANAGER:

_____

_____

_____

Indicate below whether the members of the company are to be personally liable for its debts and obligations under 11 VSA,3043(b): no

List name and address of each organizer: Gregory C. Damman, 117 N. 6th St., Seward VT 68434

SIGNATURE OF ORGANIZER(S): _____

The articles must be typewritten or printed and filed in duplicate. Unless a delayed effective date is specified, the document is effective on the date it is approved. A delayed effective date cannot be later than the 90th day after filing.
ANNUAL REPORT: Each LLC under this title is required to file an annual report within 2-1/2 months of the close of its fiscal year end. Failure to file this report will result in termination of the LLC. The annual report form will be mailed to your process agent when the report is due.

FEES: VERMONT DOMESTIC LLC = $ 75.00   FOREIGN LLC = $100.00

VIRGINIA

**COMMONWEALTH OF VIRGINIA
STATE CORPORATION COMMISSION
ARTICLES OF ORGANIZATION OF A
DOMESTIC LIMITED LIABILITY COMPANY**

Pursuant to Chapter 12 of Title 13.1 of the Code of Virginia the undersigned states as follows:

1. The name of the limited liability company is

   Damman Legal Research, L.L.C.

   (The name must contain the words "limited company" or "limited liability company" or their abbreviations "L.C.", "LC", "L.L.C." OR "LLC")

2. A. The registered agent's name is Gregory C. Damman
   whose business address is identical with the registered office.

   B. The registered agent is (mark appropriate box)
   (1) an INDIVIDUAL who is a **resident** of Virginia **and**
   [X] a member/manager of the limited liability company
   [ ] an officer/director of a corporate member/manager of the limited liability company
   [ ] a general partner of a general or limited partnership member/manager of the limited liability co.
   [ ] a member of the Virginia State Bar
   OR
   (2) [ ] a professional corporation, a professional limited liability company or a professional registered limited liability partnership of attorneys registered under Virginia Code Section 54.1-3902

3. The address of the initial registered office in Virginia is

   117 N. 6th St., Seward, VA 68434
   (number/street)

   Seward   VA 68434
   (city or town)   (state) (zip)

   located in the [ ] city or [X] county of Seward

4. The post office address of the principal office where the records will be maintained pursuant to Virginia Code Section 13.1-1028 is

   117 N. 6thSt., Seward, VA 68434
   (number/street)

   Seward, VA 68434
   (city or town)   (state)   (zip)

5 Signature

   _____   _____
   (organizer)   (date)

   Gregory C. Damman
   (printed name)

SEE INSTRUCTIONS ON THE REVERSE

WASHINGTON

STATE OF WASHINGTON
SECRETARY OF STATE
Ralph Munro, Secretary of State

APPLICATION TO FORM A LIMITED LIABILITY COMPANY
(Per Chapter 25.15 RCW)
FEE: $175

- Please PRINT or TYPE in black ink
- Sign, date and return original **and one copy** to:

CORPORATIONS DIVISION
505 E. UNION • PO BOX 40234
OLYMPIA, WA 98504-0234

- **Be sure to include filing fee.** Checks should be made payable to "Secretary of State"

EXPEDITED (24-HOUR) SERVICE AVAILABLE – $20 PER ENTITY
INCLUDE FEE AND WRITE "EXPEDITE" IN BOLD LETTERS
ON OUTSIDE OF ENVELOPE

FOR OFFICE USE ONLY

FILED: /   /   UBI:

CORPORATION NUMBER:

Important! Person to contact about this filing

Daytime Phone Number (with area code)

CERTIFICATE OF FORMATION

NAME OF LIMITED LIABILITY COMPANY (LLC) *(Must contain the word "Limited Liability Company" "Limited Liability Co." or "LLC")*

Damman Legal Research, L.L.C.

EFFECTIVE DATE OF LLC *(Specified effective date may be up to 90 days after receipt of the document by the Secretary of State)*

☐ Specific Date: _____   ☒ Upon filing by the Secretary of State

DATE OF DISSOLUTION *(If applicable)*   MANAGEMENT OF LLC IS VESTED IN ONE OR MORE MANAGERS

n/a   ☐ Yes   ☒ No

>>> PLEASE ATTACH ANY OTHER PROVISIONS THE LLC ELECTS TO INCLUDE <<<

NAME AND ADDRESS OF WASHINGTON STATE REGISTERED AGENT

Name Gregory C. Damman

Street Address *(Required)* 117 N. 6th St.   City Seward   State WA   ZIP 68434

PO Box *(Optional – Must be in same city as street address)* _____ ZIP *(If different than street ZIP)* _____

I consent to serve as Registered Agent in the State of Washington for the above named LLC. I understand it will be my responsibility to accept Service of Process on behalf of the LLC; to forward mail to the LLC; and to immediately notify the Office of the Secretary of State if I resign or change the Registered Office Address.

Gregory C. Damman
Signature of Agent   Printed Name   Date

NAMES ADDRESSES OF EACH PERSON EXECUTING THIS CERTIFICATE *(If necessary, attach additional names and addresses)*

Printed Name Gregory C. Damman   Signature _____

Address 117 N. 6th St.   City Seward   State WA   ZIP 68434

Printed Name _____   Signature _____

Address _____   City _____   State ____ ZIP _____

Printed Name _____   Signature _____

Address _____   City _____   State ____ ZIP _____

SIGNATURE OF EXECUTOR
This document is hereby executed under penalties of perjury, and is, to the best of my knowledge, true and correct.

Signature of Executor   Printed Name   Date

CORPORATIONS INFORMATION AND ASSISTANCE – 360/753-7115 (TDD – 360/753-1485)

WEST VIRGINIA

KEN HECHLER
Secretary of State
State Capitol, W-139
Charleston, WV 25305-0770
(304) 558-8000
FAX (304) 558-0900

FILE IN DUPLICATE
ORIGINALS FEE: $10.00

West Virginia Articles of Organization of a Limited Liability Company

The undersigned, acting as organizer(s) of a limited liability company under Chapter 31, Article 1A, of the West Virginia Code, adopt(s) the following Articles of organization.

1. The undersigned agree to become a West Virginia limited liability company by the name of
   Damman Legal Research, Limited Liability Company
   (The name of the corporation shall contain the words: limited liability company, without abbreviation.)

2. The address of the principal office will be
   605 South 14th street, in the city, town
   or village of **Lincoln**, county of **Lancaster**.
   State of **West Virginia**, Zip Code **68508**

3. Purpose of organization: **Any lawful purpose**

4. Name and address of the initial registered agent for service of process.
   Name **Gregory C. Damman**
   Address, Street or P.O. Box **605 S. 14th St., Ste. 412**
   City **Lincoln**, State **WV**, Zip **68508**

5. List the name and addresses of the members organizing and/or members in this limited liability company: (NOTE: Foreign corporations must also apply for a certificate of authority)

Name	Address
Gregory C. Damman	3794 H St., Lincoln, WV 68508
Susan C. Damman	3794 H St., Lincoln, WV 68508

   (attach additional sheets if necessary)

6. Period of Duration: **thirty (30) years**
   (may not be perpetual)

_____
Manager or member
authorized to sign by the limited liability Co.

Form I-LLC

WEST VIRGINIA

Acknowledgment

I (We), the understand, for the purpose of organizing a limited liability company under the laws of the State of West Virginia, do make and file this "Articles of Organization"

In witness whereof, I (we) have accordingly hereunto set my(our) respective hands this _____ day of _____ , 19 _____ .

(All organizers must sign below. Names and signatures must appear the same throughout the Articles of organization.)
PHOTOCOPIES OF THE SIGNATURES OF THE ORGANIZERS AND THE NOTARY PUBLIC **CANNOT BE ACCEPTED.**

State of _____

County of _____

I, _____ , a Notary Public, in and for the county and state aforesaid, hereby certify that (names of all organizer(s) as shown above must be inserted in this space by official taking acknowledgment)

whose name(s) is(are) signed to the foregoing Articles of organization, this day personally appeared before me in my said county and acknowledged his(her)(their) signature(s).

SEAL

My commission expires

(Notary Public)

Articles of organization prepared by _____

whose mailing address is _____

WISCONSIN

ARTICLES OF ORGANIZATION
Limited Liability Company
(Organized under Chapter 183 of the Wisconsin Statutes)

Executed by the undersigned for the purpose of forming a Wisconsin Limited Liability Company under Chapter 183 of the Wisconsin Statutes:

Article 1. (See instruction 1 for required words or abbreviations.)
  Name of Limited Liability Company: Damman Legal Research, L.L.C.

Article 2. The street address of the initial registered office is:
  (The complete address, including street and number, if assigned, and ZIP code. P.O. Box address may be included as part of the address, but is insufficient alone.)

Article 3. The name of the initial registered agent at the above registered office is:

  Gregory C. Damman

Article 4. Select appropriate choice below. (See information on reverse.)
  Management of the limited liability company shall be vested in:

  ( ) a manager or managers.
  OR
  (X) its members.

Article 5. Date executed _____.

  Name and complete address of each organizer:

  1) Gregory C. Damman   2) Susan Damman
     117 N. 6th St.   117 N. 6th St.
     Seward, WI 68434   Seward, NE 68434

  _____   _____
  (Organizer's Signature)   (Organizer's Signature)

This document was drafted by _____
  (name of individual is required by law)

FILING FEE - $130
SEE REVERSE for Instructions, Suggestions, Filing Fees and Procedures

WYOMING

ARTICLES OF ORGANIZATION

Wyoming Secretary of State
Corporation Division
The State Capitol
Cheyenne, WY 82002-0020

Phone (307) 777-7311/7312
Fax: (307) 777-5339
E-Mail: Corporations@missc.state.wy.us

I. The name of the limited liability company is: Damman Legal Research, L.L.C.

II. The period of its duration is: perpetual

III. The purpose for which the limited liability company is organized is: any lawful business

IV. The name and address of its registered agent is: Gregory C. Damman
117 N. 6th St., Seward, WY 68434

(The registered agent may be an individual resident in this state or a domestic or foreign corporation authorized to transact business in this state, having a business office identical with such registered office. Do not use a Post Office Box or Mail Drop Box)

V. The total amount of cash and a description and agreed value of property other than cash contributed is: $10,000.00

VI. The total additional contributions, if any, agreed to be made by all members and the times at which or events upon the happening of which they shall be made are: none

VII. The right, if given, of the members to admit additional members, and the terms and conditions of the admission are: majority vote of members

WYOMING

VIII. The right, if given, of the remaining members of the limited liability company to continue the business on the death, resignation, expulsion, bankruptcy or dissolution of a member or occurrence of any other event which terminates the continued membership of a member of the limited liability company: _____
Upon majority vote of members _____
_____
_____

IX. **Complete either item #1 or item #2**

1) The limited liability company is to be managed by a manager or managers. The names and addresses of the managers who are to serve as managers until the first annual meeting of the members or until their successors are elected and qualify are:

_____
_____
_____
_____

2) The management of the limited liability company is reserved to the members. The names and addresses of the members are:

Gregory C. Damman	Susan C. Damman
117 N. 6th St.	117 N. 6th St.
Seward, WY 68434	Seward, WY 68434

Date: _____

Signed: _____

_____

_____

_____

(Must be originally signed by at least one organizer)

If you have enjoyed this book and would like to receive a free catalog of all Self-Counsel titles, please write to:

>Self-Counsel Press Inc.
>1704 N. State Street
>Bellingham, WA 98225
>USA

Or visit us on the World Wide Web at *www.self-counsel.com*